THE SENSE OF CREATION

What kind of experience might help to confirm and make sense of the puzzling belief in divine creation, so central to the main monotheistic religions? Anselm and Aquinas developed a philosophical understanding of 'Creation' as an asymmetrical relationship between the world and God, that is, that the world is really related to God in a relationship of total dependence but God is in no way really related to or modified by this created world. This idea of an asymmetrical relationship is the key concept unifying all aspects of this book which discusses the three main inter-related questions in a philosophical discussion about God – the question of meaning, the question of existence, and the question of co-existence.

The book explores various 'ciphers' of this asymmetrical relationship in our pre-philosophical lived experience. These are experiences such as that of the relationship between our knowledge and what we know, or our sense of obligation to our vulnerable neighbour. It argues that deciphering such experiences helps to make sense of the 'asymmetrical' relation of creation and that it in turn makes sense of them. Masterson argues further that this idea of asymmetrical relationship provides insight into the main questions of philosophy of religion and is an illuminating source of critical dialogue with contemporary Anglo/American and Phenomenological approaches in philosophy of religion.

ASHGATE PHILOSOPHY OF RELIGION SERIES

Series Editors

Paul Helm, King's College, University of London, UK
Linda Zagzebski, University of Oklahoma, USA

The *Ashgate Philosophy of Religion* series spans many critical debates, and presents new directions and new perspectives in contemporary research and study within the philosophy of religion. This series presents books by leading international scholars in the field, providing a platform for their own particular research focus to be presented within a wider contextual framework. Offering accessible, stimulating new contributions to each topic, this series will prove of particular value and interest to academics, graduate, postgraduate and upper-level undergraduate readers world-wide focusing on philosophy, religious studies and theology, sociology or other related fields.

Titles in the series include:

Problems of Evil and the Power of God
James A. Keller

Religion and Morality
William J. Wainwright

God and the Nature of Time
Garrett J. DeWeese

Rationality and Religious Theism
Joshua L. Golding

God and Realism
Peter Byrne

Religious Diversity
A Philosophical Assessment
David Basinger

The Sense of Creation
Experience and the God Beyond

PATRICK MASTERSON
University College Dublin, Ireland

ASHGATE

© Patrick Masterson 2008

All rights reserved. No part of this publication may be reproduced, stored in a retrieval system or transmitted in any form or by any means, electronic, mechanical, photocopying, recording or otherwise without the prior permission of the publisher.

Patrick Masterson has asserted his moral right under the Copyright, Designs and Patents Act, 1988, to be identified as the author of this work.

Published by
Ashgate Publishing Limited
Gower House
Croft Road
Aldershot
Hampshire GU11 3HR
England

Ashgate Publishing Company
Suite 420
101 Cherry Street
Burlington, VT 05401-4405
USA

Ashgate website: http://www.ashgate.com

British Library Cataloguing in Publication Data
Masterson, Patrick
  The sense of creation: experience and the God beyond. –
  (Ashgate philosophy of religion series)
  1. Creation 2. Transcendence of God 3. Religion – Philosophy 4. God
  I. Title
  213

Library of Congress Cataloging-in-Publication Data
Masterson, Patrick.
  The sense of creation: experience and the God beyond / Patrick Masterson.
      p. cm. – (Ashgate philosophy of religion series)
  Includes bibliographical references and index.
  ISBN-13: 978-0-7546-6426-0 (hardcover : alk. paper) 1. Transcendence of God. 2. Creation.
  3. Religion–Philosophy. 4. God. I. Title.
  BL205.M335 2007
  213--dc22

2007036260

ISBN 978-0-7546-6426-0

Printed and bound in Great Britain by MPG Books Ltd, Bodmin, Cornwall.

For Frankie

Contents

Preface		*ix*
Acknowledgements		*xi*
Introduction		1
1	Describing God	5
2	World and God	11
3	Idea and Existence of God	19
4	God and Grammar: Echoes of Wittgenstein	23
5	Knowledge and Transcendence	41
6	Morality and Transcendence	59
7	Analogy and Transcendence	85
8	Co-Existence and Transcendence	107
9	Phenomenology and Transcendence	121
Conclusion		139
Bibliography		*145*
Index		*151*

Preface

The central theme of this book has preoccupied my mind over the years in which I took a prolonged sabbatical (as a university president first in Dublin and then in Florence) from my primary vocation as a professor of philosophy.

Since retiring from the public dimension of academic life I have been able to revisit in a more sustained way this preoccupation, namely, how to make some sense of the puzzling idea of creation by comparing it with more familiar everyday experiences.

The book was written mainly in the quiet Languedoc village of Puisserguier where my wife and I now spend much of our time and where I have my library and computer. During the time we spend in Dublin I am able to engage in more detailed library research through the gracious welcome afforded me by the library of my alma mater University College Dublin. Here, as I appreciate some fine point in Aquinas's *Summa Contra Gentiles or* Merleau-Ponty's *Phenomenologie de la Perception*, I can look, with relief, across the lake at "my" office in the Admin. Building where a successor now has the task of formulating university policy!

The book, in some ways, reflects my own philosophical itinerary. My undergraduate studies in University College Dublin were mainly, but not narrowly, Thomist in inspiration and historical in exposition. They began with the pre-Socratics and terminated with Kant—apart from some excursions into more recent moral philosophy and symbolic logic.

My Ph.D. programme in Louvain (where Mercier had pioneered a critical Thomist renewal and where Edmund Husserl's archives had been recently housed) was much more contemporary in orientation. The emphasis was on recent continental philosophy, especially phenomenology. But I also recall an eye-opening course on the philosophy of C.S. Peirce.

In my subsequent career I became actively interested in and familiar with developments in contemporary British philosophy of religion.

The influence of these various strands of philosophy, Thomism, Phenomenology, and contemporary British philosophy of religion, are evident in the following pages and I recall with gratitude former teachers and colleagues from whom I have learnt so much.

More recently, various people have encouraged me in this undertaking through discussions and, in some cases, by reading or commenting on parts of the work. For this I thank, *inter alia*, Michael Nolan, Brendan Purcell, Fran. O'Rourke, Dermot Moran, Ger. Casey, Kevin Rafferty, William Desmond, Richard Kearney, and John Caputo. It would be convenient to attribute any flagrant philosophical errors in the book to the them, but unfortunately this is not the case—indeed the contrary!

My editor at Ashgate Publishing, Sarah Lloyd, deserves a special word of thanks. In the first place for her confidence and, I like to think, judgement in recommending the publication of my book. And secondly for the professionalism and consideration with which she guided me through the various hoops which one must navigate in order to deliver a final text.

There remains now the enjoyable opportunity of thanking my family for their support. Our four children, Rosemary, Laurence, Lucy, and Naomi, have been encouraging in an amused and benignly tolerant fashion occasionally enquiring laconically how "Son of Atheism" is coming along (a humorous reference to a book on atheism which I wrote some time ago). It is to my beloved Frankie that my deepest gratitude is gladly expressed. Over many years she has so positively encouraged me in my various undertakings. In recent times she has created such an agreeable ambience for writing that I had no inclination to avoid the challenge of putting black on white—she is my cipher of transcendence.

Acknowledgements

Chapter 4 is a revised and extended version of my article "God and Grammar", *Philosophical Studies*, 29 1972, pp. 7–24.

Chapter 7 is a revised and extended version of my article "Ethics and Absolutes in the Philosophy of E. Levinas", *Neue Zeitschrift fur Systematische Theologie und Religionsphilosophie*, 25. Band, 1983, pp. 211–23.

An extended version of Chapter 9 of this work entitled "Richard Kearney's Hermeneutics of Otherness" is published in *Philosophy & Social Criticism*, 2008, 34, pp. 247–65.

Introduction

The belief that the world was created by God is fundamental to the major monotheistic religions. It is primarily a religious belief rather than a philosophical conclusion. Nevertheless, it has been widely maintained over many centuries that this religious belief is capable of rational confirmation or justification.

However, this is a claim which is not so widespread today in view of the pervasive presumption that atheism, or at least a robust agnosticism, is the philosophical position most in harmony with contemporary cultural sensitivity. Even convinced religious believers are inclined to accept this view and seek, as we shall see, to insulate their "faith" from the deception of philosophical arguments. This can expose them to another dilemma, namely, a "double-truth" dilemma according to which what is true from the perspective of religious faith is false from the perspective of philosophical reason—a view mirrored by Heidegger"s insistence upon the irreconcilable difference between theology and philosophy and the impossibility of a "Christian philosophy."[1]

A number of years ago, in a book entitled *Atheism and Alienation*, I explored the philosophical roots of contemporary atheism.[2] I argued that contemporary atheism has effected a remarkable inversion of the traditional relationship between the concepts of atheism and alienation. This involved a noteworthy reversal of the pre-modern conviction that the atheist was the prototype of the alienated or estranged individual—"the fool says in his heart there is no God"—to the current conviction that the theist is the individual who is philosophically alienated or estranged from the context of contemporary culture.

I argued that this reversal has evolved from the philosophical consequences which were drawn on the one hand from the modern scientific revolution of the sixteenth and seventeenth centuries, and on the other from Descartes momentous exploration of the *cogito*. These consequences included on the one hand the presumption that all true knowledge was limited to what could be established by means of empirical science, and on the other hand the presumption that the ultimate foundation of all meaning and value was located within the resources of human subjectivity.

Notwithstanding these widespread (sometimes mutually reinforcing and sometimes mutually opposing) presumptions of contemporary atheism I propose to revisit the claim that "God created the world" is capable of rational confirmation or justification. This will involve both clarifying what it means to say that "God created the world" and adducing reasons in support of the truth of this assertion. The account proposed in each of these stages is somewhat controversial.

---

1   Cf. M. Heidegger, *An Introduction to Metaphysics*, trans. R. Manheim, New York, 1961, p. 6.

2   Cf. P. Masterson, *Atheism and Alienation: The Philosophical Sources of Contemporary Atheism*, Harmondsworth, 1973.

The first stage, concerned with meaning, follows insights derived from Anselm and Thomas Aquinas about the related ideas of divine perfection and creation. It advances a viewpoint which is incompatible with what is often intended or implied in some contemporary accounts of the relationship between these ideas. In particular, it is incompatible with the view which describes God and his creation as realizing a process of mutual fulfillment as, for example, in certain versions of process theology, or the view that it is more appropriate to speak of God in terms of "possibility" rather than in terms of actuality.

The second stage, which seeks to provide rational argument in favor of the claim that God created the world, is at odds with the views of both unbelievers and many believers that such a project is a futile and indeed a misconceived undertaking. In Chapter 4 I consider the views of those believers who maintain that any attempt to "prove" his existence involves a misconception of the grammar of an affirmation of God.

From these remarks it will be evident that, in its basic orientation, this work attributes enduring significance and value to the, currently unpopular, form of metaphysical enquiry characteristic of traditional natural theology. As such it may be portrayed as discredited and superseded by more contemporary and relevant forms of enquiry in philosophy of religion such as phenomenology and Wittgensteinian linguistic philosophy.

However, it is a fundamental thesis of the book that the relationship between these more recent approaches and the more metaphysical line of enquiry which it advocates is not one of opposition but rather of complementarity. It is argued that these more recent initiatives in philosophy of religion require as a counterpart a dimension of metaphysical qualification if the precious insights they disclose are not to crystallize into oversights.

If there is something original, or at least newly formulated in my line of argument, it is in presenting particular features of experience as suggestive illustrations of the sort of relationship which creation involves and of which, in turn, the idea of creation makes best sense. These features of experience I call, adapting a term of Karl Jaspers, "ciphers of transcendence." They are "ciphers" in the sense that they are experiential clues that enable us to attain a rational or philosophical affirmation of God. But they are ciphers which, as such, cannot directly disclose his existence. They have to be "deciphered" by philosophical argument which argues that his existence can be affirmed as a theoretical truth condition of these features of experience.

The basic proposal is that relationships such as those involved in human cognition, in ethical response, in our experience of different degrees of being or perfection, manifest a thought-provoking asymmetry. It is an asymmetry which in a way resembles what is envisaged by the notion of creation. It is argued that these relationships are illuminated and rendered more comprehensible by the affirmation of a divine creator which is achieved through an indirect argument from these "ciphers of transcendence." It is as though the experienced relationships, or ciphers, provide an experiential foothold or basis for the idea of creation which, in turn, provides them with an intelligible basis or foundation. This, as we shall see, involves a conception of philosophy according to which our pre-philosophical lived experience provides the basis or foundation of our philosophical reflection which, in turn, provides the intelligible foundation or ground of this lived experience—a circular process, perhaps, but not viciously.

The argument for the existence of God developed in Chapter 7, based on the analogical character of the finite beings of our experience, is somewhat different in kind to those developed in Chapters 5 and 6. Whereas they relate to familiar features of our intellectual and moral life, its context and perspective are more distinctively and exclusively metaphysical. It is, in effect, an extended interpretation of Aquinas"s fourth argument for the existence of God. Some readers may find it somewhat "abstract" and remote and may prefer to defer consideration of it until they have read the rest of the book which, hopefully, will indicate its relevance.

In a philosophical discussion about God there is, besides the questions of *meaning* and *existence* mentioned above, a third general question which must be addressed. This is the question of how to understand the *co-existence* of God and humans. Some issues concerning this co-existence of God and humans, which arise from our arguments in Chapters 5–7 for the existence of a divine creator, are discussed in the final two chapters. Chapter 8 considers some general issues on this topic and Chapter 9 addresses a conception of this *co-existence* which is very much at variance with the account defended in this book.

However, before we consider these arguments and issues, we must address the first theme of our undertaking, namely, the meaning of the related ideas of divine perfection and creation.

CHAPTER 1

Describing God

Most people who affirm the existence of God do so primarily in the context of a pre-philosophical religious faith. Their affirmation is part of the discourse of the way of life into which they have been born, or "born again" through religious conversion. The language in which God is described or addressed at this level of religious faith is typically rich in self-involving metaphor derived usually from a sacred text and religious tradition proclaiming an eventful salvific interaction between man and God.

Precisely as metaphorical we understand that this language is not to be taken literally. It needs to be tempered by some appreciation or comprehension of how God is to be more appropriately envisaged if idolatry is to be avoided. In religious discourse and worship God may be un-problematically addressed as a "rock of ages" or invoked as a "kindly light" provided we do not expect to unearth him or find him literally in a beautiful sunrise. Our language of presence must be tempered by that of absence and transcendence which distinguishes God from the world of experience and the things which compose it. What is needed is a way of describing God which applies properly and only to God.

Sacred texts such as the Bible do indeed address this issue from a religious perspective. For example, when Moses asks how he is to name God to the Israelites he gets the response *ehyeh asher ehyeh*—usually (but not un-controversially) translated as "I am who am." The text suggests that God is to be understood as existing in a unique way, utterly unlike any particular determinate being. The history of monotheistic theologies, Jewish, Christian, and Muslim, is one of seeking to articulate and elaborate what this might mean.

An important contribution to this project of understanding what we should mean when we talk of God was made by the eleventh-century theologian St Anselm of Canterbury. He provided a description of God which described him, properly and uniquely, in terms which both believers and unbelievers could accept as appropriate. Thus, although himself a theologian working within the context of religious faith, Anselm contributed significantly to the creation of philosophy of religion where rational debate about God could obtain irrespective of religious faith or its absence. That Anselm proceeded to argue from this conception of God to his actual existence and thereby provide an argument which has fascinated philosophers right up to the present day is of secondary relevance to our present discussion. This famous argument will be considered later in Chapter 3. What is of immediate interest is his uniquely identifying description of God—which is an issue of meaning or significance rather than a proof of existence.

Let us consider the description of God provided by Anselm. This consideration will lead us on to a discussion of the related idea of creation elaborated more comprehensively two centuries later by Thomas Aquinas.

6 *The Sense of Creation*

In his book *Prosologion* Anselm develops a description of God as "something than which a greater cannot be conceived."[1] He argues that if we wish to describe God in a rationally convincing way, which adequately distinguishes him from an idol, we must envisage him as that than which nothing greater or better is conceivable. (Anselm uses the terms "greater" and "better" equivalently—"I do not mean physically great, as a physical object is great, but that which, the greater it is, is the better or more worthy."[2])

This orientates our thought to understanding that God is not to be identified with any one or number of finite things which happen to exist, however great or perfect. For in such cases an even greater perfection is always conceivable. God, as envisaged by Anselm, cannot pertain to the order of finite beings. It is only by having such a false or inadequate notion of God, "either giving it no meaning at all or some alien meaning," that the fool is able to say in his heart there is no God.[3]

Underlying Anselm's idea of God as that than which nothing greater or better is conceivable is the intuition of an intimate bond between reality and goodness disclosed through our experience of degrees of goodness, i.e. that some things instantiate a better, more desirable or comprehensive, way of being than others. This experience of reality as manifesting a hierarchy of existential perfection enables us to form an idea of God as its greatest conceivable expression. This idea of divine perfection has thus a foundation in our experience of degrees of perfection. Wherefore, in reply to the objection that we cannot frame any reliable idea of God he writes:

> Everything that is less good, in so far as it is good, is like the greater good. It is therefore evident to any rational mind that by ascending from the lesser good to the greater we can form a considerable notion of a being than which a greater is inconceivable.[4]

This intensive bond between reality and goodness, developed by Anselm from Platonic sources, has remained a powerful inspiration in philosophical thought about God, although it is perhaps not so obvious to a contemporary secular outlook.[5]

For Anselm, God described thus as a being than which no greater can be conceived must be understood to be of unlimited perfection and such that "it is impossible to think of it as not existing."[6] In other words, God thus described must be understood

---

1 Anselm, *Prosologion*, ch. 2. Unless otherwise mentioned the translation used is that by A. McGill in *The Many-Faced Argument: Recent Studies on the Ontological Argument for the Existence of God*, ed. J. Hick and A. McGill, London, 1968. Cf. also, *St Anselm's Prosologion*, trans. with introduction and commentary by M. Charlesworth, Notre Dame, 1979.

2 Anselm, *Monologium*, ch. 2, in *Saint Anselm—Basic Writings*, trans. S. Deane, La Salle, 1962.

3 Cf. Anselm, *Prosologion*, ch. 4.

4 Ibid., Reply VIII.

5 An illuminating discussion of this theme is provided by Iris Murdoch in her discussion of the Ontological Argument. Cf. I. Murdoch, *Metaphysics as a Guide to Morals*, London, 1992, ch. 13.

6 Anselm, *Prosologion*, ch. 3.

Describing God

as existing necessarily and not just contingently as a matter of fact. Anselm argues that to think otherwise would involve a contradiction.

> Something such that we cannot conceive of it as not existing ... is greater than something which we can conceive of as not existing. Therefore, if that than which a greater cannot be conceived could be conceived not to be, we would have an impossible contradiction: That than which a greater cannot be conceived would not be that than which a greater cannot be conceived. Therefore, something than which a greater cannot be conceived so truly is that it is impossible even to conceive of it as not existing.[7]

Hence, the divine perfection, thus conceived, must be envisaged as transcending both limiting determination and merely contingent existence—in other words, as necessarily existing infinite perfection, *verissime et maxime esse*.[8]

This assertion that God, understood as that than which nothing greater can be conceived, must be understood as necessarily existing infinite perfection enables Anselm to affirm that God must exist in reality and not just as an object of our understanding. This is the famous Ontological Argument according to which God's necessary existence must obtain in reality since such existence is greater than merely thought about necessary existence and is therefore required to fulfill the condition of that than which nothing greater can be conceived. This argument has had and still has its famous champions. Its validity has also been widely challenged, correctly in my opinion as I will indicate in Chapter 3.

However, as has been, mentioned, what interests us at this stage of our discussion is an issue of meaning rather than of existence. In other words, we want to focus on the development of what is meant by the description of God as a being than which nothing greater can be conceived. We have seen that for Anselm this description of God involves understanding him to be necessarily existing unlimited perfection— the highest good requiring nothing else, *nullo alio indigens*.

This understanding of divine perfection involved in the description of God as that than which nothing greater can be conceived implies a further important consideration which has a significant bearing on our understanding of the closely related concept of creation. It is the consideration that God plus the world, or God plus any creature, cannot be conceived as "greater" or "better" than God alone. If the created world constituted an additional perfection to that realized in God he would not be that than which nothing greater can be conceived. For God plus the world would be conceivable as a greater perfection than God alone.[9]

Anselm's description implies a conception of how the relationship between other beings and God is to be understood. It involves the idea that even if the world and its components did not exist, or ceased to exist, there would be no diminution of goodness or perfection—"things can in no way exist without You, though You do not

---

7   Ibid.

8   Ibid.

9   Cf. R. Sokolowski, *The God of Faith and Reason*, Notre Dame, 1982, p. 9. The implications of this understanding are further developed by the author in *Christian Faith and Human Understanding*, Washington, DC, 2006.

8 *The Sense of Creation*

exist any the less even if they return to nothingness."[10] God is not "better" because of the world nor is there "more" perfection than God's because of creation. The infinite perfection of God and the finite perfection of the world are incommensurable. The latter should be thought of as participating in (dependently, and in a limited way, and without adding to), the infinite perfection of God.

This conception of the relationship between the world and God has its pre-philosophical foundation in the Judaeo-Christian doctrine of creation. Anselm's account provides a perspective from which it can be developed philosophically. This development, as we shall see, was carried through very effectively a couple of centuries later by Thomas Aquinas in his account of creation. It involves a very different view of the relationship between the world and God (or gods) from that developed in Greek and Roman religions and philosophy (and indeed from some contemporary views of the relationship).

The gods of Greek and Roman religions, although revered as the best and most independent beings, were certainly part of the world and never thought of as possibly existing in the absence of the world. They were expressions of the necessities which human beings encounter in the world, which they must respect and which control their destiny.

Even when the religious-poetic conception of the gods as implicated in human fate was philosophically purified in the Greek enlightenment by philosophers such as Plato and Aristotle the divine realities remained part, albeit the most perfect part, of the world.:

> No matter how Aristotle's god is to be described, as the prime mover or the self-thinking thought, he is part of the world and it is obviously necessary that there be other things besides him, whether he is aware of it or not.[11]

Indeed it was natural to take the given world as the ultimate context and to seek to understand it as a unified structure of lesser or dependent and greater or more perfect constituents. Such, for example, is the distinction, within a unified context, between Aristotle's "divine" First Mover and lesser mutable beings, or similarly, Plato's distinction between the One and the many. As Robert Sokolowski observes:

> Both the philosophical and religious thinkers of antiquity took the whole of things, the cosmos, as the ultimate setting for their thought. They did not conceive of the possible nonexistence of the cosmos; its factual givenness was quite properly taken for granted, and the divine principles, the god or the gods, were thought of as the highest and best entities within that setting.[12]

The modern term "cosmetic" provides a suggestive indication of the Greek conception of the "cosmos" as a hierarchically unified totality rendered "beautiful" in virtue of the harmonious interrelationships of its parts. This finite totality was what was taken to exist necessarily and such explanatory distinctions as might be

---

10 Anselm, *Prosologion*, ch. 20 (trans. Charlesworth).

11 Sokolowski, *The God of Faith and Reason*, pp. 15–16.

12 Sokolowski, *Christian Faith and Human Understanding*, pp. 13–14.

discovered were to be sought within it. The divine being or god was seen as the highest internal principle of this finite totality, not as its transcendent source. In the Greek conception there was an equivalence between the notions of "being," "finitude," and "perfection." The idea of an infinitely perfect being would have seemed a contradiction in terms.

The Judaeo-Christian idea of God and creation proposes a very different conception of things. The finite world of our experience and all its constituents is understood to be the totally dependent outcome of a free decision of an infinitely perfect God to originate it into existence. This primarily religious understanding is given philosophical focus in Anselm's description of God as that than which nothing greater or more perfect can be conceived. This description implies that the world must be understood in relation to God's transcendent perfection in such a manner that this divine perfection is neither enhanced nor relativized by that of the world. For otherwise God would not be that than which nothing greater could be conceived.

The conception of creation implicit in this description by Anselm of God as that than which nothing greater or more perfect can be conceived embodies a significant philosophical insight which is explicated and developed by Thomas Aquinas, in way which we will consider further in the next chapter.

CHAPTER 2

World and God

In the preceding chapter we have indicated that implicit in Anselm's description of God is an assertion that the created world of our experience is a freely willed expression of God's goodness. It is a world which, although a reality with its own distinct existence, its *esse proprium*, is neither required by, nor enhances, nor relativizes the divine perfection.

However, although Anselm's conception of God has these important implications for the idea of creation it does not, as such, involve this idea. Being that than which nothing greater can be conceived does not include being the creator of the world. Thus one might ask of what significance for the human predicament is the idea of such transcendent and self-sufficient perfection? The point is illustrated dramatically by Sartre in *The Flies* where he has Orestes declare to Jupiter

> What have I to do with you or you with me? We shall glide past each other, like ships in a river, without touching: you are God and I am free; each of us is alone and our anguish is akin.[1]

The relationship between the idea of creation and that of an infinitely perfect God must, in Aquinas's view, be established by an *a posteriori* argument which shows that the finite world of our experience requires as its ultimate creative source the infinitely perfect God envisaged by Anselm. His development of the idea of creation elaborates this relationship between the finite world and its infinitely perfect source.

Central to this conception of creation is the claim that it is not a change in some presupposed indeterminate stuff. It is not an action by God on some pre-existing thing to re-form it into something new. Creation does not mean that God brings it about that something which exists becomes an x, e.g. a man. It means rather that God brings it about that there exists something which is a man. "In creation the thing created does not undergo change, and is not passive to divine action."[2] It originates absolutely and totally.

Likewise, just as creation does not presuppose something, however ephemeral, in which it happens, neither is it a required development, prolongation, or alienated expression of God's own being. This Neoplatonic conception of creation, which has various modern idealist counterparts, is explicitly rejected by Aquinas. If the world, in some inchoate form, is not presupposed by creation neither does it arise as a necessary manifestation, expression, or realization of the divine being. Creation is *ex nihilo* and freely enacted, not formed from some pre-existing milieu, nor

---

1   J.P. Sartre, *The Flies*, trans. S. Gilbert, New York, 1947, p. 159.
2   P. Geach, *God and the Soul*, London, 1969, p. 89.

as an inevitable self-externalization of the divine being. It is the un-necessitated outcome of an act of divine freedom—a newly existing order of finite being arising as freely initiated by the wholly independent infinite perfection of God. Creation "participates" in this infinite perfection in a limited and wholly dependent manner. And as such it possesses its own proper existence as other than a moment of divine self-knowledge.[3]

An important consequence of this is that God is not and need not be invoked as an intrinsic explanation, a *deus ex machina*, of the world. Aquinas insists that the world has its own distinct and coherent being, its self-possessed intrinsic intelligibility, its *esse proprium*. It depends on God not as on a constitutive component but as the transcendent cause of its distinctive existence and activity as the world which it is—of the fact that it is and is such as it is, even though it need not have been at all.

For Aquinas, this attempt to outline the nature of the relationship between God and the world, which emphasizes divine transcendence vis-à-vis his creation, need not lead to a conclusion that God is unaware, of or indifferent to, the circumstances of the created world.

Our human experience of knowledge and sympathy involves features of passivity and feeling. We are affected and modified by that which is distinct from us. The desire to proclaim God's interest in and love for the world leads some thinkers to envisage him as somehow likewise affected and associated with us through "com-passion." This conception, which implicates the divine being intrinsically in the history of the world, leads naturally to a view of God as subject to a process of development, as an evolving potentiality rather than unchanging actuality "a God who may-be." In this context one could refer to the work of process theologians such as Whitehead and Hartshorne or to the more recent interesting work of Richard Kearney which we will consider in Chapter 9.[4] Even some eminent Thomist philosophers, in dialogue with process theology, propose a development which defends an account of God as really related to the world and, therefore, in a sense, mutable and enriched in virtue of this relationship.[5]

This conception is incompatible with the description of the creator God proposed by Anselm and developed by Aquinas which we have been outlining here, namely, a God envisaged as pure act of infinite perfection. Such a God cannot be in any way passive with respect to the world. For this would imply a limiting co-relativity with the world. If God is changed by what happens in the world he will be simply another component of the world and not its creator. Hence, for Aquinas, God's knowledge of and solicitude for the world should be conceived as identical with his conscious act of creation through which the world exists and endures as a finite participation in his infinite perfection. It is through this relationship of creation, involving no passivity on his part, that God is said to be more intimately present to creatures than they can be to each other. Unlike them he is not to be envisaged as moved from ignorance to

---

3   Cf. Aquinas, *Summa Theologiae*, 1, q. 18, a. 4, ad 3. trans. Blackfriars edn, London, 1964–74 (hereafter *S.T.*).

4   Cf. R. Kearney, *The God Who May Be*, Bloomington, 2001.

5   For example, cf. W. Norris Clarke, *The Philosophical Approach to God*, Winston-Salem, 1979, pp. 66–109 and *Explorations in Metaphysics*, Notre Dame, 1994, pp. 183–210.

World and God 13

knowledge or from indifference to concern.[6] His presence in and concern for them is not as an interactive participant in their affairs them but as the transcendent source of their entire existence and activity.

Undoubtedly, this issue of the co-existence of finite and infinite, of creatures and God, gives rise to many philosophical problems and is a focus of contemporary debate among theists and between theists and atheists. However, the history of modern philosophy suggests that an atheistic conclusion tends to follow as a consequence unless this co-existence is understood in terms which maintain that God's infinite perfection is neither modified, enhanced, nor relativized by the created existence of the finite world. I have argued this point in the concluding chapters of *Atheism and Alienation* and I add some further observations on this issue of the co-existence of God and creation in Chapters 8 and 9 of this work.

In his major works Aquinas devoted detailed attention to the wide range of issues which a full discussion of creation involves. His account has been extensively analyzed and commented upon and I do not propose to re-examine all its various aspects.[7] However, there is one central feature of this account which must be further considered. For in many ways it is the key to the various other aspects of his overall treatment of the topic—and it is crucial to the further argument of this book. This central feature is his insistence that the relationship between creatures and God is a non-mutual real relation. In other words, that there is a real relationship of dependence of creatures upon God but no real relationship of God to creatures. We will begin by briefly situating this idea of the relationship between creatures and God in the context of Aquinas's more general account of the ways in which any objects can be said to be related.[8]

In his discussion of this topic he takes up and develops Aristotle's account of objects which are related as "things that in their very being pertain in some way to something else."[9] They are in some way or condition oriented or ordered towards another. He saw the extra-mental constituents of the world as really related to each other in virtue of their quantitative or qualitative features or their active or passive potencies and thereby establishing the cosmic order or system. He writes that:

> The perfection and good which are in extra-mental things follow not only upon something inhering in things absolutely, but also on the order of one thing toward another, as also the good of an army consists in the order of the parts of the army, for to this order the

---

6   An illuminating development of this theme is to be found in H. McCabe, *God Matters*, London, 1987.

7   Cf., for example, A.D. Sertillanges, *L'Ideé de Creation*, Paris, 1945; R. Swinburne, *The Coherence of Theism*, Oxford,1977; B. Davies, *An Introduction to the Philosophy of Religion*, 3rd edn, Oxford, 2004; D. Turner, *Faith, Reason and the Existence of God*, Cambridge, 2004; R. te Velde, *Aquinas on God*, Aldershot, 2006, and *Participation and Substantiality in Thomas Aquinas*, Leiden, 1995; N. Kretzmann, *The Metaphysics of Theism: Aquinas's Natural Theology in* Summa Contra Gentiles I, Oxford, 1997.

8   On this topic see ch. 2 of the excellent study by M. Henninger, *Relations: Medieval Theories, 1250–1325*, Oxford, 1989.

9   Cf. Aquinas, *Summa Contra Gentiles*, trans. English Dominicans, London, 1924, Bk 2, ch. 12.

14   *The Sense of Creation*

> Philosopher compares the order of the universe. Therefore it is necessary that in those
> (extra-mental) things there be certain relations according to which one (thing) is ordered
> to another.[10]

He would have considered contradictory the notion of an isolated finite individual without any real relationships to anything else. The relationships of things to each other are real features of their being—just as real as their own intrinsic natures. They really exist independently of our knowing or supposing that they do—even though, as we shall see, not every relationship which we affirm, is real in this sense.

A helpful way of speaking about relations and distinguishing between real and "unreal" relations is to say that this distinction is indicated by the consideration that some relational propositions latch onto reality in a way that others do not.[11] Only some propositions predicate a "real" relation. For example, it is natural to view the proposition "Edith envies Herbert" as indicating an actual condition of Edith involving a real relation on her side in a way that it would be unnatural to regard the logically equivalent proposition "Herbert is envied by Edith" as indicating an actual condition of Herbert involving a real relation on his side. This presupposes, contrary to what is sometimes supposed, that relational propositions admit of subject–predicate analysis. As Peter Geach remarks:

> If a relational proposition indeed made no predications about A or B, but only affirmed a
> relation "between" them, then it would be quite unintelligible how, if true, the proposition
> could correspond to a reality in A rather than in B.[12]

For a real relationship to obtain there must be two distinct extra-mental objects in one of which (A) there is a real extra-mental foundation (e.g. this weight, this color, this activity) in respect of which it is oriented towards the other (B). Likewise, where the relationship is mutual, in this other B there is a real extra-mental foundation of the same type (i.e. quantity, quality, active or passive potency) in respect of which it is oriented towards the other object (A).[13] Thus being the husband of a wife, being older than one's daughter, being the artisan of a statue, being the key of a lock are real features of the associated objects and not just our way of considering them. Neither can be affirmed as such without implying the other. Admittedly, their real relationship is an "accidental" feature of their being. The husband's humanity is not identical with being a husband, or his wife's with being a wife. The artisan's humanity is not identical with his being an artisan. Nevertheless, considered not simply as human, but as a husband, a wife, or an artisan, they really pertain to and imply something else which in turn really pertains to and implies them.

Aquinas was well aware that not all relations are like these mutual real relations. Some relations are only relations of reason which are caused by and dependent for

---

10   Aquinas, *De Potentia / On the Power of God*, trans. English Dominicans, London, 1932–4, q. 7, a. 9.

11   Cf. P. Geach, "God's Relation to the World," in *Logic Matters*, Oxford, 1972, p. 318. The whole of this article pp. 318–27 is a valuable contribution to the topic.

12   Ibid., p. 320.

13   Cf. Aquinas, *On the Power of God*, q. 7, a. 10.

World and God 15

their existence upon our minds. A relation is one of reason if (1) one or both terms of the relation are not extra-mental realities, e.g. my relation of temporal priority to future non-existent generations, or the logical relation between the concepts of genus and species; (2) the terms of the relation are not really distinct, e.g. the relation of self-identity of the Eiffel Tower to itself; (3) there is no extra-mental foundation of the relationship, e.g. the claim that A is to the left of B where the affirmed relation depends simply upon my situated viewpoint.[14]

Thus Aquinas distinguishes clearly between mutual real relations and relations of reason. Mutual real relations are those which obtain between distinct exta-mental objects, where the real relationship or orientation of one object (A) to another object (B) implies a correlative relationship of (B) to (A) based on a foundation in each of the same type or order.[15] Relations of reason on the other hand have no reality independent of our minds construction of them. They arise through the activity of a mind instituting a comparison of some kind and when no such comparison is entertained by a mind no relationship obtains.

However, besides the mutual real relationships between extra-mental objects and the relationships of reason instituted by our minds there is another kind of relation, highlighted by Aquinas, and in terms of which he describes the relationship between creatures and God. This is a relation which is real in respect of one of its terms but only a relation of reason in respect of the other. In other words what is involved is a "non-mutual" real relationship. And this, as I have mentioned, is the nature of the relationship which he adduces in his account of creation. Creatures, he argues, are really related to God in a relationship of radical dependence upon him for their being but God is only imagined as, but cannot really be or be truly represented as, reciprocally related to creatures. Thus although it is true both that "God providentially created the world" and that "the world is providentially created by God," only the second of these propositions predicates a "real" relation.[16]

This follows from the conception of God outlined in the previous chapter, according to which, God as infinitely perfect being transcends and is incommensurable with whatever, through his free decision, exists as a created participation in his infinite being. He does not enter into composition or correlation with his creation, nor does this creation in any way enhance his being, or somehow express an alienated aspect of himself.

Because we understand creatures to be really related to God as his dependent creation we naturally imagine him, their creative cause, as reciprocally related to them. But we should understand, in view of the conception of God involved, that the envisaged relationship is only one of reason arising from our usual way of thinking about causes and effects. For in our experience of the finite order of things we usually apprehend real causes and effects as mutually related. Thus Aquinas remarks:

> Since God is altogether outside the order of creatures, since they are ordered to him but not he to them, it is clear that being related to God is a reality in creatures, but being

---

14 Cf. Aquinas, *S.T.*, 1, q. 19, a. 7.

15 Cf. Aquinas, *On the Power of God*, q. 7, a. 10.

16 Cf. Geach, "God's Relation to the World," p. 318.

16 *The Sense of Creation*

related to creatures is not a reality in God. We say it about him because of the real relation in creatures. So it is that, when we speak of his relation to creatures, we can apply words implying temporal sequence and change, not because of any change in him but because of a change in creatures.[17]

This account of the relation between creatures and God highlights the uniquely transcendent nature of God envisaged as creator in the main monotheistic religions of Judaism, Christianity, and Islam. This "non-related" creator of the world is clearly distinguished from the cosmically related deities of paganism and classical philosophy. And although it gives rise to its own issues for topics such as God's knowledge of and interest in his creation (and in particular for an account of the Christian doctrine of incarnation) it is nevertheless the basic perspective from which such topics should be addressed rather than the reverse. For to subordinate the understanding of creation to an initially more attractive view of the co-relative co-existence of finite and infinite will ultimately undermine the religious significance of this co-existence. That this is so is amply illustrated in the development of such an approach in Hegelian philosophy and its consequent dissolution into various forms of atheism.

Although this idea of a non-mutual real relation applies in a very particular sense to creation it is not, for Aquinas, an idea arbitrarily devised to meet just this particular case. It is, he maintains, an idea for which we have some empirical basis. He cites the example of the relationship between our knowing and what we know as an analogical instance of such a non-mutual real relationship.

Knowing, for Aquinas, is an immanent activity, i.e. an activity whose result remains within and enriches the agent who performs it. It differs from transitive activity which results in the modification of something other than the agent, e.g. when a fire heats a kettle of water. This immanent activity of knowing achieves knowledge of something other than itself. By means of this knowledge the knower is really related to this other—to "what is known." But what is known is, as such, related only by reason to the knower, for it is not made or modified by being known. It has a certain non-correlative transcendence or independence of the knowing. What is known is of a different order of reality to the knowledge which is dependent upon it. The knowledge, achieved through a non-material activity of a subject, has intentional (cognitional) reality, the object known has extra-mental natural or physical reality. Contrary to Berkeley's belief its *esse* is not *percipi*. (For Berkeley the being of things consisted in their knowing or being known.) Unlike the real relation of the knower to what is known, the relation of the known to the knower is one of reason whose only basis is the intellect's grasp of the relationship of the act of knowledge to what is known.[18]

Thus, for Aquinas, in this account of knowledge as a non-mutual real relationship between a knower and a known we have an analogical parallel of the non-mutual real relationship between creatures and God. Just as the knower is really related to

---

17 Aquinas, *S.T.*, 1, q. 13, a. 7.

18 Cf. Aquinas, *On the Power of God*, q. 7, a. 10; also *S.T.*, 1, q. 13, a. 7.

World and God

the known but not vice versa, so likewise creatures are really related to God but not vice versa.[19]

One may speak of this transcendence of the object known vis-à-vis the knower as a cipher of the transcendence of God vis-à-vis creation. In subsequent chapters of this book we will consider how this and some other such ciphers of transcendence within experience might be developed into arguments for the existence of God as transcendent creator. However, before doing so we must consider a couple of objections to the enterprise of seeking to develop any argument for the existence of God from such features of our lived experience. The objections maintain that the project of providing such an argument is either unnecessary or altogether misconceived.

The view that such an undertaking is unnecessary is proposed because, it is claimed, the existence of God can be established *a priori*, independently of our lived experience, by an analysis of the implications of our idea of God. In the next chapter we will briefly consider this much discussed view, which is usually referred to, since Kant, as the Ontological Argument.

The view that seeking to provide an argument for the existence of God is radically misconceived is often loosely, and controversially, referred to today as Wittgensteinian Fideism. We will consider this view in Chapter 4.

---

19 Cf. Aquinas, *Quaestiones disputatae de veritate / Truth*, trans. R. Mulligan, Chicago, 1952, q. 4, a. 5.

CHAPTER 3

Idea and Existence of God

The most famous *a priori* argument for the existence of God, of which others are variations in one way or another, is the argument, mentioned in Chapter 1, which was proposed by Anselm in his work *Prosologion* and named by Kant seven centuries later the Ontological Argument. It is an argument which claims that from a true understanding of what is meant by God we can pass directly to an affirmation of his existence. The basic formulation of the argument is provided in chapter 2 of the *Prosologion.* A further refinement is provided in chapter 3 of the same work.

In the basic formulation God is described as that than which nothing greater or more perfect can be conceived. Even the fool who says in his heart there is no God can understand in his mind (*in intellectu*) that this is what is meant by the term "God." Anselm makes a distinction between such existence in the understanding (*in intellectu*) and actual extra-mental existence in reality (*in re*). Actual existence in reality, he remarks, is a greater perfection than existence only in the understanding.

Appreciating this we can (unlike the fool) argue directly from our understanding of God as that than which nothing greater can be conceived to his actual existence (*in re*). For if he did not exist in reality but only in our mind *(in intellectu)* he would lack an important quality or perfection, namely, real extra-mental existence. As such he would not be that than which nothing greater could be conceived. For to exist in reality *and* in the intellect is greater than to exist in the intellect alone. Therefore if, as indeed is the case, God is that than which nothing greater can be conceived, he must exist not only in the mind but also in extra-mental reality. Otherwise we would be in the ridiculous situation of conceiving something greater than that than which nothing greater can be conceived. In Anselm's words:

> That than which a greater cannot be conceived cannot stand only in relation to the understanding. For if it stands at least in relation to the understanding, it can be conceived to be also in reality, and this is something greater. Therefore if "that than which a greater cannot be conceived only stood in relation to the understanding then that than which a greater cannot be conceived" would be something than which a greater can be conceived. But this is impossible. Therefore, something than which a greater cannot be conceived undoubtedly stands both in relation to the understanding and exists in reality.[1]

The refinement in *Prosologion* chapter 3 of this basic formulation of the argument elaborates further the feature of our idea of God as that than which nothing greater can be conceived. It notes that that than which nothing greater can be conceived

---

1   Anselm, *Prosologion*, ch. 2, trans. A. McGill, in *The Many-Faced Argument: Recent Studies on the Ontological Argument for the Existence of God*, ed. J. Hick and A. McGill, London, 1968.

20 *The Sense of Creation*

must be understood to exist, not only in reality as well as in the understanding, but also to exist necessarily and not just as a matter of fact. For what has necessary existence has greater perfection than what just happens to exist but might not have. Therefore, in thinking of God as that than which nothing greater can be conceived we can and should think him to be such that he cannot be conceived not to exist. For to exist in a manner that it is impossible to be thought of as not existing is to be greater than something which we can conceive of as not existing.

Therefore, since God is that than which nothing greater can be conceived he must be conceived to exist necessarily, i.e. such that he cannot not exist. From this his real extra-mental necessary existence follows. For a non-existent necessarily existing perfect being would be a contradiction in terms. To avoid this contradiction we must affirm that the real extra-mental existence of God is implied by our idea of him as necessarily existing perfect being. Anselm again:

> For if that than which a greater cannot be conceived could be conceived not to be we would have an impossible contradiction: that than which a greater cannot be conceived would not be that than which a greater cannot be conceived. Therefore, something than which a greater cannot be conceived so truly is that it is impossible even to conceive of it as not existing.[2]

This refinement of the idea of that than which nothing greater can be conceived focuses on its necessary existence. Stated simply it advances from the claim that the greatest conceivable must exist extra-mentally as do other things such as tables and chairs to the further claim that, unlike these contingent beings, it is such that it cannot not exist. It exists necessarily eternally and independently—unlike the finite contingent realities of our experience. In this way the refinement of *Prosologion* chapter 3 anticipates and refutes the objection of Anselm's fellow-monk Gaunilo who claimed that on Anselm's reasoning one could argue from the idea of the most perfect island to its real existence on the grounds that unless it really existed it would not be the most perfect conceivable island. Anselm's point in *Prosologion* chapter 3 is that the idea of God as that than which nothing greater can be conceived is entirely different to ideas of contingent things which can be conceived of as not existing. For God so envisaged cannot even be conceived not to exist in reality. He must be conceived as existing not just in the mind but also in extra-mental reality, and not just as a contingent fact but in the more perfect manner of necessary existence—of inconceivable non-existence.

Anselm's famous argument has fascinated philosophers throughout the ages and, in various forms, has had its defenders such as Descartes and Leibniz and its critics such as, most notably, Kant. In the twentieth century it enjoyed a revival of interest with defenders such as Barth, Hartshorne, Malcolm, and Plantinga, and critics such as Flew, Findlay, Russell, and Ryle.[3] In this more recent discussion it is the refinement of *Prosologion* chapter 3 which has attracted most attention, i.e. the claim that God as that than which nothing greater can be conceived exists necessarily. Defenders

---

2   Ibid., ch. 3.

3   For a discussion of both defenders and opponents cf. Hick and McGill, *The Many-Faced Argument*, pp. 35–356 and J. Barnes, *The Ontological Argument*, London, 1972.

Idea and Existence of God 21

maintain that this conception not only identifies God uniquely but also shows that his non-existence is inconceivable. Critics have argued that the idea of necessary extra-mental existence is self-evidently absurd since necessity is only a logical property of statements and cannot be a feature of extra-mental existence. Thus J. Findlay remarks:

> It was indeed an ill day for Anselm when he hit upon his famous proof. For on that day he not only laid bare something that is of the essence of an adequate religious object, but also something that entails its necessary non-existence.[4]

This criticism that necessity can only be a logical property of statements and never of an existing reality has been vigorously, and I think rightly, rejected. There is nothing self-evidently meaningless about the idea of a necessarily existing reality understood as one existing eternally and non-dependently. And as Geach remarks:

> since what is "necessary" is what "cannot" not be to say that "necessary" can only refer to logical necessity is equivalent to saying that what cannot be so, *logically* cannot be so—e.g. that since I cannot speak Russian, my speaking Russian is logically impossible: which is absurd.[5]

However, there are other considerations which count against the validity of Anselm's argument. The most common refutation of the argument is one which denies that in saying that something exists one is predicating an additional property or perfection of the thing. One is saying rather that whatever is involved in the concept of the thing is truly predicable of something or other. A real hundred dollars does not *mean* something different to a thought about hundred dollars. It signifies rather that what we mean by a hundred dollars is true of something or other. Similarly if I say that blindness, which is an absence or privation, "exists," I do not signify that it has the attribute of existing. I signify rather that what I mean by blindness is truly predicable of some eyes. Likewise, to say that God exists is not to predicate existence of him but rather to say that "God," however conceived, is truly predicable of something. It remains an open question whether "God," conceived even as necessarily existing, is truly predicable of anything.

I think that this objection can be developed further along lines which concentrate not so much on the issue of whether existence is a predicable attribute. (For "existence" in the technical medieval understanding of *esse* is not simply a univocal term signifying only that some feature is truly predicable of something or other. Understood in the sense of "actuality" it can indeed function as a predicate.)[6] An

---

4   J. Findlay, "Can God's Existence be Disproved?" in *New Essays in Philosophical Theology*, ed. J. Flew and A. MacIntyre, London, 1955, p. 55.

5   P. Geach, "Aquinas," in *Three Philosophers*, Oxford, 1961, p. 114.

6   The verb "to be" is used in two ways: one way signifies the act of existing, the other way signifies the formation of a proposition which the mind accomplishes by uniting predicate to subject. Understood in the first sense we cannot know the existence of God any more than we can know his essence. In the second sense we can because we know that the proposition which we frame about God when we say that he exists is true. And we know this to be true from his effects. (Aquinas, *S. T.*, q. 3, a. 4, ad 2, my trans.) Cf. also, D. Turner, *Faith, Reason and the Existence of God*, Cambridge, 2004, pp. 170–90.

22   *The Sense of Creation*

equally fundamental issue is whether we can be sure *a priori* that the idea of God proposed by Anselm is altogether coherent.

If we could be sure, *a priori* from a consideration of the idea of God as necessarily existing infinite perfection, that this idea is a coherent, positively possible—i.e. non-contradictory, idea—then, I believe, we could say that it does indeed imply the real extra-mental existence of God so conceived. Because if God, conceived as necessarily existent infinitely perfect being does not exist he *could not* exist. For a necessarily existent being is not such that it might or might not exist. Hence, on the supposition that God does not exist, the idea of him as necessarily existent would be a contradictory idea. It would be an idea of what could not be, in other words a contradictory or positively impossible idea.

The idea of God as necessarily existent infinitely perfect being would indeed distinctively and uniquely describe God if it is truly predicable of anything. The difficulty is that we cannot know, *a priori*, by simply considering the idea as such, whether or not this idea is a genuinely non-contradictory idea. In other words, we cannot know *a priori* whether or not it *could* be truly predicable of anything. The Greeks who equated the ideas of being, perfection, and finitude would certainly have considered the idea of an infinitely perfect being contradictory. The proposition describing God as necessarily existing infinite being may indeed, in-itself, be analytically and necessarily true, but we cannot know *a priori* that this is the case. As Aquinas remarks in his discussion of Anselm's argument, the proposition is self-evident in-itself (*per se*) but not to us (*quoad nos*). [7]

The most one can claim *a priori* is that this idea of God is negatively possible, i.e. we do not know whether it is positively possible, i.e. coherent and non-contradictory, or positively impossible, i.e. incoherent and contradictory. We have to *prove* that the heuristic idea of a necessarily existent infinitely perfect being is positively possible, i.e. non-contradictory. In other words we do not prove the existence of God, *a priori*, from the validity of the idea of God. We prove the validity of the idea of God, by proving his existence by *a posteriori* argument from features of our experience.

In subsequent chapters we will consider how such *a posteriori* arguments for the existence of God might be developed. However, before addressing this topic of *a posteriori* arguments, we must appraise an influential contrary approach which, drawing inspiration from the later thought of Wittgenstein, claims that any project of providing a philosophical argument for the existence of God is entirely misconceived.

---

7   Cf. Aquinas, *S.T.*, 1, q. 2, a. 2. This distinction is convincingly defended by M. Dummett in *Frege: Philosophy of Language*, London, 1973, p. 118.

CHAPTER 4

God and Grammar:
Echoes of Wittgenstein

Introduction

An influential approach to the question of the existence of God is one which maintains that it is a serious mistake to think that an affirmation of his existence can be independently justified by rational or philosophical argument. This, it is claimed, involves a radical misconception of the true significance of an affirmation of God. It implies that the affirmation is of an additional being beyond the range of ordinary experience for which a rational person would rightly demand supporting evidence by way of argument which did not beg the existence of the being in question. However, the truth of the matter, according to the view under consideration, is that the logic of an affirmation of God precludes such evidence.

The person who appreciates this fact, it is claimed, will confine discussion of the existence of God to its role within the religious form of life and language where alone it makes sense. The speculative or philosophical vindication of this approach will consist chiefly in arguing the inappropriateness of seeking a philosophical justification or proof for an affirmation of the existence of God. One would insist that one's affirmation was uncompromisingly and exclusively a religious affirmation of the God of Abraham, of Isaac, and Jacob, the God of Jesus Christ or of Mohammed, and not at all the problematic God of philosophy.

This view is representative of a Protestant theological tradition espoused, for example, by Kierkegaard and Barth, which (because of a certain conception of grace and human nature) mistrusts the claims of natural theology and insists on the indispensability of the gift of faith for knowledge of the existence of God. However, it is also representative of an Anglo-Saxon style of philosophy of religion in the latter half of the twentieth century which claims inspiration from the later thought of Wittgenstein. (It is sometimes known as Wittgensteinian Fideism but this designation has been vigorously repudiated by at least one of its principal proponents, D.Z. Phillips, whose views we consider later in this chapter.)[1] It is a view which maintains that the affirmation of God is a function of involvement in or commitment to a religious form of life which establishes its own internal criteria of rationality but which is logically unamenable to any external assessment or confirmation. It is with philosophers from this latter school of thought that this chapter is concerned (although interesting parallels could be drawn with contemporary continental post-

---

1   Cf. D.Z. Phillips, *Belief, Change and Forms of Life*, London, 1986, ch. 1. and *Religion and the Hermeneutics of Contemplation*, Cambridge, 2001.

24 *The Sense of Creation*

modern thought).Their views are well exemplified in the proceedings of a conference sponsored by the Royal Institute of Philosophy entitled *Reason and Religion*.[2]

Exponents of this view include N. Malcolm, C. Lyas, D.Z. Phillips, and P. Winch. Its guiding inspiration is the Wittgensteinian suggestion that many seemingly deep problems are not metaphysical issues about what really exists or how things are but rather conceptual problems about appropriate linguistic usage. In the case of theistic beliefs or assertions it is argued that such beliefs are intrinsically but non-problematically groundless and are to be understood as primarily grammatical rather than ontological assertions. We will consider these aspects of groundlessness and grammar in turn.

Groundless Belief—Malcolm and Lyas

A forthright defense of the non-problematic groundlessness of theistic beliefs is provided by Norman Malcolm.[3] His strategy is to indicate that there is nothing exceptional about claiming that religious beliefs are groundless since most of our important beliefs are similarly groundless and it is merely a malaise of thought which impels us to seek grounds and justifications which are both unnecessary and unavailable.

Nobody is surprised at the way in which children accept what they are told without asking for grounds. It is less commonly appreciated that fundamental beliefs of our adult lives are equally groundless. Consider, for example, our belief that familiar material things, such as watches, shoes, and wallets, do not cease to exist without some physical explanation, even though we all have had the experience of things getting lost and not turning up again. One could imagine a society which held the opposite belief, namely, that things occasionally "vanish into thin air." Each of the views is compatible with ordinary experience. But the theories and practice of the two groups would be significantly different. The second group would differ from ourselves, for example, in their attachment to things, in their persistence in searching, in their appraisal of evidence of theft, in their attitude to experiments.

Although the different beliefs have such very different consequences, we never try to support with grounds our fundamental conviction that things don't simply cease to exist without trace. It is tacitly accepted as an unquestioned element of the fundamental framework of our thinking about material things. Such frameworks or systems provide the boundaries *within* which we form hypotheses, conduct tests, and seek grounds. They are not invented or proved. They are conveyed to us through assimilation into a human community. They form the way in which we think. They do not rise or fall on the basis of evidence or grounds. "We are taught, or we absorb, the system within which we raise doubts, make enquiries, draw conclusions. We grow into a framework. We don't question it. We accept it trustingly."[4]

Malcolm cites various other examples of groundless fundamental beliefs such as our belief in the continuity of nature, the validity of mathematical calculation,

---

2   S. Brown (ed.), *Reason and Religion*, Ithaca and London, 1977.

3   Cf. N. Malcolm, "The Groundlessness of Belief," in Brown, *Reason and Religion*, pp. 143–59.

4   Ibid., p. 147.

the reliability of our images and feelings, the basic trustworthiness of science. In view of such pervasive acceptance of groundless belief there should be nothing surprising or disconcerting about the claim that religious belief is also an instance of groundless belief. However, here perhaps even more than with other language games the pathological urge for justification makes itself felt—as evidenced by the preoccupation with "proofs" for the existence of God.

This obsessive concern with proofs reveals the assumption that for religious belief to be intellectually respectable it *ought* to have a rational justification. *That* is the misunderstanding. It is like the idea that we are not justified in relying on memory until memory has been proved reliable.[5] Religious belief is a perspective on reality which is not like a hypothesis for or against which evidence can be marshaled. We cannot prove its truth to others, we can only invite them to share the vision and nurture it by illuminating examples, In brief: "religion is a form of life, it is a language embedded in action—what Wittgenstein called a 'language game'. Science is another. Neither stands in need of justification, the one no more than the other."[6]

Colin Lyas argues, more circumspectly, that Malcolm's claim needs to be refined since he tends to fudge the obvious assertion that we have beliefs for which we *do not in fact* seek grounds, with the far less obvious assertion that such grounds *could not* be sought because to attempt to do so would be to misunderstand the nature of the beliefs. However, Lyas agrees that there are groundless beliefs in this stronger conceptual sense and that religious theistic belief is arguably a case in point.

Before discussing the groundless nature of theistic belief he indicates how in science we also encounter groundless framework principles. To elucidate this point he distinguishes amongst the framework principles of science between *constitutive* principles and *regulative* principles. The former are formal principles which articulate what it means to engage in rational empirical enquiry. They include principles such as "It is wrong to ignore the results of a properly conducted experiment," "If there is a contradiction in a scientific theory it is worthless." To call such principles into question is to call science itself into question.

The regulative framework principles are of more material import and signify basic principles which scientists accept, operate with, and by which they regulate their activities. As possible examples he cites "Nature is continuous," "Things don't just disappear." One can envisage changes in such principles without calling science as such into question. Such changes would amount to fundamental theoretical innovations *within* science rather than a change in the very meaning of science. Such changes, when they occur do not do so groundlessly and likewise the regulative principles involved are not wholly independent of any possible justification. By contrast, the constitutive framework principles of science "are groundless in that our only reply when asked to justify them is that without them justification makes no sense. They are what 'justification' means."[7]

---

5   Cf. ibid., pp. 154–5.

6   Ibid., p. 156.

7   C. Lyas, "The Groundlessness of Religious Belief," in Brown, *Reason and Religion*, p. 169.

26 *The Sense of Creation*

In the light of this distinction between constitutive and regulative framework principles Lyas turns his attention to a consideration of why one might come to a conclusion that religious belief is groundless. He begins by discussing why a religious belief might be characteristically such that "it not merely *does not*, but *could not*, rise or fall on the basis of grounds or evidence and *could not* later be withdrawn in the light of new evidence."[8] He suggests that this could be so because a genuinely theistic religious belief is distinctively such that it enables one to respond to the vicissitudes and contingency of the world with an assurance that one has recourse to a source of security, which comes to one not from anything in oneself or the world, and which guarantees one's safety whatever may happen in the world.

Such a belief could not be a belief merely in the *probable* existence of God based on the indications of worldly evidence. For, if God only probably exists, it might turn out that there is no God and then one would not be adequately secured from the vicissitudes of what might happen. Moreover, if a person's religious belief is based upon evidence, he must allow that other evidence might come to his attention which could change his belief and leave him once again at the mercy of events. Hence, if religious belief is such as has been described, attempts to produce evidence for the probable existence of God involve a conceptual misconception of what believers themselves take to be involved in religious belief.

For Lyas, if one's belief is in a *religiously adequate* God, then there are certain constraints upon what one can say when speaking about God. One is precluded from coherently attempting to establish by indirect evidence the probable existence of a religiously adequate God. For such evidencing procedures could not yield an affirmation of God such as he is envisaged in religion, namely, a certain and assured basis for one's life which does not depend on anything that might exist or happen in the world. One cannot maintain *both* that a religiously adequate God must be such as has been described *and* that adducing indirect evidence for his probable existence is an appropriate activity. One might say that the affirmation of God is a groundless constitutive framework principle of religion in the sense that to seek argued justification of the affirmation is incompatible with what is envisaged in religion.

Lyas's discussion highlights the way in which a believer's affirmation of God might be considered chiefly from a conceptual or grammatical point of view. Moreover, it suggests how the grammar of a religiously adequate affirmation of God might be invoked to support the claim that such an affirmation is necessarily groundless. Central to Lyas's presentation is the view that all so-called indirect theistic proofs are at best probabilistic and therefore fall short of a religiously adequate affirmation of God who must be envisaged as the unquestionably reliable source of ultimate security.

However, a theist might dispute either the antecedent or the consequent of this contention. He might dispute the antecedent by questioning the, admittedly prevalent, presumption that all theistic proofs are at best probabilistic. Thus he might argue that we can by indirect argument have *certain* knowledge of the existence of God as religiously conceived. On the other hand, he might dispute the consequent by arguing that even a probabilistic proof is not *ipso facto* only an argument for what

---

8   Ibid., pp. 172–3.

might not exist and therefore not be adequately trustworthy. For, as Basil Mitchell has pointed out, such a proof even if it did not place the existence of God beyond all doubt could nevertheless put a person's mind at rest that he had good reason to believe in the absolutely trustworthy God envisaged in religion:

> Should there, after all, be no God, as remains for him logically possible, his peace will, indeed, have proved illusory; but it would not then follow that the God he believed in was not trustworthy, even necessarily trustworthy; only that the trustworthy God he believed in did not exist.[9]

Grammar—Phillips and Winch

A view similar to that of Lyas concerning the groundlessness of theistic belief, based upon grammatical considerations, is proposed by D.Z. Phillips, one of the most articulate proponents of the Wittgensteinian turn in philosophy of religion.[10] He argues that whether there is a God is not something anyone could find out by way of arriving at a matter of fact answer. God's existence is not a matter of fact which might conceivably not have been. It therefore cannot be established as though it were a matter of fact. It makes no sense to envisage God's existence as either a fact or not a fact to which some process of rational argument might be relevant in deciding which alternative is true.

The question of the reality of God is a question of the possibility of sense and nonsense, truth and falsity *in religion.* The criteria of what can sensibly be said of God can be found only within religion. It is a mistake to look for external reasons for believing in God as though one could settle the question of his existence without referring to the religious form of life of which belief in God is a fundamental part.

Philosophy can explore the meaningfulness of talk about God only by reference to the presupposed context of religion and "religious reactions to various situations cannot be assessed according to some external criterion of adequacy." [11] In coming through religion to see that there is a God one does not come to see that an additional being exists whose existence might be independently established. One comes rather to see a new meaning in one's life and to attain a new kind of understanding. Discovering that there is a God is not like establishing that something exists within a familiar universe of discourse. It is rather a discovery of a new universe of discourse. We must not impose an alien conception of rationality on religious discourse nor assume that the distinction between the real and the unreal comes to the same in every context. We must not suppose that God's reality is to be construed as an existent amongst existents. As Kierkegaard put it: "God does not exist. He is eternal."

---

9   B. Mitchell, "Remarks," in Brown, *Reason and Religion,* p. 185.

10   His exposition of this approach is only implicit in his contribution to this conference where he discusses the problem of evil. It is more fully developed in his other writings e.g. in D.Z. Phillips, *Faith and Philosophical Enquiry*, London, 1970 and *Belief, Change and Forms of Life*.

11   Phillips, *Belief, Change and Form of Life*, p. 12.

28   *The Sense of Creation*

Seeing that there is a God is synonymous with seeing the possibility of eternal love. If one rises above the dimensions of contingent temporal love such as self-love, erotic love, and friendship to an acknowledgment that there is an eternal love which will not let one go whatever happens, one thereby attains the affirmation of God. In the context of religion, which is the only one appropriate to a discussion of God, belief, understanding, and love can be equated. What it means to affirm the reality of God can only be apprehended in and through the context of a lived religious commitment to eternal love. Such commitment precludes any distinction between the commitment and the grounds for the commitment.

For Phillips the arguments of natural theology are both irrelevant and potentially misleading. They are neither a necessary theoretical basis for a subsequent commitment, nor a means of establishing the possibility of God. The commitment has an absolute priority and it is through it alone that the reality of God is attained. The truths of theistic discourse arise within a religious form of life and it is a mistake to look for philosophical argument which would establish their truth or even their possible truth. It is a basic mistake to suppose that "the relation between religious beliefs and the non-religious facts is that between what is justified and its justification, or that between a conclusion and its grounds."[12]

There are no trans-field criteria of rationality through which the truths of theistic discourse, which arise only in religion, could be evaluated. They can be fully understood and assessed only through an insider's grasp of the religious form of life of which they are a part. "Religious language is not an interpretation of how things are but determines how things are for the believer."[13] There can be no philosophical justification of commitment to God outside the religious form of life of which it is a part.

Further interesting developments of this viewpoint are provided by Peter Winch in an article entitled "Meaning and Religious Language."[14] Winch's aim is to undermine the view that a religious belief is lacking in meaning and rationality unless it involves theological presuppositions which commit the believer to verifiable or at least falsifiable existential claims. He suggests that, rather than seeking to explain religious belief and practice in terms of belief in the truth of certain theological doctrines or presuppositions, such doctrines or presuppositions should be understood in the context of their application within the more fundamental and autonomous domain of religious worship and practice. Religious worship and practice, involving certain characteristic uses of language, is a primitive human response to certain distinctive human situations and predicaments. The application of theological doctrines must be understood within the context, and within the grammatical constraints of the language of such worship and practice. It would be a mistake to understand them as articulating *a theory* about the nature of the world to which one is committed by one's religious practice and language.[15]

But how can any sense be made of religious practices and beliefs unless their adherents are committed to certain theoretical, theological presuppositions? For

---

12 Phillips, *Faith and Philosophical Enquiry*, p. 101.
13 Ibid., p. 101.
14 Cf. ibid., pp. 193–221.
15 Cf. ibid., p. 201.

example, surely praying to God presupposes that there is a God to pray to, just as sending a petitionary letter to the ambassador of Yugoslavia presupposes that such a person really exists. (Winch's article was written when there still were Yugoslav ambassadors!)

Winch argues that this analogy is misleading because there is a difference in grammar between "asking something of God" and "asking something of the Yugoslav ambassador." There are internal connections of a sort obtaining between ceasing to believe in God's existence and ceasing to see any point in prayer which do not obtain between ceasing to believe in the ambassador's existence and ceasing to see any point in writing to him. To question the existence of the Yugoslav ambassador does imply questioning the point of sending letters to him but not the general practice of sending letters. Moreover, questioning the point of writing *to him* is more a *consequence* of independently ceasing to believe in his existence, than an *aspect* of ceasing to believe. In the case of God, however, reflection which may lead to a cessation of belief in his existence cannot be separated from ceasing to see the point of prayer and worship. For these are the terms in which reflection on God's existence must take place since they constitute the context within which an affirmation of God finds its application. Seeing or ceasing to see any point in prayer and worship are *constitutive aspects* of believing or ceasing to believe in God.[16]

Winch acknowledges that his opponent might, nevertheless, rightly insist on the importance of confronting religious beliefs with reality if we are to avoid insulating such beliefs from any relation to ordinary life or to our understanding of the world. However, he insists that such confrontation with reality must not be represented in terms of adducing evidence for God's existence or non-existence. The world of experience has a bearing on religious belief by way of the factual circumstances in which religious language is applied. These include general facts such as the conditions of dependence of people upon nature and upon each other, and more "internal" facts such as the varied responses which may be elicited when religious language is used, say, in encounter with affliction. This does not mean that the expression "God" refers to such facts but rather that the reality which it expresses is to be found in the conditions of its application. He quotes approvingly Simone Weil's remark: "Earthly things are the criterion of spiritual things ... Only spiritual things are of value, but only physical things have a verifiable existence. Therefore the value of the former can only be verified as an illumination projected onto the latter."[17]

To further illustrate his point he refers to the relationship between geometry and the properties of spatial objects. Thus, although terms as used in geometry such as "circle" and "triangle" do not describe the properties of empirical structures, they do have application in such descriptions and make possible ways of thinking and techniques (e.g. of measurement) in dealing with them which would not otherwise be possible. Their relation to reality consists in this application rather than in being a description of some other non-empirical realm of reality. Winch writes:

---

16 Cf. ibid., pp. 206–9.
17 S. Weil, *First and Last Notebooks*, London, 1970, p. 147.

Religious uses of language equally, I want to say, are not descriptions of an "order of reality" distinct from the earthly life with which we are familiar .... These uses of language do, however, have an application in what religious people say and do in the course of their life on earth and this is where their "relation to reality" is to be sought.[18]

When we speak of God's power of love or goodness as infinite or incapable of failing we are not extrapolating from some empirical experience of these qualities to their realization in the nth degree (n =infinity), any more than to think (geometrically) of perfect sphericity is to make an extrapolation from an experience of very finely produced ball bearings. Rather, we are making a conceptual or grammatical move in each case. Such moves enable us to articulate a standard from the point of view of which features of experience may be assessed and come to terms with. In each move there will be repercussions on how we speak and act in connection with, say, human power and love or the sphericity of ball bearings. But in neither move are we dealing with mere extrapolations from the original empirical observations which suggested the moves.

According to Winch, one can indicate how the "grammatical" conception of God as all powerful and good—carrying with it the idea that to him and to him only we owe absolute obedience—has various applications to earthly situations. Thus it may qualify our conception of the obedience due to earthly authorities. Or it may induce us to approach moral questions and enterprises in a very different spirit to, say, that of utilitarianism. It may lead us to adopt trustingly a demanding course of action which goes beyond that warranted by a balancing of likely consequences. It is in such circumstances involving the application of the notions of God's infinite power and goodness that we come to see the point of the "necessity" with which such notions are predicated of God.[19]

The upshot of Winch's argument is that a proper philosophical appraisal of religious discourse will disclose that its "relation to reality" is to be understood in terms of its application within lived experience rather than in terms of its reference to a problematic "different order of reality" beyond such experience. This is not, he assures us, to deny that the believer may in the expression of his belief have recourse naturally and unconfusedly to expressions such as "a different reality," "a higher reality" or "not of this world." For religious rituals and practices characteristically involve a demeanor of worship, detachment, and reverence which in a way marks them off from everyday secular activities, even though their ultimate aim is to achieve a fundamental perspective on such activities. However, it is up to the philosopher or speculative theologian to show that what is at issue in the use of such expressions is their proper application in our this-worldly lives in accordance with the grammar of religious discourse, rather than their reference to some mysterious non-empirical entities.

---

18 P. Winch, "Meaning and Religious Language," in Brown, *Reason and Religion*, p. 214.
19 Cf. ibid., pp. 216–19.

Remarks

The Wittgensteinian "family resemblances" between the views of the four writers described above are apparent. They are chiefly twofold. Firstly, that it is a misconceived venture to seek a philosophical proof or argument for the affirmation of God, which is seen rather as an un-problematically groundless belief attained only through a religious form of life. Secondly, that the groundlessness of such belief is to be understood in terms of certain conceptual or grammatical considerations rather than in terms of metaphysical accounts of what really or actually exists. Malcolm and Lyas tend to highlight the theme of the groundlessness of the affirmation of God whereas Phillips and Winch emphasize the conceptual and grammatical considerations.

It is this latter theme which is of particular interest and which gives a distinctive inflection to the associated theme of groundlessness. For whereas there is nothing particularly new or disconcerting for a traditional theist about the claim that the existence of God cannot be established by philosophical argument, the defense of the claim in terms of grammatical considerations has far-reaching consequences which constitute a serious challenge to the traditional understanding of Judaeo-Christian theistic belief. It is important, therefore, to appreciate why this is so and to discuss the adequacy of the grammatical approach.

One principal misgiving about the grammatical approach as elucidated by Phillips and Winch is that it appears to call in question the transcendent and independently possessed being of God. Thus, for Phillips, coming to see that God exists is not a matter of coming to see that an additional being exists but rather of coming to see a new meaning in one's life.[20] Similarly, Winch insists that "religious uses of language … are not descriptions of an order of reality distinct from the earthly life with which we are familiar."[21]

A traditional monotheist could agree with Phillips that it is a mistake to affirm God as an extra being on a par with the finite beings of our experience. But this would not be because the affirmation is a matter of seeing a new meaning in life, but rather because the divine being as infinite must be understood as being of an essentially different order of perfection to that of the finite realities of our experience. Likewise, he would agree with Winch that a religious affirmation of God has connections with earthly life but would emphatically deny that it is not about a transcendent order of reality distinct from this life.

If then ordinary or traditional monotheistic language characteristically involves the affirmation of God as an independently existing reality, it would seem that the "grammatical" account of such language is inadequate and even incorrect. For on this account such an affirmation appears to be called in question.

However, Winch claims to meet this objection by observing that it is not so much the expressions that believers use which he disputes as a particular philosophical or theological interpretation of them. Thus he admits that, in expressing their beliefs, believers very naturally use expressions such as "a different reality" and "not of this

---

20   Cf. Phillips, *Faith and Philosophical Enquiry*, pp. 17–18.

21   Winch, "Meaning and Religious Language," p. 214.

32   *The Sense of Creation*

world," since religion is characteristically an activity of reverential detachment from everyday preoccupations in order to see them in ultimate perspective. His objection is to the theoretical elaboration which tends to ontologize or reify the force of such expressions by taking them to refer to the nature or properties of some independently existing divine entity. (There are interesting similarities between this objection and post-modern critique of onto-theology which we consider in Chapter 9.)

Instead he offers an account which claims to reformulate the true content of religious language in its appropriate philosophical, i.e. grammatical, form. He is not, he claims, repudiating ordinary religious language. Nor, he would say, is he repudiating its philosophical or theological elaboration as such, but only their misleading metaphysical versions. These he replaces with the proper sort of philosophical and theological approach to religious language, i.e. philosophy and theology as grammar. This approach by disclosing the proper application within religious discourse of expressions such as "a higher reality" puts out of play, at the level of critical reflection, the misleading and inappropriate application of them to refer to an independently existing transcendent being.

This is a neat solution and one reminiscent of Hegel's reformulation of ordinary religious language about God into the appropriate philosophical idiom of Absolute Spirit. However, doubts concerning its adequacy remain and the grounds upon which it rests need to be examined more closely. For it may transpire that what is involved is not so much a greater sensitivity to the logic of religious discourse but rather a restrictive limitation of such discourse arising from the constraints of a particular philosophical viewpoint.

The central thesis in the grammatical approach is the important insight that if we want to understand how theistic discourse is related to reality we should begin by examining its actual application in the life of the believer rather than by focusing our attention primarily on the question of the existence of a divine entity supposedly referred to by it. It is reasonable to maintain that the primary context of the application of such discourse is that of religion, in which the believer seeks to articulate a salvific resolution of the mystery and paradoxes of his lived experience. Thus before it is an object of detached philosophical appraisal the affirmation of God is a self-involving religious affirmation with profound implications for the believer in terms of attitude and action. The affirmation latches onto reality by making ultimate sense of his world or, as Winch remarks, it serves to "articulate a standard from the point of view of which the disorder and wretchedness which so largely characterise human life in its fundamental aspects may be assessed and come to terms with."[22]

This being so, one can appreciate the philosophical grammarian's contention that reflection on a religiously adequate God must take the form of reflection on existential concern, prayer, worship, and the like, since it is primarily in such contexts of experience that the affirmation of his existence has application. These are the contexts which condition and give point to the affirmation of God.

However, to this claim it can be responded that an affirmation of God, even if prompted by phenomena such as existential concern, worship, and prayer, and even granted that it must be such that it can find application in these contexts, must

---

22   Ibid., p. 221.

nevertheless be understood to involve something more—a more fundamental reality reference.

More generally, I would say that to know the meaning of an affirmation is to know its truth conditions (i.e. what would have to obtain for it to be deemed true) and that in formulating the truth conditions of some affirmations one can distinguish between their application conditions and their theoretical truth conditions. The application conditions are, broadly speaking, the empirical states of affairs which must obtain if the affirmation is to be true. The theoretical truth conditions are the non-observational states of affairs which must obtain if the affirmation is to be true. Thus, for example, one could say that the application conditions of the Ptolemaic system of astronomy are that the relative position of the planets observable at different times are found to conform to the predictions of the system. A theoretical truth condition would be that a geocentric state of affairs obtains. A different system of astronomy, e.g. the Copernican, could have the same application conditions but would have different non-observational truth conditions.

In the case of the affirmation of God, quite apart from appreciating that its application conditions require that it be internally related to assertions about phenomena such as existential concern, worship, and prayer, there is the further issue of its theoretical truth conditions which refer to the non-observational requirements of the truth of the affirmation. Traditional theism sees this issue as committing the believer to a different theory about the nature of the world from that to which an unbeliever would subscribe—a theory involving the dependence of the world upon the higher and independently possessed reality of God.

Philosophical grammarians such as Phillips and Winch are at pains to deny that such a theoretical commitment is involved. Thus although Winch admits that one whose thoughts are couched in religious language has, in a sense, a very different *view* of the world from one who does not think in this way, he explicitly denies that this amounts to accepting an alternative *theory* about the world, involving a description of an "order of reality" distinct from the earthly life with which we are familiar.[23] Likewise according to Phillips, "to say that God created the world would not be to put forward a theory, hypothesis, or explanation of the world."[24] Even more explicitly he insists: "Religious language is not an interpretation of how things are, but determines how things are for the believer. The saint and the atheist do not interpret the same world in different ways. They see different worlds."[25]

Inasmuch as the affirmation of God is thus understood in terms of "having a view of" in explicit distinction from "accepting a theory about" the world, it is problematic what existential significance should be ascribed to the affirmation. Perhaps the most benign interpretation is that it connotes a commitment to live in and regard the world of experience in all its factual circumstances *as though* it were a divine creation but eschewing any affirmation (or denial) of God as an independently existing reality. As Winch puts it, whatever his existence amounts to is expressed in the way people apply the language they speak in activities such as worship, prayer, and interpersonal

---

23 Cf. ibid, pp. 201, 203 and 214.

24 Phillips, *Faith and Philosophical Enquiry*, p. 56.

25 Ibid., p. 132.

34 *The Sense of Creation*

relationships.[26] Likewise Phillips observes that when he speaks of religion as turning away from temporal powers towards the eternal, he is not making an epistemological claim but referring to the way in which the concept of the eternal can play a role in very many human relationships.[27]

However, this bracketing of the issue of God's independent existence by substituting an "attitudinal" or "viewpoint" theory of belief-related sentences, which restricts their range of reference to the circumstances of their empirical application, is not, in the final analysis, satisfactory. At least it is not satisfactory as an account of what most religious believers have traditionally meant and still mean by their theistic assertions. An impartial survey of what believers actually mean when they affirm the existence of God would surely confirm that more is involved than articulating a particular viewpoint from which human life in its fundamental aspects must be assessed and come to terms with. As reflectively articulated and practically applied in prayer, worship, and the like, the ordinary believer's affirmation of God is of a really existing infinite and transcendent personal creator of the universe of finite beings which stand in a real relationship of absolute dependence upon him. We are motivated to pray because we believe in God and not vice versa.

This traditional account of God and the world is intended as an affirmation of what actually exists, of how things really are, whether or not somebody adopts this viewpoint, believes it, recognizes it, or is committed to its being so. Thus the affirmation of God involves the assertion that although the finite beings by which he is known cannot be without him, he would nevertheless exist if they did not and must be affirmed as existing independently of their reality and of being known by them.

This account of the affirmation of God—leaving aside the issue of how such an affirmation might be justified—certainly has the sort of attitudinal implications of which Phillips and Winch speak. But it also has theoretical implications which they deny. Thus not only is it incompatible with certain existential claims, for example, the claim that only empirical things exist. It also comprises positive existential assertions about the independent existence and nature of God, which clearly mark it off from other theories about the world.

Perhaps, it may be replied, the grammatical approach does not so much wish to deny these existential implications as to bracket them, or put them (phenomenologically?) out of play as involving an *unnecessary* metaphysical complication of the meaningfulness of religious belief. These existential implications involve, it might be argued, problems of verification and awkward confrontations with other general theories about the world which it would be better to avoid if possible. What further meaning or reference is required for an affirmation of God than that it embodies effectively a viewpoint in accordance with which people can live a life invested with a sense of ultimate meaning and value? The affirmation is internally related to the life of the believer as that which, in Lyas's words, "makes him safe whatever happens in the world."

On this view to affirm the existence of God is simply to affirm that life can be lived most meaningfully if lived in accordance with the outlook or response that

---

26 Cf. Winch, "Meaning and Religious Language," p. 200.

27 Cf. Phillips, *Faith and Philosophical Enquiry*, p. 21.

God and Grammar: Echoes of Wittgenstein 35

it is under the providence of a loving creator. His existence shows itself—not in the form of an impersonal metaphysical truth about a divine being—but through its profoundly illuminating congruity with the deepest exigencies of our life. It shows itself, for example, as the appropriate elaboration and concomitant, *though not explanation*, of worship which, according to Winch "is a primitive human response to certain characteristic human situations and predicaments ... part of the natural history of mankind."[28] Those who see the issue in this light will recognize the inappropriateness of formulating the question of God's existence in impersonal theoretical terms.

However, notwithstanding the sophisticated simplicity of this anti-metaphysical approach to the meaningfulness of an affirmation of God, certain objections still remain. Firstly, there is the objection that in consciously putting the metaphysical issue of God's independent existence out of play, one is not really leaving it an undecided and open question but rather implicitly deciding it in a way which poses a formidable threat to the coherence of any affirmation of God. It can be argued that a similar difficulty presents itself in the phenomenological tradition of philosophy where the phenomenological *epoché* claims to merely put into parentheses the independent existence of the objective world by considering it simply as it appears to consciousness.[29] The difficulty is that the seeming impartiality of this transcendental-phenomenological reduction vis-à-vis the alternatives of realism and idealism may in fact involve an implicit judgment in favor of idealism. The difficulty becomes acute, as we shall argue in Chapter 9, in a phenomenology of religion where, as in the case of the grammatical approach which we are considering, the meaning of an affirmation of God is insulated from the question of his independent existence.

The grammatical approach, by precluding theoretical assertions about God's ontological status and interpreting the affirmation exclusively in terms of its application conditions in human experience, provokes the objection that it is excessively anthropocentric. For if one precludes the traditional claim that religious beliefs, such as belief in the existence of God, are true or false in an impersonal way one seems committed as S. Brown remarks, to making their truth "dependent on there being people who are able to hold them and to whose lives such a belief would have a relevance."[30] Now, whereas it is uninterestingly obvious that the *recognition* of the truth of such beliefs is dependent upon there being people who recognize them, it is an altogether different matter to claim that the truths themselves are so dependent. Would the truth cease to obtain if there had been no natural history of mankind or if this natural history had been different—if there were no people or even if people ceased to hold the belief or experience its relevance? If so, what defense would there be against an objection, such as that of Merleau-Ponty, that theological discourse is inherently mercurial to the point that one can never be sure whether it is God who sustains men in their human reality or vice versa, since his existence is

---

28 P. Winch, *Reason and Religion*, p. 202.

29 Cf. E. Husserl, *Cartesian Meditations,* trans. D. Cairns, The Hague, 1960, pp. 18–23.

30 S. Brown, "Religion and the Limits of Language,", *Reason and Religion*, pp. 246–7.

36 *The Sense of Creation*

affirmed only via their own.[31] In other words is the grammatical approach not just another version of anthropocentric reductionism?

Exponents of the approach would vigorously deny the charge of reductionism and certainly they are not reductionist in the way that Feuerbach or Marx or Freud are expressly so. Indeed they would argue that they are defenders of the specifically religious character of theistic discourse against certain reductive tendencies of philosophy and science. They would not accept that the God who is acknowledged as the object of religious worship can be adequately envisaged as a projection, extrapolation, or useful fiction. Thus Winch insists that the believer's conception of God carries with it the idea that we owe him an absolute obedience and that where an act has the character of being done out of obedience to God's will, care for the good rests with the one who commands, not with the will of the one who obeys.[32]

Likewise for Lyas, it is characteristic of a theistic response that those who make it not merely find a way of coming to terms with the world's contingency but feel themselves to have a source of security that comes *to* them and not from them or anything in the world.[33] And for Phillips, the reality of God, attained in activities of contemplation, thanking, living, and the like, is independent of the believer, not indeed as a separate biography but "independent of the believer in that the believer measures his life against it."[34]

Such sentiments indicate that exponents of the grammatical approach wish to acknowledge the receptivity and dependence of mankind vis-à-vis the reality of God and to deny that this reality is ultimately identical with that of man or of the world.

However, there remains the difficulty: can they coherently hold this position while at the same time precluding any meta-anthropological or metaphysical statements about the existence and nature of God such as the one we have just noted Phillips explicitly denying, namely, that God's independent reality is that of an independent separate biography? If the religious affirmation of God is an affirmation of him as effectively operative in a person's life—as a source of grace and security, which as Lyas puts it, the believer maintains comes *to* him not *from* him—then surely the believer is committed, whether or not he realizes it, to an account of the ontological status of God and his activity. He is committed to some idea of the ontological state of affairs which must obtain if this religiously crucial affirmation of God is to be true rather than false, illusory, or meaningless.

An unreflecting believer may not advert to or elaborate the ontology implicit in his religious belief in God as the worshipful standard which measures and sustains his life. But it is an entirely different matter, once this topic of God's own ontological status is raised as an issue by reflective consciousness, to reject it or put it out of play as unnecessary or misguided. For to do so inevitably exerts pressure on the initial belief and provokes critical enquiry concerning just what kind of reality is to be attributed to the God affirmed by the believer. Nor at this point is it an adequate reply to the charge of anthropocentric reductionism simply to reiterate that the divine

---

31 Cf. M. Merleau-Ponty, *Éloge de la philosophie*, Paris, 1953, p. 38.

32 Cf. Winch, *Reason and Religion*, pp. 216 and 218.

33 Cf. Lyas, "The Groundlessness of Religious Belief," p. 174.

34 D.Z. Phillips, *Death and Immortality*, London, 1970, p. 55.

God and Grammar: Echoes of Wittgenstein

reality is affirmed from a viewpoint which envisages it as a source of security and grace which comes *to* man and as not identical with him. For the question remains, how can it be such if one does not allow the legitimacy of any statement about its mode of reality other than those which express it in terms of relationships which correspond to the exigencies of human experience?

If from the religious viewpoint the divine reality can be legitimately spoken of only in terms of its bearing upon the human condition, then the assertion that he is envisaged as a supervenient source of grace and support is inadequate to allay the suspicion that whatever his reality amounts to it is dependent upon that of man. For, as R. Bambrough points out, whereas it is true that activities such as worship and prayer are modes of intentionality which require an object, it can be asked "do they require merely 'grammatical' objects—internal accusatives—or is it envisaged that these emotions are directed at something external to and independent of human beings?"[35] If the former, then the divine reality is more plausibly interpreted idealistically as a function of man's inherent capacity or natural tendency to constitute for himself an object of consciousness, which appears to the intentionality of believing consciousness as a given ideal in accordance with which he can regulate his life. If the latter, then some ontological account, in terms of theoretical or metaphysical truth conditions of the divine object envisaged as external to and independent of human beings, should be available if the proposal is to stand as a genuine alternative not prey to re-absorption within the anthropocentric idealism of the former possibility. For if such an account is, in principle, not available then perhaps God as an object of worship, even if envisaged as really external to and independent of man may possibly only appear as such to believing consciousness and in fact have no reality other than as thus appearing.

The upshot of these reflections is that if the affirmation of God's existence is to be understood only in terms of its applicability to the circumstances of human life, and if all metaphysical statements about God's own and independently possessed and transcendent mode of being are precluded as illegitimate, then the divine reality for what it is worth is indeed, as Merleau-Ponty suspected, dependent upon that of man. This seems to be the conclusion to which the grammatical approach is, perhaps unwittingly, implicitly committed notwithstanding its attempt to interpret the significance of worship and prayer in a contrary sense.

There is indeed one way in which this conclusion that the divine reality must be understood as somehow dependent upon that of man could be maintained without endorsing an explicitly anthropocentric reductionism such as that of Feuerbach, Marx, or Freud. It is the way of Hegelian absolute idealism which argues that the reality of God as absolute spirit, although in a way dependent upon man, is not simply identical with him or totally derived from him. It sees the relationship between God and the whole finite order including man as a necessary and reciprocal one. The material world and man are seen as the necessary medium of God's progressive self-realization in the dual sense of becoming actual and attaining self-consciousness. This self-realization is finally fully attained in and through man's highest activities, namely, art, religion, and philosophy. Thus although the divine reality finds full

---

35 R. Bambrough, "Introduction," in Brown, *Reason and Religion*, p. 15.

38 *The Sense of Creation*

expression only through the mediation and in terms of a human context, it is not reducible to this context because it constitutes, as it were, the whole rationale and ultimate significance of this context. In Hegel's own words:

> It is equally true that God exists as finite and the Ego as infinite .... But this separate existence of the finite must not be retained; it must, on the contrary, be abrogated. God is movement towards the finite, and owing to this He is, as it were, the lifting up of the finite to Himself. In the Ego, as in that which is annulling itself as finite God returns to Himself, and only as this return is He God. Without the world God is not God.[36]

In many respects this Hegelian system, or some variation of it, is the one which appears to make most sense of the seemingly conflicting statements of the grammatical approach to theistic discourse which we have been considering. Thus it provides an account of how it might make sense to say that the divine reality, which an affirmation of God expresses, is to be found only in the circumstances of human experience, yet is not entirely identical with or reducible to these circumstances.

However, there is little doubt that Hegelianism is a *metaphysical* system in the fullest sense of the term involving theoretical assertions about the existence, nature, and activity of God known only by speculative reason. In this respect it is difficult to reconcile it with the grammatical approach which is at pains to deny that the affirmation of God involves a theory, particularly a metaphysical theory, about the nature of God and the world. Moreover, although it is not our intention to embark here on a discussion of the claims of Hegelianism, it does seem doubtful that it is able to safeguard adequately the irreducible significance of an affirmation of God. Suffice it to say, as has often been pointed out, that the Hegelian system has not fared well in the subsequent history of thought and that many of the explicitly atheistic views which hold sway today can be seen as reductive reversals of its basic viewpoint.

Conclusion

Our conclusion must be that the grammatical approach, even if dubiously reinforced by a Hegelian interpretation, is not a satisfactory approach to the meaning of an affirmation of God. Notwithstanding its many important insights about the grammar of theistic discourse and its application conditions, it does not adequately encompass all the conditions of the meaning of such an affirmation. Notably, it fails to do justice to the theoretical or metaphysical truth conditions which refer to the non-observational state of affairs which must be postulated concerning the divine reality. In particular, and assuming that there are good reasons for not adopting an Hegelian position, it fails to do justice to a basic traditional claim about divine transcendence.

This basic traditional claim is the claim, highlighted as we have seen by Anselm, that although the finite world of human experience is wholly dependent upon the creative decision of God, he possesses his infinite perfection of being in absolute independence of creatures. Consequently, whereas they could not be were he not, he

---

36 G.W. Hegel, *Lectures on the Philosophy of Religion*, trans. E. Spiers and J. Sanderson, London, 1968, vol. 2, pp. 199–200.

would exist even if they did not. Moreover, the fact that they exist as God's creation does not constitute any real relational modification of the divine being. In other words, as we have discussed in Chapter 2, between finite beings and God there is a non-mutual real relation. Their being as creatures is wholly relative to his but his is in no real sense but only notionally relative to theirs.

It is this metaphysical conception of a non-mutual real relationship, representing a crucial truth condition of the traditional theistic affirmation of God, which is neglected in the grammatical approach. Its treatment of theistic discourse concentrates exclusively on the internal relationships between such discourse and our lived experience. It provides a grammar of divine immanence rather than of divine transcendence—an account of the way in which the circumstances of human existence condition how we must speak of God in these circumstances, e.g. as worshipful, dependable source of security, worthy of gratitude.

All of this is of great interest and importance but it does not include a treatment of God's absolute transcendence which is ultimately a more fundamental consideration. It is more fundamental because it is a theoretical truth condition of the meaningfulness of talk about divine immanence and its exclusion tends to undermine the irreducibly theistic significance of such talk and to open the way to a reductionist anthropocentric account of it.

The foregoing remarks indicate that an adequate account of the truth conditions of an affirmation of God must include a reference to God's own transcendent mode of being and not merely to his relevance to human life. The formulation of these conditions can be seen as a grammatical exercise though in a somewhat different and larger sense than that suggested by the writers we have considered above. Inasmuch as these truth conditions include a reference to God's absolute and independently self-possessed being, which is not empirically given in the circumstances of human experience, there arises the difficult problem of showing that they are actually satisfied, i.e. that such a being truly exists. This cannot be solved by an account of the grammatical considerations applicable within experience but only, if at all, by the "grammar" of metaphysical argument. In the following three chapters we will consider various contexts in which such argument might be developed.

CHAPTER 5

Knowledge and Transcendence

Realism

Our cognitive life opens us, through the windows of perception, to a threefold presence— a presence to the world, to other people, and to ourselves. This pre-reflective lived experience is developed to a greater or lesser extent by rational reflection. Through such reflection we aim at deeper comprehension or explanation of our lived experience. In this undertaking we resort, inter alia, to literary, historical, scientific, artistic, philosophical, and religious considerations.

A remarkable feature of this reflection is that it can move from the "first-person" perspective in which it originates—from how things are "for me" or even "for-us" to thoughts, principles, arguments, and judgments, which are ascribed an impersonal, universal and, in some cases, even unconditional validity. Their validity is taken as independent of any first person singular or plural perspective. What makes them valid or true is not our thinking them or agreeing that they are so. Their validity is not relative to my history, my language, my form of life, or my culture. Our knowledge is relative to their objective validity—not their validity relative to our knowledge.

We are aware that our knowledge, although originating and terminating within ourselves and not affecting anything external to it, nevertheless attains an object which is more than just an object of consciousness. We attain valid affirmations about how things truly are in a world which exists independently of our representations of it. Their truth or validity is grounded in an intelligibility which is deeper than, independent of, and which enables our affirmations.

Of course, since our knowledge is a human product as well as a discovery, psycho-physical, historical, cultural, and personal factors are involved in coming to know objective truths. And they can often influence us to ascribe objective truth to what is only a culturally conditioned presumption or prejudice: e.g. the pre-modern conviction that the sun revolves around the earth. But this does not undermine our assurance that genuinely rational reflection can and does, with varying degrees of insight and certainty, give us access to truths which are so quite independently of our making, enabling, or claiming them to be so. They are had by us but do not derive from us. Even when we judge ourselves to be mistaken in ascribing objective validity to an argument or claim, we correct ourselves by means of arguments and claims which we take to be objectively valid.

This is a realist or rationalist position as opposed to a subjectivist or relativist one. It is realist in claiming that a world exists independently of our "intentional" representations of it, and rationalist in claiming that some of our representations successfully describe how things are in this independently existing world. It is the view accepted, but not arbitrarily, in this study. To accept it does not presuppose a theistic commitment. It is a view convincingly defended in various ways by a wide range of philosophers including those with no theistic convictions.[1]

Our knowledge of objective principles, arguments, truths, and realities will vary in scope and certainty depending upon whether we are dealing with the purely formal realm of mathematics and logic or the more empirically rooted disciplines of experimental science and philosophy.

Irrespective of our language, the state of our brain, our ideological convictions, or our very existence, it remains objectively valid that 4+4=8. Descartes thought that God might have made to be the case what we perceive to be contradictory, e.g. that it is not true that 4+4=8.[2] However, earlier Aquinas had argued, more plausibly, that not even God can make what is contradictory to be the case, because what is contradictory is precisely what cannot be the case.[3]

Similarly, and more fundamentally, the basic principles of logic, e.g. "If, if p then q, and if not q, then not p (*modus tollens*)" although perhaps not immediately evident are objectively valid, and indeed even self-evident, whether or not I or anyone else agrees. Correspondingly, what is not self-evident may indeed, for somebody, be experientially evident and undeniable.

Experimental science and philosophical reflection envisage objectively valid judgments about an independently existing extra-mental world. Where they have to revise these judgments they proceed by way of objectively valid arguments and conclusions about what is the case independently of our thinking it to be so. Even socially constructed realities such as marriage or money, which unlike mountains and atoms do not exist independently of *all* representation, nevertheless, as Searle remarks, require a reality which is independent of all representation:

> The simplest way to show that is to show that a socially constructed reality presupposes a reality independent of all social constructions, for there has to be something for the construction to be constructed out of. To construct money, property and language, for example, there have to be the raw materials of bits of metal, paper, land, sounds, and marks, for example.[4]

Against this general epistemological background let us seek to advance towards a consideration of the particular case of rational argument for the existence of God.

---

1   Cf., for example, T. Nagel, *The Last Word*, Oxford,1997; The *View from Nowhere*, Oxford, 1986; J. Searle, *The Construction of Social Reality*, London,1995; R. Bhaskar, *A Realist Theory of Science*, 2nd edn, Hassocks, 1977; R. Trigg, *Reason and Commitment*, Cambridge, 1973; D. Davidson, *Enquiries into Truth and Interpretation*, Oxford, 1984; M. Baghramian, *Relativism*, London, 2004.

2   Cf. *The Philosophical Works of Descartes*, trans. E. Haldane and G. Ross, Cambridge, 1967, vol. 2, Reply to Objection VI, section 8.

3   Cf. Aquinas, *Summa Contra Gentiles*, trans. English Dominicans, London, 1934, Bk 2, chs 22, 25.

4   Searle, *The Construction of Social Reality*, p. 190.

Rationality

One thing seems clear, namely, that the transcendent God of Judaeo-Christian belief, the God whom "no man hath seen at any time" is not an object of direct experience. Nor, as we have seen, can his existence be established through an analysis of our idea of him. Moreover, he cannot be discovered by means of experimental science which is limited to knowledge about what can be, however indirectly, an object of sense experience. Therefore, if we are to affirm the existence of God, otherwise than through faith, it will have to be by way of "non-scientific" yet rational or philosophical argument from some features of our lived experience.

Like all philosophical issues, an argument for God's existence is rooted in a pre-philosophical experience, from which it unfolds and develops by way of rational reflection, culminating in an affirmation of his existence, which, it claims, provides an ultimate foundation or explanation of this experience.

Pre-philosophical experience is "prior" to philosophy in a threefold sense. It is temporally prior inasmuch as our lived experience precedes philosophical reflection. Secondly, it has a logical or foundational priority in that it is the foundation or basis of philosophical reflection. Thirdly, it is prior in the sense of being provisional—awaiting from philosophical reflection its critical elucidation, appraisal, and explanation.

One can see in all of this a non-vicious circularity according to which our pre-philosophical lived experience provides an originating foundation for philosophical reflection which, in turn, seeks to provide an ultimate foundation for this lived experience. Let us consider how this idea can be developed with reference to the idea of "proof" or "argument" for the existence of God.

The idea of "proof" envisages a movement of thought from one affirmation held to be true to another affirmation also held to be true in virtue of the rational structure of the movement of thought or argument from the original affirmation. Hence, in a proof or argument for God, the affirmation of his existence is said to be achieved by a rational or logical process of thought developing from the affirmation of some features of our experience. The process of thought is claimed to be rational or logical in the sense that it is a valid and coherent discourse, rooted in the beings of our experience, and which achieves a deeper comprehension of their nature and existence.

It is important to bear in mind that the basic aim of human reasoning is to achieve a deeper comprehension of extra-mental reality. Our reasoning must, of course, conform to the principles and rules of formal logic—e.g. it must not contradict itself. But it must also respect and seek to disclose or discover what may be called the material logic or intelligible structure inherent in the constituents of the external world of our experience.

The simple elements, principles, and processes of logic and mathematics are independent of the contingencies of our concrete experience. They are clear, evident, and intrinsically undeniable. We cannot attempt to question them without, in the process, presupposing them.[5]

When we try to reason about the extra-mental realities of our experience the situation is very different. Here nothing is fully transparent. We certainly do not

---

5   Cf. Nagel, *The Last Word*, ch. 4.

44   *The Sense of Creation*

have a comprehensive knowledge of the beings of our experience. We perceive their extra-mental being from a particular perspective. In affirming their being as existing independently of our knowledge of them we affirm that there is more to them than meets the eye, more than is explicit in our initial perception of them. In the thrust of our minds towards further knowledge of them we seek to go beyond simply providing an extended list of empirically observed facts. We seek in various ways to uncover and discern aspects of the "material logic" or "trans-phenomenal underlying structure" of their independently possessed being. We are seeking to disclose spheres of natural, as distinct from logical, necessity, e.g. when we account for the pre-scientific phenomenal features of water by way of its chemical analysis in terms of H_2O.

The "phenomenal" appearance of things is apprehended as the appearing or self-manifestation within experience of their extra-mental reality itself. We apprehend things as they are in themselves for us. The phenomenon is the manifestation of a structured reality which is accessible to us and partly understood by us. As one writer puts it:

> It is possible to go beyond facts, because facts are phenomena, not just undecomposable data, but a process of manifestation. It is possible to go back towards the principles because the phenomenon itself ... as the unfolding of a principle, gives us the leading thread which enables us to rediscover this principle, to grasp again the origin behind the self-manifestation and in it, ... Once we have undertaken the regressive movement ... we realize that we are penetrating into a vast region of reality the structure of which is very complex. We are then in the field of principles, but we reach them not as *a priori* elements—as if they were purely logical elements, premises assignable to possible deductions—but as concrete elements which belong to the very texture of reality.[6]

This inherent intelligibility of the extra-mental objects of our experience has a certain pre-linguistic or pre-predicative character. It is given expression by us in the particular contingent languages we happen to speak. It enables us to live in a world which is not just mine or yours but everyone's. The culturally conditioned languages by means of which we are able to express this intelligibility of things are not the foundation of this intelligibility. This intelligibility is independent of the particular languages in which we seek, with varying degrees of success, to give it expression. The order of explanation here is from the fundamental intelligibility of things to language, not the reverse.[7] As Michael Dummett remarks:

> even though the language we speak is our language in the sense that it is we that have given our words the meaning that they bear, it is nevertheless part of any realist interpretation of language that that meaning is such that we grasp what it is for a given sentence to be true independently of the means we have for knowing it to be true.[8]

---

6   J. Ladrière, "Preface" to C. Winckleman de Cléty, *The World of Persons*, London, 1967, p. xiii.

7   Cf. Nagel, *The Last Word*, pp. 34–41.

8   M. Dummett, *Frege: Philosophy of Language*, London, 1973, p. 118.

Knowledge and Transcendence 45

To sum up: our discourse about the external world seeks to express an intelligibility constituted not just by our language, or by its conformity with the laws of formal logic. It is constituted more fundamentally and chiefly by the pre-linguistic logic or intelligible structure of reality itself.

This intelligibility becomes known by us to the limited, historical, developing extent that our limited, temporal, personal mode of being can achieve. We have to work at this inherent intelligibility of reality to achieve a modest, culturally conditioned, measure of insight into it. (And the effort is not only theoretical as when we seek to understand the natural laws of the physical world. It is also, as we shall discuss in the next chapter, practical and ethical, as when we seek to treat other people whom we encounter appropriately, as beings who exist not simply for us—but also in and for themselves.)

The theoretical interrogation of the intelligibility of the world can take various forms and it functions at different levels of enquiry. Thus at one level it operates through the modalities of empirical science. At another, more fundamental level, it operates by way of philosophical or metaphysical reflection. This latter level of enquiry arises as a self-involving exigency, which is at once speculative and existential, for light and truth concerning the ultimate significance of being in general and of human existence in particular. It is, as we shall see, at this level of reflection that the philosophical issue of the existence of God arises.

The various regional areas of intelligible reality, which different forms of pre-philosophical enquiry explore, give us information limited to various aspects of the internal structure and operation of the world of experience including ourselves Thus, for example, physics, chemistry, biology, psychology, and anthropology reveal to us aspects of the intelligibility of this world. Basic to this realist view of such sciences is the principle that perception gives us access to things, and experimental activity gives us access to structures, that exist independently of us. Although this experimental activity often involves a complicated framework of idealizing mathematical models, sophisticated technology and indirect experiment, the envisaged intelligibility is not a mental construct but rather an objective extra-mental structure of reality however obliquely and incompletely portrayed. In their different ways the various sciences disclose and confirm the intrinsic analogical intelligibility of reality itself.

The intelligibility disclosed by such particular forms of empirical enquiry is confined to the *intrinsic* nature, principles, and operation of the physical world. Their method of procedure requires them to operate as though the natural world of our experience is the ultimate context of scientific enquiry. As such they are methodologically atheistic or at least agnostic. They do not include any reference to God as a feature or source of the intelligible structure which they discern and elucidate. This intelligibility is taken, un-problematically, as something given -- a factual feature, one might say, of the experienced world. It is explored by a form of understanding and explanation which not only originates in experience but also, by means of verifiable experiment, terminates in experience.

46 *The Sense of Creation*

Metaphysical Enquiry

The metaphysical interrogation of reality envisages a more fundamental kind of intelligibility than the various particular and limited domains of scientific intelligibility disclosed through our human enquiry as a cognitive openness to the world, to ourselves, and to other people. This cognitive openness and the threefold reality which determines it constitute our world of lived experience. The metaphysical interrogation of reality makes this world of lived experience—this cognitive openness and all that it discloses and discovers—an object of further and deeper reflection. It seeks some account or comprehension, however indirect, of how this extra-mental world disclosed in cognitive experience, and our understanding of it, can themselves have arisen and be constituted so as to present themselves as they do—as factually intelligible reality "intentionally" or cognitively accessible to our finite minds. It seeks to make sense of the *existence* of this state of affairs. For, although it undoubtedly exists, it is difficult to understand how it can do so. As Husserl remarked:

> Can we be satisfied simply with the notion that human beings are *subjects for the world* (the world which for consciousness is their world) and at the same time are objects in this world ... the juxtaposition "subjectivity *in* the world as object" and at the same time "conscious subject *for* the world" contain a necessary theoretical question, that of understanding how this is possible.[9]

This is not just a matter of trying to understand how a mindless material universe of corruptible contingent things can embody such a remarkable and abiding framework of intelligible physical laws. (Although this is indeed mysterious notwithstanding Bertrand Russell's dismissive assertion "I should say that the universe is just there, and that's all."[10] It does not seem unquestionably adequate simply to assert that the existence and orderly interaction of mindless material bodies is ultimately, coincidentally, and unsurprisingly how things have always been.)

More fundamentally, the issue is one of how we, finite contingent natural organisms, can exist as self-conscious rational subjects to whose intentional cognition the independent objective intelligibility of the natural world is, to some extent at least, accessible. Stated simply, the sequence of physical events in the natural world, including those intimately related to the development and operations of our brains, does not as such explain the existence or nature of our consciousness. In particular it does not explain the openness in virtue of which we transcend our initial first-person-singular perspective on the world and attain an impersonal partial understanding of its objective intelligible structure. As Thomas Nagel remarks "the

---

9   E. Husserl, *The Crisis of European Sciences and Transcendental Phenomenology*, trans. D. Carr, Evanston, 1970, pp. 180–81. Or as Sartre enquires: "What is the synthetic relation we call being-in- the-world? What must man and the world be in order for a relation between them to be possible?" J.P. Sartre, *Being and Nothingness*, trans. H. Barnes, New York, 1966, p. 34.

10   Cf. J. Hick (ed.), *The Existence of God*, London, 1964, p. 175.

physical story, without more, cannot explain the mental story, including consciousness and reason."[11]

Nor can this mental story be explained, as is popularly supposed, by some version of the theory of evolution through natural selection. The basic reason why this is so is that such explanation is only a more sophisticated version of the self-defeating reductionist interpretations of reason in terms of contingent psychological, cultural, or linguistic conditioning. The idea that our rational capacity is the product simply of natural selection would leave us no more grounds to trust the results of our reasoning (including the theory of evolution) than if this reasoning were simply the product of our psychological conditioning. As Nagel remarks:

> An external understanding of reason as merely another natural phenomenon—a biological product, for example—is impossible. Reason is whatever we find we must *use* to understand anything including itself. And if we try to understand it as merely a natural (biological or psychological) phenomenon, the result will be an account incompatible with our account of it and with the understanding we have of it in using it.[12]

With regard to evolution, our capacity for objectively valid thinking about the world may be seen as a *post hoc* but not exclusively *propter hoc* occurrence. In other words, even if it is by biological evolution that we have developed into organisms able to claim some objective understanding of the world, the validity of this claim depends upon knowing that this exercise of understanding is intrinsically and independently trustworthy and not *merely* a consequence of this evolution. It is an emergent rather than a resultant feature of our biological evolution. A naturalistic account of our reason and understanding is incompatible with their use and our understanding of their use.

The issue was anticipated by Aristotle when he asked "At what moment, and in what manner, do these creatures which have this principle of Reason acquire their share in it, and where does it come from? This is a very difficult problem which we must endeavour to solve ..."[13] He is convinced that this "difficult problem" is not to be solved by a naturalistic account of our power of reasoning and understanding. "It remains then, that Reason alone enters in, as an additional factor, from outside, and that it alone is divine, because physical activity has nothing whatever to do with the activity of Reason."[14]

In other words, brain-cells clicking off each other do not make it to be the case, and known to be the case, that "If, if both P then Q and not-Q, then not-P." Even if there are non-contingent systematic relationships between the phenomenological features of such consciously exercised rationality on the one hand, and specific neuro-physiological states of our brain on the other (and granted the validity and importance of research into such relationships), nevertheless the former are irreducible to the latter. Any attempt at a radical conceptual reduction of the mental to the physical or neuro-physiological is unavailing because it effectively eliminates what is

---

11 Nagel, *The Last Word*, p. 138, cf. also *The View from Nowhere*, pp. 7–8.
12 Nagel, *The Last Word*, p. 143.
13 Aristotle, *Generation of Animals*, Loeb edition, trans. A.L. Peck, London, 1984, 736b.
14 Ibid.

48 *The Sense of Creation*

distinctive and undeniable about the mental—its conscious rational subjectivity. As Nagel remarks: "so long as the mental states remain characteristically subjective and radically emergent, there is no basis for describing them as physical or physically constituted."[15]

This refusal of a naturalistic account of our reason and understanding is the counterpart of our earlier implicit rejection of idealism. This rejection of idealism is embodied in our realist claim that the intrinsic intelligibility of the external world, which we come to understand to some extent, exists independently of, and is not relative to or created by, our understanding. Correspondingly, a rejection of a naturalistic interpretation of reason is embodied in our claim that a reductionist interpretation of our rational life is incompatible with our understanding of it.

This complex state of affairs—comprising a non-naturalistic account of human understanding and a realist, as opposed to an idealist, account of the intelligible structure disclosed by our understanding—gives rise to the metaphysical level of enquiry mentioned above. We affirm an illuminating harmony or fit between the profound intelligibility of the physical world and the resourceful openness of our understanding. But what is not at all evident is how this state of affairs can exist, which it undoubtedly does. The question naturally arises: "How must reality ultimately be in itself if an explanatory account of this puzzling, even mysterious, state of affairs is to be provided?"

There are various possible responses to this question. The first and simplest is that there is no answer to it. One just accepts that this is how things are and have always been and that there is nothing further to be said. This termination of the process of enquiry is more like a blunt decision than a convincing insight. It would tend to be confirmed only to the extent that no more satisfactory answer is available. As Schopenhaeur remarked, you cannot pay off a line of enquiry like a cab when it has taken you as far as you choose to go.

Another possible response (suggested somewhat diffidently by Nagel) is to accept a hypothesis according to which the existence of minds capable of partly understanding the universe is made possible by certain unknown fundamental mind-like laws of the universe of a different order to, but compatible with, the beautiful laws of fundamental physics. These hypothetical laws are invoked to explain the *possibility* of intelligent life in general. Their efficacy in achieving the particular actualization of *human* intelligence would further require the right specific initial conditions of the primordial state of our universe which, given its general laws, enable the formation of molecules, galaxies, organisms, consciousness, and finally intelligence.[16]

This answer is an attempt to provide an ultimate account of our objective knowledge of the external world solely in terms of parameters intrinsic to this world, its regular system of laws, constants, and initial conditions. Its claim to explanatory ultimacy involves an exclusion of any theistic reference or implication.

15　T. Nagel, "The Psychophysical Nexus," in *Concealment and Exposure and Other Essays*, New York, 2002.

16　Cf. Nagel, *The Last Word*, ch. 7, also *The View from Nowhere*, pp. 51–3.

Knowledge and Transcendence 49

However, that it does indeed satisfy the philosophical quest for ultimate rationally satisfying explanation is certainly not evident.

Undoubtedly our experience of to some extent actually understanding an intelligible world presupposes the possibility of this understanding. Further, it may be granted that this possibility involves the felicitous congruity of (a) the general physico-chemical laws operational in the formation of the physical universe; (b) the corresponding, unknown but supposedly different order, laws which make possible the occurrence of rational minds; (c) the appropriate initial physical conditions which enable the combined operation of these laws to produce or develop actual human intelligence.

That this complex set of possibilities does obtain may be granted given the *actuality* of the experience of which they are alleged to be a precondition. But the fact that these possibilities are thus implicated in our actual experience of the world does not explain the existence of these contingent possibilities and the felicitous and valuable congruity of their differing orders of intelligible laws and initial physical conditions which enable the existence of our human understanding of the external world.

This hypothetical regular state of affairs, although certainly intelligible, appears to be neither self-explanatory nor necessary. It is a contingent regularity and intelligibility. It does not appear as an account for which no further or more comprehensive explanation might even be sought. It is indeed a more developed answer to the question of how to explain the harmony between our intelligence and the objective intelligible structure of the universe than the first answer mentioned above which precludes any explanation. It outlines hypothetical intrinsic preconditions of the possibility of this harmony. But (unless one simply asserts that this is the ultimate inexplicable basis of all explanation) the same quest for understanding and explanation of this harmony reappears at this deeper level in terms of the why and wherefore of these contingent felicitously interrelated preconditions, possibilities, and regularities. The presumption that regularity of occurrence is self-explanatory is mistaken.

At this point one may be tempted to seek to eliminate the problem by reverting either to some form of idealism, which absorbs the external world within the ambit of mind, or to some form of naturalistic empiricism, which explains mind in terms of evolution through natural selection. Or if one retains a realist viewpoint one might simply maintain that postulating the existence of the intrinsic diverse law-like possibilities and initial physical preconditions of the harmony of mind and nature, however problematic or mysterious, is as far as our enquiry can extend. One would simply accept that the existence of these various preconditions of all consciously affirmed meaning and value constitute a most felicitous accident. But, just as in the case of the first response considered above, this response would tend to be confirmed only to the extent that no more satisfactory answer is available.

The quest for this more satisfactory answer may indeed be prompted by the contention that to acquiesce in the inexplicable ontological ultimacy of this felicitous accident may in fact undermine the very affirmations of meaning and value it is intended to sustain. This point is intimated by Wittgenstein in the *Tractatus* where he writes:

50 *The Sense of Creation*

The sense of the world must lie outside the world. In the world everything is as it is and happens as it does happen. *In* it there is no value—and if there were it would be of no value. If there is a value which is of value, it must lie outside all happening and being so. For all happening and being so is accidental. What makes it non-accidental cannot lie *in* the world, for otherwise this would again be accidental. It must lie outside the world.[17]

Let us consider how this possibility might be developed in terms of a theistic argument.

Adequate Explanation

By means of our contingent, psycho-physically conditioned, minds we develop a cognitive relationship to the external world. We achieve some objective and impersonal understanding of its independently possessed underlying structure. How can there be this cognitive fit between us, contingent individual subjects, and the trans-empirical intelligible structure of the world? Some explanation of it is needed if our cognitive claims are not to appear groundless and ultimately unintelligible. As Thomas Nagel (though not himself a theist) remarks:

> When we use our minds to think about reality, we are not, I assume, performing an impossible leap from inside ourselves to the world outside. We are developing a relation to the world that is implicit in our mental and physical set up, and we can do this only if there are facts we do not know which account for this possibility. ... But without something fairly remarkable, human knowledge is unintelligible ... I believe that unless we suppose that they [our beliefs] have a basis in something global (rather than just human) of which we are not aware, they make no sense—and they do make sense.[18]

Within our human experience we are intellectually satisfied when an orderly but puzzling state of affairs can be explained or accounted for in terms of the free decision of a rational agent. Consider, for example, the story related by the logician Peter Geach about a Russian soldier standing guard at a particular spot on a lawn of the Tsar's palace. When the Tsar asked why this was so he was told that this is how it had always been. Not satisfied with this reply he enquired further until he discovered that several hundred years previously a young Tsarita, wishing to protect a snowdrop from being trampled, had ordered a soldier to stand on guard at the spot and the order had never been revoked. This explanation, in terms of the free decision by a rational agent, made adequate sense of the puzzling phenomenon and is intellectually satisfying in a way that explanation of the form "That's how things *always* happen" is not.[19] Once again, mere regularity of occurrence is not self-explanatory!

The story provides a clue to the kind of explanation which may be required to account for the puzzling state of affairs which we are considering. This state of affairs is the relationship whereby a contingent individual subject achieves some impersonal and objectively valid understanding of an independently existing world.

---

17 L. Wittgenstein, *Tractatus Logico-Philosophicus*, London, 1922, 6. 41.

18 Nagel, *The View from Nowhere*, pp. 84–5.

19 Cf. P. Geach, *Providence and Evil*, Cambridge, 1977, p. 74.

Knowledge and Transcendence 51

Here the puzzle is not just the contingent intelligibility of the world or the emergent rationality of individual bits of it, namely, ourselves. It is rather how to account for the relationship between our understanding of the world of which we are a part, and the world itself as object of our understanding, in a way which neither reduces the known world to our knowledge of it, or our knowledge to only a physico-chemical product of the world. Our knowledge is relative to the physical world which we know, but not reducible to or deducible from it. And the intelligible structure of the world which we know is not relative to our knowledge of it but is disclosed by it as that to which this knowledge is asymmetrically related.

We claim that our human understanding provides naturally reliable knowledge of an independently intelligible external world. In calling it "naturally" reliable knowledge we emphasize that we are not, like Descartes, invoking God *as a presupposition* to enable us to affirm the existence of the intelligible external world. The affirmation of God is not required as an intrinsic component or step in our realist claim and conviction. The argument to be made is rather that the existence of God is required as a non-observational theoretical truth condition of the realism which we naturally and, we believe, rightly maintain. It is similar to Kant's moral argument, which we will consider in the next chapter, according to which the existence of God is affirmed, not as a presupposition of moral action, but as a practical implication of its rational coherence. The argument which we are proposing involves the claim that the realist view of knowledge which we have been discussing requires a teleological, and ultimately a theistic, justification.

A graphic introduction to the sort of argument involved is provided by Richard Taylor in his book *Metaphysics*.[20] Suppose, he says, that you observe an arrangement of stones on a hill portraying the message "THE BRITISH RAILWAYS WELCOMES YOU TO WALES." You would be inclined to believe that it had been so arranged to inform you of your imminent arrival in Wales. However, the arrangement of stones might have come about accidentally through the chance interaction of natural forces operating in accordance with physico-chemical laws. In which case, it could provide no information other than what might be inferred from the stones' own physical structure and composition. But if, solely for the reason that the stones were so arranged, you were to conclude that you were indeed entering Wales you could not, consistently with that, suppose that the arrangement of stones was accidental. You would be implying that they were thus arranged by an intelligent being for the purpose of conveying information concerning something other than themselves.

This illustration can be developed analogically in an argument from the reliability of our knowledge of the external world. We rely upon our variously influenced cognitive activity to attain knowledge of non-evident truths about the structure of the world which are affirmed to be true independently of our cognitive activity. Taylor argues that if we have no stronger foundation for saying that our cognitive ability reliably discloses the nature and existence of an external world than we would have in saying that a non-purposefully arranged pattern of stones reliably disclosed

---

20 Cf. R. Taylor, *Metaphysics*, Englewood Cliffs, 1963, ch. 7, also R. Creel's defense of Taylor in "A Realist Argument for Belief in the Existence of God," *International Journal for Philosophy of Religion*, 10, 1979, pp. 233–53.

52   *The Sense of Creation*

the proximate reality of Wales, then we could not rationally, i.e. for good reason, confirm the reliability of our knowledge. We might claim to be intuitively aware that it is reliable but would be unable to show how it could be so. Like the purported message of the arrangement of stones, our purported knowledge could be rationally confirmed to disclose what we think it does, namely, the inherent intelligible structure of an independently existing world, only on the supposition that it is intentionally fashioned to do so by an appropriately capable agent.

The insight which underlies Taylor's argument is that we may not speak in a contradictory way about our cognitive ability and that we would do so if we denied its purposeful origin. For to claim that it achieves reliable knowledge of independently existing intelligible structure implies that it is purposefully ordered to do so, and this contradicts the claim that it is of non-purposeful origin. To illustrate why the realist conception of our cognitive ability implies its purposeful origin, Taylor adduces the comparable but simpler case of the arrangement of stones being taken to convey objective truth about Wales. Here the requirement of purposeful agency is obvious and mediates insight into the more complicated case of our claim to objective knowledge of the external world.

Taylor's illustration is illuminating. However, it needs to be developed by further elucidation of the metaphysical basis of its epistemological realism. This elucidation can be expressed as follows.

Nothing can be the adequate explanation of something intrinsically independent of it. For this would involve the contradiction that the object both is and is not independent of it. But, according to epistemological realism, our cognitive ability achieves knowledge, or intentional understanding, of intelligible structure which exists independently of our knowledge of it. What is known is not an effect or an inferred or constituted object of our cognitional capability. It is something which intrinsically has a genuine independence and transcendence vis-à-vis this capability. The sun's gravitational field *really does* obey an inverse square law. This is not something which we invent. We discover it.

The realist claims that intelligible extra-mental being, although attained by our knowledge, reveals itself, in its very signification, as not dependent upon the cognitive act which grasps it. The existence and intelligibility of what we know is irreducible to being known either actually or potentially by the human spirit. Our understanding is really dependent in its activity upon what is known. But what is known is not similarly dependent upon our knowing. Between our understanding and extra-mental being there is a real relationship, between being and our understanding only a logical one. This is the asymmetry to which we have referred above.

That our cognitive ability should be relied upon intuitively as providing dependable insight into what thus exceeds and is independent of its intrinsic constitution would be paradoxical if this cognitive state of affairs is viewed as having an exclusively natural mechanistic non-purposeful origin. For, in this case, its alleged reliability would be ultimately as groundless as the claim to be entering Wales would be if based only on an accidental arrangement of stones.

It would involve the contradictory contention that our mind can be relied upon to provide deep knowledge of extra-mental reality, that it has a natural capacity for such reliable knowledge, but that this claim is groundless. It is groundless because

Knowledge and Transcendence 53

no account of why the realist claim is reliable is available if our cognitive capacity, which appears to be purposefully ordered or fitted to know the external world, is in fact either not purposefully ordered or embodies a purposeful ordering which is irreducible and unintelligible.

Should such groundlessness be the case, the harmonious fit affirmed to obtain between the deep structure of extra-mental being and the human mind, and presupposed by objective knowledge, would lack explanation or justification and the realist position would be thereby undermined. A non-purposeful, naturalistic, account of the origin of our cognitive capacity is, as we have argued, incompatible with affirming the reliability of epistemological realism. One would be axiomatically denying what one operationally affirms—operationally affirming the reliability of our knowledge but axiomatically denying any rational explanation of this reliability. Alternatively, to say that there just happens to be a purposeful fit between our mind and the world but that this is irreducible and unintelligible is to retain the mystery but again preclude any adequate explanation of how it can be so. One would thereby revert to the unsatisfactory first response discussed above, which terminates enquiry by simply asserting that this is how things inexplicably are.

Therefore, if the realist claim to objective knowledge of what transcends and is independent of this knowledge is to be upheld as justifiably reliable it requires a further and different level of explanation. Instead of the unavailing attempt to explain away, in exclusively naturalistic non-purposeful terms, the apparently purposeful or teleological origin of such knowledge, or simply to accept it as an unintelligible brute fact, we must consider whether, and how, a different explanation which accounts for its purposeful character can be argued.

From Teleology to Theism

Undoubtedly there are many phenomena in the world which can and should be explained teleologically, i.e. as occurring in order to achieve a particular goal or purpose. Thus it is wholly appropriate to speak of refrigerators being there in order to keep food cool or hearts being there in order to pump blood. The question remains, however, whether such explanation is basic as denoting an irreducible feature of the world. Most people, whether atheists or not, consider this idea of inexplicable purpose altogether unsatisfactory. Teleological explanation, it is generally agreed, is not basic and must be reducible to some other kind of explanation. Such alternative explanation might be either a mechanistic explanation in terms of efficient causation as natural science requires, or an explanation in terms of a design, either one immanent to a rational agent who intends it or one formulated by an extrinsic purposive agent.[21]

---

21 Cf. A. Kenny, "The Argument from Design," in *Reason and Religion: Essays in Philosophical Theology*, Oxford, 1987, pp. 69–84. Also, B. Davies, *An Introduction to the Philosophy of Religion*, 3rd edn, Oxford, 2004, pp. 74–97. However, although not definitively accepting it Nagel seeks to present the case for irreducible natural teleology, on the presumption of the non-existence of God, in an interesting article "Secular Philosophy and the Religious Temperament," available from www.law.nyu.edu, accessed Sept. 11, 2005.

54   *The Sense of Creation*

To maintain that there is a harmonious fit between our minds and extra-mental reality *in order that* we may have reliable objective knowledge is to provide a purposeful or teleological explanation. To maintain that we have reliable objective knowledge *because* there is a harmonious fit between our minds and extra-mental reality is to give a naturalistic explanation in terms of efficient causality. The difference might be described as saying that in the first case we have explanation of form in terms of function and in the second we have explanation of function in terms of form. There is no reason why both types of explanation cannot be availed of as useful, compatible, and mutually complementary just as we can validly claim that veins have got valves in order that blood might flow to the heart *and* that blood flows to the heart because veins have valves. As Peter Geach remarks: "'A happened in order that B should' is in nowise in conflict with 'B happened because A did.'" [22]

However, the harmonious fit between mind and reality, a fit which is teleologically adapted to achieve reliable objective knowledge, is not something that *can* be comprehensively explained in terms of an exclusively naturalistic account of it. Thus it is not enough to say that we have reliable objective knowledge because it has always been the case that our minds and extra-mental reality are harmoniously related. This is no more satisfactory than the explanation that the Russian soldier stands where he does because this is how it has always been the case. Nor, as we have argued, is it satisfactory to claim that the harmonious fit between our minds and reality is adequately explained as having been caused exclusively by some prior natural process such as biological evolution giving rise to determining systematic relationships between specific neuro-physiological states and our exercise of rational consciousness.

In the light of such dead-ends it is reasonable to explore the possibility of a satisfactory explanation of the dependable but puzzling harmony between our minds and reality, not simply in naturalistic terms, but rather in terms of an intelligent free decision. In other words that the purposeful or teleological fit between our minds and extra-mental reality which obtains *in order that* we may have reliable knowledge implies an intelligent designer.

In teleological explanation the specifying good to be achieved through the purposeful and dependable fit of our minds with extra-mental reality, namely reliable knowledge of extra-mental reality, *does not exist* prior to the purposeful fit which accomplishes it. Such explanation, which is essentially explanation in terms of a good or beneficial result to be achieved differs from Darwinian naturlalistic explanation which also essentially involves a reference to what is good or beneficial. This latter explanation explains how a good outcome, e.g. a better-adapted species, is produced as *a result* of the circumstances and structures of natural selection. Teleological explanation, on the contrary, "explains" the anterior circumstances and structures, e.g. the felicitous harmony of mind and reality, by reference to the yet to be achieved good outcome, i.e. reliable knowledge.

But this poses the formidable question "How can this purposeful fit be determined by a goal which *does not yet exist?*" It is in seeking a response to this genuine difficulty that the move from discussion of purpose to discussion of design arises

---

22   P. Geach, *Reason and Argument*, Oxford, 1976, p. 86.

Knowledge and Transcendence   55

with the claim that the difficulty can be met if the specifying good pre-exists in the mind of an intelligent designer.[23] Moreover, our own immanent intelligence cannot be the source of this intelligent design since its existence and exercise presupposes the design.

More specifically, the paradox that a finite contingent subject is teleologically or purposefully capable of knowledge which is incapable of exclusively natural non-purposeful explanation, could be resolved by reference to the purposive intention of an intelligent creator. This postulated creator is envisaged as causing to exist and naturally to be such as they are, both the intelligible extra-mental world and our ability to understand it—and also the asymmetrical non-mutual relationship in which they stand to one another. Such an account provides an ultimate *rationale* of a teleological account of our objective knowledge in a way which an exclusively naturalistic account cannot. It is also more satisfactory than simply accepting this teleological account as a paradoxical and inexplicable mystery.

As I have indicated with the story of the Tsarita, we have an analogue for this theistic explanation in the appeal to intentional human agency to explain an orderly state of affairs which is problematic if considered in exclusively non-purposeful terms. In our experience, the existence of any contingent, but not naturally occurring, orderly system, for example the first atomic bomb, is accounted for in terms of human intelligence freely deciding to devote activity to the realization of this rather than some other (more intelligent) possibility. In an analogous way, the naturally occurring but not naturalistically explicable orderly fit of our contingent minds with the extra-mental intelligibility of the physical world is accounted for by the affirmation of a creative intelligence whose free decision brings into being this contingent but remarkable state of affairs.

The analogy holds good because in each case a contingently intelligible or orderly state of affairs obtains which finds its requisite explanation in terms of a free decision of a rational agent. However, it is only an analogy because notwithstanding the similarity of the two cases there are also distinctive differences. The finite human agent is itself contingent and the artificial intelligibility which it establishes presupposes the contingent natural intelligibility of the world. The divine agent, on the other hand, exists non-contingently, and freely causes to exist, *ex nihilo*, both the contingent intelligible universe of which we are a part and our rational ability to understand, at least to some extent, its objective extra-mental intelligible structure.

Envisaged as understanding all possibilities and willing into existence the contingent order which actually obtains, God is affirmed as the requisite explanation of the universe, namely, the creative cause of the contingently intelligible order which involves the purposeful fit between our finite minds and the universe of which we achieve, to some extent, objective knowledge. God is understood not to require similar explanation because he exists independently of the contingent order which he explains, i.e. he exists non-contingently or necessarily. His free intelligent creative act explains the paradoxical existence of the contingent intelligible universe, which includes our partial objective understanding of it. But this creative act has no

---

23   Cf. Kenny, "The Argument from Design," pp. 82–3.

56 *The Sense of Creation*

explanation distinct from the sovereign free intelligence which God necessarily, i.e. non-contingently, is.

In summary, we affirm the existence of God as the intelligent source which makes sense of an account of objective knowledge in terms of the teleologically understood harmony between our minds and the world. It is worth mentioning that this affirmation of God is not reached by an appeal to the principle of sufficient reason which, as formulated by Leibniz, is the principle

> in virtue of which we hold that there can be no fact real or existing, no statement true, unless there be a sufficient reason why it should be so and not otherwise, although these reasons usually cannot be known by us.[24]

For not only is this principle inherently questionable. It also implies unacceptable consequences for theism such as the denial of God's freedom in respect of creation.

The line of argument which we have been advancing does not depend upon the grandiose and dubious principle that our understanding the intelligible structure of the extra-mental physical world requires the existence of God as sufficient reason why it must be so and not otherwise. It relies rather on the more modest claim that this state of affairs would be incoherent or contradictory in the absence of an affirmation of an intelligent creator. In other words, we suggest that the fundamental metaphysical principle operative in philosophical argument for the existence of God is not the principle of sufficient reason but rather the principle of non-contradiction. The argument seeks to show that the state of affairs which we have been considering requires, in ultimate analysis, the affirmation of God as its creative source if we are to avoid incompatible and contradictory affirmations about it. These would be affirmations such as "Our claim to knowledge of the world is reliable" and "Our claim to knowledge of the world has no reliable basis."

Conclusion

The foregoing discussion illustrates how an argument for the existence of God can be developed by reflection upon our ability to understand the intelligible structure of the extra-mental world. This intelligibility obtains independently of our limited knowledge which discloses it and which is judged to stand in a non-mutual relationship of real dependence upon it. This paradoxical relationship is a cipher within experience of the analogous relationship of non-mutual real dependence of the world upon God. It serves as a perspicuous source of argument from a "transcendence" manifest within our cognitive experience to the "beyond-experience" absolutely transcendent God.

The non-mutual relationship between our knowledge and the world is a kind of negative mirror image of the relationship between the world and God. It is a relationship which enables a "reflection" from a humanly experienced asymmetry to the ultimate asymmetry which is the relationship between God and the world. The similarity of the relationships was noted by Aquinas who writes:

---

24 G. Leibniz, *Monadology*, 32, in *Leibniz Selections*, ed. P. Wiener, New York, 1951, p. 539.

Knowledge and Transcendence 57

Now the relations that God is said to bear to creatures though represented mentally as existing in God, really exist not in God but in the creatures, just as things are called objects of knowledge not because they are related to knowledge, but because knowledge is related to them.[25]

The chapter began with a description of our knowledge as establishing a threefold presence to the world, to other people, and to ourselves. It concentrated mainly on the cognitive relationship between ourselves and the world. It mentioned various regional areas of understanding which we attain by different forms of phenomenological, historical, and scientific enquiry. It indicated how these specific domains of knowledge, which disclose areas of the intrinsic intelligible structure of the world, give rise to a different level of enquiry, namely, philosophical or metaphysical enquiry. At this level of enquiry the question arises how the world and our knowledge of it must themselves be ultimately understood to be, given that they manifest themselves within our experience as they do. The enquiry gave rise to a reflection on the asymmetrical relationship between the world and our understanding of it which culminated in an affirmation of the existence of God as the requisite explanation of this relationship. The asymmetry between the world and our knowledge of it is a cipher of, and is explained by, the creative asymmetry between God and the world.

The main focus of this chapter has been on a discussion of how the asymmetry involved in our *theoretical knowledge* of the world can be understood as a cipher of the asymmetry between the world and its transcendent creator. In the next chapter we will continue this discussion of asymmetry but in the more *practical* and existential domain of our moral relationship with other people. This move from the impersonal objective viewpoint, characteristic of theoretical reason, to the self-involving viewpoint of practical reason involves concentrating attention on another fundamental feature of human existence. This is the irreducibly first-person-singular character of each human subject—myself and the other individual subjects with whom I find myself in direct inter-personal encounter. In Chapter 7 we will revert to a more impersonal mode of discourse and consider how the sort of asymmetry we are exploring reveals itself also in a metaphysical analysis of the analogical character of the objects of our experience.

---

25 Aquinas, *S. T.*, 1, q. 6,a. 2, ad 1, Blackfriars edn, London, 1964–74.

CHAPTER 6

Morality and Transcendence

Introduction

In this chapter I wish to discuss how one might argue that the implications of morality suggest an affirmation of God envisaged as infinitely perfect transcendent creator.

The history of philosophy provides a rich variety of views on the relationship between morality and belief in God. They range between the extremes of those who maintain that genuine morality is impossible without belief in God and those who maintain that genuine morality is incompatible with such belief.

The latter extreme is exemplified in various forms of atheistic humanism such as Marxism, some versions of existentialism, and scientific humanism. The former can trace its ancestry back to the debate in Plato's *Euthyphro* about whether deeds are good because approved by the gods or approved by the gods because they are good. Some medieval thinkers, notably Ockham, maintained that morality without belief in God is impossible since they held that any ascription of goodness or badness, rightness or wrongness, to actions can be validly made only if it is explicitly recognized that God has decided this to be the case.[1] Even heroes of the Enlightenment such as Locke and Berkeley maintained that without belief in God morality is impossible, because belief in God is the basis of the moral law. As Locke puts it: "that God has given a rule whereby men should govern themselves, I think there is nobody so brutish as to deny … This is the only true touchstone of moral rectitude."[2] The denial of God insofar as this is a real possibility, which Locke was inclined to doubt, is a clear indication of moral blindness and a powerful source of wickedness.

Here, I will be concerned with these antithetical positions only incidentally. I want rather to present an argument for an intermediate position. This is one which holds that, although acceptance of a certain view of morality does not explicitly involve or presuppose an affirmation of God, a case can be made out that this affirmation is implicit in such a view of morality and that it can be made explicit by rational argument. In other words, when one reflects upon a particular conception of morality, which one accepts as compelling, one comes to the realization that an affirmation of God is ultimately required as the vindication, in a sense to be explained, of its rational cogency.

The sort of argument involved can be called a transcendental one in the sense that, if you accept a particular conception of morality, which even though it does not intrinsically involve an explicit affirmation of God, you must, nevertheless, if you would be rational, accept this affirmation because it is a rational implication of the

---

1   Cf. F.C. Copleston, *Medieval Philosophy*, New York, 1962, pp. 133–4.

2   J. Locke, *An Essay Concerning Human Understanding*, ed. A. Fraser, New York, 1959, Bk 2, ch. xxviii, 8.

60 *The Sense of Creation*

conception of morality which you have accepted. It would, in the final analysis, be irrational both to accept the view of morality and be an atheist, although this is not immediately evident and must be argued.

Kant

An important illustration of this line of thought is to be found in Kant's "moral argument" for the existence of God. Although he was convinced that there could be no valid theoretical argument by way of speculative reason for the existence of God, Kant maintained that belief in his existence as a postulate of morality can be rationally justified. However, he very explicitly insists that this belief in no way compromises our moral autonomy. It is not at all required in order to recognize our moral responsibility and to act upon it. He writes:

> So far as morality is based upon the conception of man as a free agent who, just because he is free, binds himself through his reason to unconditioned laws, it stands in need neither of the idea of another Being over him, for him to apprehend his duty, nor of an incentive other than the law itself, for him to do his duty ... Hence for its own sake, morality does not need religion at all whether objectively as regards willing, or subjectively, as regards ability to act; by virtue of pure practical reason it is self-sufficient.[3]

According to Kant, in order to act morally a man must require of himself to pursue not some selfish or pragmatic end but an unconditioned one, the *summum bonum* or highest good. This constitutive goal of all truly moral action is a complex one involving the combination of two intrinsic but specifically distinct elements. In the first place it involves the supreme unconditioned condition of all moral action, namely, a dutiful will or virtue whose only aim is morally right behavior. However, besides this necessary but incomplete component of the *summum bonum* there is a further component, namely, the enjoyment of happiness in due proportion to virtue. Although the pursuit of happiness cannot be the criterion of moral action, nevertheless to act morally or virtuously is to behave in such a manner as to be worthy or deserving of happiness. He who so behaves should be able to hope for and expect happiness. Thus a truly moral person will have as his abiding moral goal a virtuous life and the happiness which any impartial rational appraisal would judge to be appropriate to such a life: "For to need happiness, to deserve it, and yet at the same time not to participate in it, cannot be consistent with the perfect volition of a rational being."[4]

But here Kant encounters a dilemma, namely, that it cannot be conceived to be within man's power to realize this complex goal which he recognizes he must pursue in order to live a fully moral life. For it by no means follows that dutiful behavior, which is within his resources and which is the *sine qua non* of morality will produce

---

3   Kant, *Religion Within the Limits of Reason Alone*, trans. T. Green and H. Hudson, New York, 1960, p. 3. Cf. also R. Arp, "Vindicating Kant's Morality," *International Philosophical Quarterly*, 47, 2007, pp. 5–22.

4   Kant, *Critique of Practical Reason*, trans. T. Abbott, London, 1963, par. 246–7.

Morality and Transcendence

the due happiness which is the further intrinsic component of the highest good. Happiness depends upon the harmony of the course of nature with a man's wish and will. Since the human will cannot dictate the course of natural events neither can it ensure the necessary connection between virtue and happiness intrinsic to the *summum bonum.*

It would appear therefore that the project of a moral life is undermined by the consideration that it involves a requirement to pursue the seemingly impossible and unattainable. If the attainment of the supreme good is not possible, "then the moral law also which commands us to promote it is directed to vain and imaginary ends, and must consequently be false."[5] Since it cannot be a rational duty to pursue the impossible, reason "would have to regard the moral laws as empty figments of the brain."[6]

However, what may be impossible from the perspective of natural human resources alone may not be absolutely impossible. That this is so can be known by pursuing the distinctive and legitimate question of our ultimate basis of hope.

According to Kant:

All the interests of my reason, speculative as well as practical.
Combine in the three following questions:

1. What can I know?

2. What ought I to do?

3 What may I hope?

The first question is merely speculative ...The second question is purely practical .... The third question—If I do what I ought to do, what may I then hope—is at once practical and theoretical, in such a fashion that the practical serves only as a clue that leads us to the answer to the theoretical question, and ... arrives finally at the conclusion that *something is* (which determines the ultimate possible end) *because something ought to happen.*[7]

Pursuing this third question about hope, Kant argues that the systematic unity of ends envisaged in the *summum bonum*, and which we maintain should obtain, would not be impossible if we postulate the existence of God as a provident creator who could, in the fullness of time, bring it about that happiness is enjoyed in due proportion to virtue. Moreover, although we can have no speculative knowledge concerning the existence of such a being neither can we claim to know that such a being does not exist.[8] This, combined with the fact that only on the condition of his existence can we conceive the attainability of the *summum bonum*, which must be the object of our moral endeavor, entitles us to affirm his existence as a postulate of morality. Thus the existence of God is postulated in the context of practical reason not as a presupposition of morality but as a condition of the due fulfillment of its rational requirements. It is a meta-ethical condition of an ethical imperative justifiably affirmed under pain of violation of our moral sentiment.[9] In Kant's own words:

---

5   Ibid., par. 252.

6   Kant, *Critique of Pure Reason*, trans. N. Kemp Smith, London, 1968, par. A 811.

7   Ibid., A 805–6.

8   Cf. ibid., A 641.

9   Cf. Kant, *The Critique of Judgement*, trans. J. Bernard, New York, 1968, par. 87.

62 *The Sense of Creation*

Now it was seen to be a duty for us to promote the *summum bonum*; consequently it is not merely allowable, but it is a necessity connected with duty as a requisite, that we should presuppose the possibility of this *summum bonum*; and as this is possible only on the condition of the existence of God, it inseparably connects this supposition with duty: that is, it is morally necessary to assume the existence of God.[10]

The existential and self-involving character of Kant's affirmation of God is highlighted by his insistence that it is inappropriate to impose the impersonal mode of discourse upon a statement of theistic certainty. The latter is essentially personal since it is through reflection upon my own subjectivity in its moral dimension that I draw my theistic belief:

I am certain that nothing can shake this belief, since my moral principles would thereby be overthrown, and I cannot disclaim them without becoming abhorrent in my own eyes … No, my conviction is not *logical* but *moral* certainty; and since it rests on subjective grounds (of the moral sentiment), I must not even say, "*It is* morally certain that there is a God etc.", but "*I am* morally certain etc." In other words, belief in a God and in another world is so interwoven with my moral sentiment that as there is little danger of my losing the latter, there is equally little cause for fear that the former can ever be taken from me.[11]

It is noteworthy that Kant, who is so adamant in rejecting any speculative argument for the existence of God is equally adamant that a rational argument, arising from practical reason in its moral dimension, enables us to affirm a rational belief in, and personal certainty of, his existence.

Various difficulties can and have been raised about Kant's particular formulation of an argument for the existence of God from the implications of morality. For example, not everyone would concur with his specific account of the *summum bonum* as the defining goal of morality. Or, it might be asked, why must the highest good, however defined, be an attainable goal rather than an ideal towards which we should approximate as best we can given the limitations and vicissitudes of our natural condition? Again, clarification can be required about Kant's idea of God effecting in a future life a reconciliation between virtue and due happiness.

However, instead of dwelling upon how Kant would have energetically responded to such difficulties, I propose instead to concentrate, in a more contemporary context, upon his basic insight that an affirmation of God can be achieved as a rational implication of certain moral considerations.

An important feature of the moral theory which underpins Kant's theistic argument is its insistence upon the objectivity and absolute or categorical character of moral imperatives. To be moral an action must be objective, i.e. regarded as universally valid for all rational beings. Its performance must also be absolutely or unconditionally required, i.e. simply because it is an objectively virtuous action derived from a universal law proscribed by a rational will—and not because it happens to suit some ulterior purpose or conforms to some set of empirical facts about human inclinations. Morality must not be regarded as a set of guidelines to

---

10 Kant, *Critique of Practical Reason*, par. 267.

11 Kant, *Critique of Pure Reason*, A 828–9.

Morality and Transcendence 63

fulfill a preferred need, attitude, or desire, or to achieve some extraneous end such as general happiness, human perfection, or self-realization. It is concerned with what is objectively, universally, and unconditionally required of us.

These ideas that moral judgments refer to what is in fact objectively right or wrong and that they impose an absolute, and not merely conditional or pragmatic, requirement upon action are of focal interest not just in Kant's moral theism but also in contemporary discussions of morality. Let us see how they might be presented today in terms which, as with Kant, suggest a line of reflection that leads to an affirmation of God as their rational postulate. What we will be suggesting is that if one accepts a particular view of morality, which does not presuppose the existence of God, it can nevertheless be shown by argument that an affirmation of God is implicit in this view of morality as a postulate of its ultimate rationality.

To introduce this discussion let us consider some observations made by the American philosopher Thomas Nagel, himself not a theist, in his interesting collection of essays entitled, *Mortal Questions*.[12] We have already referred to some other works of this significant philosopher in our previous chapter.

Thomas Nagel

In an essay entitled "War and Massacre" Nagel discusses the conflict between two disparate categories of moral reasons that may be called *utilitarian* and *absolutist*. They differ in that utilitarianism gives primacy to a concern with what will *happen* whereas absolutism gives primacy to a concern with what one is *doing*.[13] Each provides moral reasons for actions and one can feel the force of both types of reason very strongly. Together they can generate powerful moral conflict, notably when a desirable end or outcome can only be achieved through reprehensible means, for example, when a disaster can be prevented only by torturing a prisoner or murdering an innocent person.

Utilitarianism can be described in a general way as claiming that one should try to maximize good and minimize evil and that, if faced with the possibility of preventing a great evil only by producing a lesser, one should choose to produce the lesser.[14] This principle can be used to justify even very large scale indiscriminate punitive action if the stakes are high enough.[15]

Absolutism proposes, as of more fundamental significance, a different kind of moral consideration. It is not a substitute for utilitarian reasoning. Rather it operates as a limitation upon it. It maintains that taking account of the consequences of one's actions, although important, is subordinate to the consideration of what one may or may not *do*:

An absolutist can be expected to try to maximize good and minimize evil, so long as it does not require him to transgress an absolute prohibition like that against

---

12 Cf. T. Nagel, *Mortal Questions*, Cambridge, 1979.
13 Cf. ibid., p. 54.
14 Cf. ibid., p. 55.
15 Cf. ibid., p. 57.

64 *The Sense of Creation*

murder. But when such a conflict occurs, the prohibition takes complete precedence over any consideration of consequences.[16]

The prohibitions which the absolutist has in mind concern what we deliberately do to people rather than what may be merely brought about or happen to people as a result of what we do. For example, although it is absolutely prohibited directly and deliberately to kill an innocent person there could not without incoherence be an absolute prohibition against bringing abut the death of an innocent person since this may be, in certain circumstances, the unavoidable consequence of any action or even inaction on our part.

Moreover, the absolutist requires not so much that we *prevent* certain actions at all costs as that we *avoid* doing them at all costs. Furthermore, the source of the absolute prohibition is not some self-centered requirement to preserve one's moral integrity, to keep one's hands clean, at all costs. For it is only if the action is already overridingly wrong that one's moral integrity could be decisively impugned. Any moral theory, including utilitarianism, which defines the right course of action in various circumstances and enjoins the performance of that action *ipso facto* asserts that one should do what preserves one's moral integrity, since such action *is* what preserves one's moral integrity.[17] Consequently, the specific source of the distinctively absolutist prohibition against doing certain actions in any circumstances whatsoever is not to be located in some general requirement of moral integrity which is a common feature of diverse moral theories.

Nagel acknowledges the difficulty of providing a fully satisfactory account of the absolutist position. He suggests, however, that it should be seen as animated by an idea of the relationship in which one should stand to other people according to which

> whatever one does to another person intentionally must be aimed at him as a subject, with the intention that he receive it as a subject. It should manifest an attitude to *him* rather than just to the situation, and he should be able to recognize it and identify himself as its object.[18]

To defend its claim to priority over considerations of utility, absolutism must hold that the maintenance of a direct interpersonal response to other persons is an absolute requirement which no advantage can ever justify one in abandoning. The approach will suggest certain, though not always clear-cut, moral guidelines for action, for example, for the hostile treatment of other persons in the case of war. It will involve the admittedly difficult task, in a state of hostilities, of discriminating between the combatant and the human person and restricting accordingly the scope of one's hostility.

Nagel offers a defense of the absolutist position which he sees as underlying a valid and fundamental type of moral judgment which cannot be reduced to or overridden by other principles. He judges it to be often the only barrier before the abyss of utilitarian apologetics for large-scale murder.[19]

---

16 Ibid., p. 58.
17 Cf. ibid., p. 63.
18 Ibid., p. 66.
19 Cf. ibid., p. 56.

Morality and Transcendence 65

However, his defense is a qualified one. For he sees its insistence that certain actions are never to be done, because no quantity of resulting benefit could justify such treatment of a person, as potentially involving one in the most acute moral dilemmas. In some extreme circumstances the utilitarian cost of refusing to adopt a prohibited course of action may be so high that whether one adopts or refrains from the prohibited course of action one cannot count oneself fully morally justified and free from guilt. What if the world or men's actions are such that they may ineluctably face a previously innocent person with an unavoidable choice between morally abominable courses of action? He is driven to the following pessimistic conclusion:

> Given the limitations on human action, it is naïve to suppose that there is a solution to every moral problem with which the world can face us. We have always known that the world is a bad place. It appears that it may be an evil place as well.[20]

The moral dilemmas arising from the tension between competing values and principles recur in subsequent essays of Nagel's book and even his qualified defense of absolutism, although never wholly abandoned, tends increasingly to yield ground to a more fragmentary view of morality.

Moral conflicts, he observes, arise from tension between various categories of value which one cannot resolve definitively by trying to establish an order of priority amongst them.[21] For example, there is a formal contrast between general rights (e.g. people's freedom from assault or coercion), specific obligations (e.g. to one's family or community), and personal commitments (e.g. to personally adopted projects) on the one hand, and utilitarian (e.g. taking account of the effect of what one does on everyone's welfare), and perfectionist (e.g. intrinsically worthwhile achievements such as scientific discovery) values on the other.

The former constitute reasons of a personal, subjective, or agent-centered kind—though the term "subjective" should not be misunderstood to mean that the general principles of obligation are matters of subjective preference which may vary from person to person. They are subjective in the sense that they are reasons which apply primarily to the individual involved as reasons for *him* to act in a certain way—even though it may also be a good thing, impersonally considered, for him to do so. By contrast, utility or perfectionist values constitute reasons which are decidedly impersonal, objective, and outcome-centered. They have to do primarily with what happens, not with what one does. It is the contribution of what one does to what happens or is achieved that matters.[22] He concludes that "this great division between personal and impersonal, or between agent-centered and outcome-centered, or subjective and objective reasons, is so basic that it renders implausible any reductive unification of ethics."[23]

In his final essay, "Subjective and Objective," he develops a comparison between disparate moral viewpoints and disparate speculative viewpoints.[24] He sees it as part

---

20   Ibid., p. 74.
21   Cf. Nagel's article: "The Fragmentation of Value," ibid., pp. 128–46.
22   Cf. ibid., p. 133.
23   Ibid., p. 133.
24   Cf. ibid., pp. 196–213.

66 *The Sense of Creation*

of a general problem of the opposition between subjective and objective points of view. We tend to link objectivity and reality, to insist that *only* what can be regarded impersonally and objectively is real. But often what appears only to a more personal and subjective viewpoint cannot be accounted for in this way. Hence it seems that either the objective viewpoint is incomplete or that the subjective viewpoint is illusory and should be eliminated.[25] The idea that persons and everything about them must be part of objective reality exercises a powerful appeal. Nevertheless, it seems impossible to accommodate within an objective viewpoint (which attempts to conceive persons completely as a kind of thing in the world), the various aspects of the internal idea of the self as a first-person agent that appears inwardly to the self-conscious subject.

For Nagel, as we have seen, in the context of ethics the contrast between objective and subjective viewpoints is illustrated by the difference between utilitarianism on the one hand, and more agent-centered or "subjective" views of right and wrong on the other.

Utilitarianism or any other purely consequentialist point of view is very demanding. It requires all actions to be justified exclusively from an impersonal outcome-centered point of view in terms of their contribution to the common good.

However, to such an approach it can be objected that it makes questions about what to do subordinate to questions about what would be best overall. Such criticism maintains that an ethical theory should be more agent-centered and allow some room for each individual to pursue his own ends and be responsive to the rights of other individuals without always subordinating such considerations to some comprehensive utilitarian goals. Thus, it is objected, that what is permitted and what is required may sometimes deviate from what might be considered impersonally to be the best overall.[26]

Although these two agent-centered considerations—of leaving room for the individual to pursue his own life interests, and of being responsive to the particular claims of other directly encountered individuals—each suggests a more personal or subjective general ethical theory than utilitarianism, they do so in different ways. The first, which refers to permissions, derives simply from the standpoint of the personal claims of the individual agent. The second, which refers to deontological or dutiful requirements, emerges when the agent considers in a certain way his own point of view together with those of the persons to whom he is directly related in action. Here the real source of the requirements or restrictions is not the agent but the potential victim whose rights are protected.

However, deontological requirements, though intended to apply universally are agent-centered. For they instruct each person to evaluate his actions in terms of their rightness and wrongness from the viewpoint of his position in the world and his direct relations to others envisaged as subjects, rather than in terms of the overall good or bad outcome of his actions for the world as a whole. This distinction between subjective and objective viewpoints, which appears in metaphysical, epistemological,

---

25 Cf. ibid., p. 196.
26 Cf. ibid., p. 202.

Morality and Transcendence 67

and ethical contexts, is a polarity which gives rise to problems because the same individual is the occupant of both viewpoints.

Difficulties arise when the objective viewpoint encounters a fact or value revealed subjectively which it cannot adequately accommodate. Problems of personal identity, mind–body relationship, free will, and disparate moral viewpoints arise because subjectively apparent facts cannot be encompassed within a more external viewpoint. The pressure towards a comprehensive objective viewpoint urges one to suppress the recalcitrant dimension of subjectivity either by reduction, elimination, or annexation.[27]

Nagel judges such moves unsatisfactory. He recognizes the force and value of the objective viewpoint but queries the tendency to dismiss deontological requirements and other non-consequentialist ethical intuitions as superstitious, selfish, or rule-bound. Instead he suggests that we simply accept the polarity of conflicting subjective and objective viewpoints, varying in detachment from the contingent self, as an irreducible fact of life. It is the aim of eventual unification that is misplaced, both in our thoughts about how to live and in our conception of what there is.[28]

Perhaps, as he conjectured earlier, in some circumstances, whatever one does, one cannot count oneself morally justified, cannot refrain from doing what is morally reprehensible. Might it not be the case that moral action can be operative only within a restricted range of human circumstances and that the alleged overriding claim of a moral viewpoint may be deprived of application conditions by the world's irreducible core of evil?

This contention, that at times the performance of gravely immoral deeds may be not merely permissible but even unavoidable is deeply corrosive of the unique significance generally ascribed to morality. Rather than simply acquiescing in so nihilistic a conclusion it is reasonable to look for some more comprehensive view of things which, though not immediately evident, might obviate it.

One way in which this pessimistic and even Manichean conclusion might be avoided would be to refuse the premise from which it is derived, namely, the irreducibility of the claims upon action of two disparate categories of moral reason, the utilitarian and the absolutist. (The term "absolutist" should not be understood as equivalent to "intolerant" but rather as "deontological agent-centered reason for action".) One could, for example, maintain that, in the final analysis, utilitarian considerations are more fundamental than absolutist claims, or one could maintain that, in the final analysis, utilitarian considerations are subordinate to absolutist claims.

In general, according to the first alternative one would accept that the overriding moral consideration is to maximize good and to minimize evil. From within such a moral perspective one could accord very great weight to the sort of prohibitions against murder, torture, tyranny, degradation, and the like characteristic of absolutism. One could acknowledge the importance, in any overall scheme for the maximization of good, of cultivating an outlook and practice in which such prohibited deeds would be habitually avoided. One might almost go so far as to maintain that the project of maximizing good and minimizing evil could never countenance such deeds.

---

27 Cf. ibid., pp. 210–11.
28 Cf. ibid., pp. 211–13.

68 *The Sense of Creation*

Almost, but I think not quite—at least without implicitly undermining the claim that utilitarian considerations are more ultimate than absolutist ones. For if one accepts that nothing which might happen could ever count as of greater good or consequence than the avoidance of certain deeds then one has effectively conceded the basic limitation on utilitarian reasoning which is distinctive of absolutism. One would have absolutism in utilitarian clothing inasmuch as one would have conceded that a necessary constraint upon action to maximize utility is that it should never happen that certain deeds are done.

The radical utilitarian will repudiate any such absolutist constraint upon his position and repudiate likewise the irreducibility of the absolutist viewpoint. He will argue that the fundamental moral consideration is the assessment of overall results or states of affairs and that in relation to this the assessment of actions is secondary. It is the contribution of what one does to what *happens* which is of decisive significance. It is the best overall state of affairs, impersonally considered, which must be the moral objective. This carries with it the implication that at times some dreadful deeds may have to be done in the interest of overall utility. At times, if the stakes are high enough, even torture and murder may be permissible if such deeds are necessary to achieve an objectively better or less evil state of affairs.[29]

Now it can and indeed does happen that people may judge that this consequence of a thoroughgoing utilitarianism is morally unacceptable. And if they are also dissatisfied with the view that there is an irreducible tension in ethics between utilitarian and absolutist considerations, they may feel impelled to explore the other alternative mentioned above. This is the alternative that, in the final analysis, utilitarian considerations concerning the beneficial outcome of action are subordinate to the morally more fundamental constraints of certain absolutist prohibitions and requirements. I propose to consider how this position might be elaborated and then go on to discuss how an affirmation of God might be relevant to a vindication of its rationality.

Perhaps it will be helpful to begin this discussion by recalling Nagel's own suggestion that if absolutism is to maintain its claim to priority over considerations of utility it must defend a specific approach to the world in general and interpersonal relationships in particular. According to this approach whatever one does to other people intentionally should be aimed at them as subjects with the intention that they receive it as subjects.[30] Rather than seeking to turn oneself into an impersonal instrument for the realization of the best outcome *sub specie aeternitatis*, each person should seek to determine the rightness or wrongness of his actions solely from the point of view of his own position in the world and his direct relations with others. This approach to ethical constraints against murder, torture, and the like, though intended to apply universally, opposes the agent's specific relations

---

29   Thus the Cambridge philosopher Elizabeth Anscombe in her famous article "Modern Moral Philosophy," *Philosophy*, 33, 1958, pp. 1–19 claims that every one of the best known English academic moral philosophers since Sidgwick "has put out a philosophy according to which e.g. it is not permissible to hold that it cannot be right to kill the innocent as a means to any end whatsoever and that someone who thinks otherwise is in error." p. 10.

30   Cf. Nagel, *Mortal Questions*, pp. 66–8.

Morality and Transcendence 69

with other people to the conception of a single end that everyone should exclusively promote. The real source of the ethical requirement is the potential victim in his concrete relationship to others through which he exercises a claim on each person not to violate his rights. It is the character of one's actions vis-à-vis the rights and requirements of others, rather than the state of the world as a whole, which must be one's primary concern.[31] The justification of one's actions must be primarily interpersonal rather than administrative.[32]

A similar line of thought is developed by the continental philosopher Emmanuel Levinas in a remarkable but enigmatic work entitled *Totality and Infinity*.[33] A consideration of this comparable development, in an idiom rather different to the more typically Anglo-American one of Nagel, is illuminating and will advance our objective of exploring how an affirmation of God might be adduced as a rational postulate of such a conception of morality.

Emmanuel Levinas

Levinas introduces his work in a vein similar to the preoccupations of Nagel's essay "War and Massacre." "Everyone", he observes, "will readily agree that it is of the highest importance to know whether we are not duped by morality."[34] This issue is borne in upon us with particular force by the permanent possibility of war, which challenges the claims of an agent-centered morality. Thus he remarks:

> The state of war suspends morality; it divests the eternal institutions and obligations of their eternity and rescinds ad interim the unconditional imperatives. ... it renders morality derisory. The art of foreseeing war and of winning it by every means—politics—is henceforth enjoined as the very exercise of reason. Politics is opposed to morality, as philosophy to naiveté.[35]

War proposes itself as the harsh truth of reality, the true face of being, making people play roles in which they no longer recognize themselves, betraying not only their commitments but also their very substance. Their significance as individuals is lost in the totality of the enterprise of war and its overriding goal of victory at any cost.

According to Levinas, morality can sustain the mocking gaze of the political man only if somehow the certitude of peace dominates the evidence of war.[36] This certitude of peace, a "prophetic eschatology" which claims supremacy over the "ontology" of war, cannot be deduced from or produced by past or present states of war. Morality cannot be founded teleologically upon politics as the intended best overall rational outcome of the impersonal politics of war. It must be seen as expressing a non-utilitarian primordial relationship with being quite different to that which has dominated the thought of western philosophy. For Levinas, as the title of

---

31 Cf. ibid., pp. 202–6.
32 Cf. ibid., p. 68.
33 Cf. E. Levinas, *Totality and Infinity*, trans. A. Lingis, Pittsburgh, 1969.
34 Ibid., p. 21.
35 Ibid., p. 21.
36 Cf. ibid., p. 22.

70   *The Sense of Creation*

his work indicates, this means defending the primacy of a concept of infinity over that of totality. He writes:

> Eschatology institutes a relation with being *beyond the totality* or beyond history and not with being beyond the past or the present. ... It is a relationship with *a surplus always exterior to the totality*, as though the objective totality did not fill out the true measure of being, as though another concept, the concept of *infinity*, were needed to express this transcendence with regard to totality, non-encompassable within a totality and as primordial as totality.[37]

Let us attempt to elucidate what Levinas might mean by this enigmatic utterance by considering briefly some of the central ideas of his profound but sometimes obscure thought.

The basic theme which Levinas argues in his work is that we must take the transcendence of the other person seriously. This means that we must not seek to "com-prehend" him as just an *alter ego*, a mere reflection of our own subjectivity, or as simply an instance, like ourselves of some englobing totality such as the species, the human race, or the State. The term "infinity" expresses this concept of the other person's irreducible transcendence of any attempts to contain him within some totality or totalitarian scheme of control.

According to Levinas, the other person as other transcends the realm of "the same." This is the egoistic realm of my self-identity and the world of objects, activities, and bodily states which are the articulations of this self-identity. The world pertains to the self as its milieu or site over which it exercises power, control, and comprehension. Its otherness vis-à-vis the self is not radical. The alterity of the world in which I sojourn falls under my sway. Not so the other person:

> He and I do not form a number. The collectivity in which I say "you" or "we" is not a plural of the "I". I, you— these are not individuals of a common concept. Neither possession nor the unity of number nor the unity of concepts link me to the Stranger (*l"Etranger*), the Stranger who disturbs the being at home with oneself (*le chez-soi*). But the Stranger also means the free one. Over him I have no *power.* He escapes my grasp by an essential dimension, even if I have him at my disposal. He is not wholly in my site (*sic*).[38]

Western philosophy, for Levinas, has most often been an ontology.[39] It aims at a theoretical comprehension of all things through the neutralizing mediation of an all-embracing concept of being. It can be seen as a manifestation of egoistic freedom expressing itself as a cognitive reduction of the, initially conceded, alterity of "the other" to the conceptual unity of "the same." It accomplishes, not a relation with the other as such, but rather a possession and domination of the other. The individual existent, which exists primarily, is converted into intelligible generality within the unifying grasp of the concept. "truth which should reconcile persons, here exists anonymously. Universality presents itself as impersonal; and this is another

---

37   Ibid., pp. 22–3.
38   Ibid., p. 39.
39   Cf. ibid., pp. 42–7.

Morality and Transcendence 71

inhumanity."[40] Ontology as first philosophy is a philosophy of power. "I think" comes down to "I can," a conceptual appropriation of what is—a matter of freedom rather than justice. It issues concretely in the tyrannical power of the State which seeks to absorb the irreducible otherness of persons within the ambit of its utilitarian and even totalitarian claims.

According to Levinas, an alternative, more critical and fundamental, metaphysics can go beyond this entrenched ontology by calling into question the egoistical spontaneity which sustains it. It will take the form of an ethics, which calls my spontaneity into question by acknowledging the transcendence of the other person, his irreducibility to my thoughts and possessions.[41] It will seek to maintain, within the anonymity of community, the true society of the I with the Other, which is a relationship irreducibly prior to any impersonal comprehension of him in some objective ontological system.[42] (Following the translator's convention, approved by Levinas, we write the term "Other" with a capital letter when it refers to the personal other "*autrui*". We use the term "other" when it refers to an impersonal other "*autre*".)

The Other cannot be encompassed as an object of thought. He or she must be envisaged rather, to use a favorite illustration of Levinas, as Descartes envisaged the divine perfection, namely, as an *ideatum* or reality surpassing its idea in us. The other person presents himself to me, not as an idea, but as a face which expresses itself and evokes a relationship of conversation. Levinas writes:

> To approach the Other in conversation is to welcome his expression, in which at each instant he overflows the idea a thought would carry away from it. It is therefore to *receive* from the Other beyond the capacity of the I, which means exactly: to have the idea of infinity. But this also means to be taught.[43]

This inter-subjective experience, in which the transcendence of the other is acknowledged, is an ethical experience which discloses that I do not have the right to demand of the Other what I permit myself to demand of myself. "Correlation does not suffice as a category for transcendence."[44] Levinas lays great emphasis upon this asymmetry which he sees as precluding the possibility of treating indifferently the self and the Other in terms of some all-embracing system, totality, or history: "this moral experience, so commonplace, indicates a metaphysical asymmetry: the radical impossibility of seeing oneself from the outside and speaking in the same sense of oneself and of the others, and consequently the impossibility of totalization."[45]

When one distils the main thrust of Levinas's rather exotic style of expression one may note a parallel between his ethical account of the Other and Nagel's account of an agent-centered ethics which ascribes irreducible significance to the claims which other individual subjects make directly upon us—by contrast with an outcome-

---

40   Ibid., p. 46.
41   Cf. ibid., p. 43.
42   Ibid., p. 47.
43   Ibid., p. 51.
44   Ibid., p. 53.
45   Ibid., p. 53.

72 *The Sense of Creation*

centered utilitarian ethics which seeks to determine impersonally and objectively the best overall outcome of a situation.

For Levinas, authentic conversation with another person will confirm and maintain his irreducible heterogeneity.[46] It will respect his quality of strangeness or freedom whereby he is in a direct interpersonal relationship with me only inasmuch as he is autonomous and enjoys a significance which is self-possessed and not by reference to a system.[47] This way of ethically regarding the other person affects my appraisal of my own freedom. Morality begins when freedom, instead of being regarded complacently as innocent spontaneity is ashamed of itself as arbitrary and violent.[48]

To welcome the other person is to put in question my freedom. Thus Levinas writes:

> The relationship with the other does not move (as does cognition) into enjoyment and possession, into freedom: the Other imposes himself as an exigency that dominates this freedom, and hence as more primordial than everything that takes place in me. The Other, whose exceptional presence is inscribed in the ethical impossibility of killing him in which I stand, marks the end of powers. If I can no longer have power over him it is because he overflows absolutely every *idea* I can have of him.[49]

To adopt this perspective is to separate oneself from the influential philosophical tradition which seeks to ground the meaning and value of one's self within *oneself.* One claims that the access to ultimate meaning and value is not achieved via an exploration of the self envisaged as a Sartrean *pour-soi.* It is achieved rather by attending to what is more basic than presence to oneself, namely, presence of the Other—which calls the egoism and arbitrariness of the self into question and invites one to aim beyond freedom to justice.[50]

This metaphysical or ethical relation with the other person differs from a cognitive relation with an object of consciousness. It differs also from the enjoyed symbiosis with our environment from which we live as embodied sensibility prior to our representational life of cognition. In such relationships the alterity of the object of consciousness, or the world as the medium in which I sojurn, is not absolute. It is, rather, either relative or correlative to myself.[51] My relationship with the other person is quite different. "the alterity of the Other is in him and is not relative to me; it *reveals* itself."[52]

Moreover, the Other does not reveal himself as just another freedom, similar to and just as arbitrary as my own, which threatens to dominate me. His alterity is manifested in a mastery which does not conquer but teaches—a teaching which finds its most concrete expression in my acknowledgment of the ethical impossibility of murdering him. He reveals himself as a teacher who addresses me, not as coexistent

---

46 Cf. ibid., p. 69.
47 Cf. ibid., pp. 74–5.
48 Cf. ibid., p. 84.
49 Ibid., p. 87.
50 Cf. ibid., p. 88.
51 Cf. ibid., pp. 122–42.
52 Ibid., p. 121, cf. also p. 297.

Morality and Transcendence 73

on the same level but, as it were, from on high disclosing and calling into question my violence and enabling me to speak the language of ethical response.[53]

Further, this ethical response to the invocation of the Other is not the fulfillment of a natural need. It is rather the initiation of an original ethical desire aroused by the presence of the Other. Such desire situates the center of gravity of my being outside itself. This distinction between need and desire is fundamental to Levinas's thought and to his rejection of totality: "desire is an aspiration that the Desirable animates; it originates from its object"; it is revelation—whereas need is a void of the Soul; it proceeds from the subject." [54] Ethical requirements vis-à-vis the Other do not stem from a prior psychological motivation. Rather they uncover or establish a specifically ethical motivational structure which is explained by the transcendent desirability of the Other that grounds these requirements. As Levinas puts it: "Desire does not coincide with unsatisfied need; it is situated beyond satisfaction and non satisfaction. The relationship with the Other or the idea of Infinity, accomplishes it."[55] (In an early work Nagel makes a comparable observation:

> There are reasons for action which are specifically moral; it is because they represent moral requirements that they can motivate, and not vice versa. If this is correct ethics must yield discoveries about human motivation ... Not just information about what people want. If ethics is not to presuppose any motivations, but must instead reveal their possibility, the discoveries must be at a more fundamental level than that.[56])

Thus the ethical solicitude and desire for the Other is not a function of a natural need for happiness. Through ethical desire for the Other the autonomous separated self surpasses itself and can sacrifice to this desire its very happiness. Through this non-egoistical preoccupation with the Other as desirable one goes beyond theoretical comprehension of being to goodness.[57]

In ethical discourse the Other as my interlocutor surpasses, as essentially transcendent, the Other taken merely as a theme to whom I myself could ascribe meaning or significance. Ethical discourse is not a product of my own thought or understanding, not merely my excogitation, but relationship with a transcendence which offers new powers to the soul, powers of welcome, of gift, of hospitality. The structure of this discourse exhibits the ethical inviolability of the Other.[58] Such discourse with the Other is not utilitarian talk about an instance but face-to-face response to a moral summons.

The Other resists and calls in question my power, not by opposing a greater force to mine within the totality of forces but by the infinity of his transcendence which, prior to any struggle or war, finds expression in his face as the primordial word: "You shall not commit murder."[59] The Other, encountered primordially as transcendent yet

---

53 Cf. ibid., pp. 100–101 and pp. 171–4.
54 Ibid., p. 62.
55 Ibid., p. 179.
56 T. Nagel, *The Possibility of Altruism*, Oxford, 1970, p. 13.
57 Levinas, *Totality and Infinity*, p. 63.
58 Cf. ibid., p. 195.
59 Cf. ibid., p. 199.

74   *The Sense of Creation*

destitute, does not limit but promotes my freedom, non-violently, by arousing my goodness. His expression ineluctably evokes my responsibility, discloses that pre-existing the plane of ontology is the ethical plane.[60]

This non-violent expressive presence of the Other as ethical discourse and signification is the very paradigm and definition of reason. Primordially the intelligible is not a concept but an intelligence, the Other as signification. The expressive presence of the Other as signification and language is not the mere manifestation of an impersonal reason nor a moment in the articulation of the rational State. The pluralism of society precedes the impersonal universal order of the State.[61]

Nor is the Other to be found as just an instance of a pre-cognized common humanity. Rather it is in my irreducible relation with the Other as ethical signification, in answering his call to responsibility and justice, that humanity is found. The third party, the whole of humanity, looks at me in the eyes of the other and is properly envisaged only in this way. The universal and irreducible range of moral imperatives, such as that prohibiting murder, is disclosed through the primordial ethical relationship established between the Other and myself. Every social relation leads back to the expressive face to face presence of the Other to the same, i.e. to myself.

Undoubtedly the human race is a biological genus, and in respect of common functions men may exercise in the world as a totality they can be considered under a common concept. But the essence of society is not like a genus that unites interchangeable like individuals, is not comparable to the collectivity of a beehive. It is "the intersubjective experience that leads to the social experience and endows it with meaning (as to believe the phenomenologists, perception, impossible to conjure away, endows scientific experience with meaning)."[62]

Society is a fraternal community of unique separated individuals, instituted as a fraternity by my ethical welcome of the Other.[63] The Other, present in relation to me as separated and transcendent, presents himself from the outset as an absolute, as one I cannot adequately represent and to whom I am obligated.[64] For Levinas, the idea of infinity, proposed by Descartes as the idea of that which is beyond my capacity to produce or comprehend, expresses this relationship: "a relation with a total alterity irreducible to interiority—a receptivity without passivity, a relation between freedoms."[65]

Implicit in this view is a repudiation of any idealist or utilitarian viewpoint in which the Other and the I function only as elements of an ideal calculus or moments in a system. Such a viewpoint ultimately reduces ethics to politics, reduces the separated will as personal ethical desire to impersonal universal reason. Its goal would be the maximization of happiness through the constitution of rational institutions in which an impersonal reason, already at work in people, is made effective and objective as the universal State.

---

60   Cf. ibid., pp. 200–201.
61   Cf. ibid., pp. 201–8.
62   Ibid., p. 53.
63   Cf. ibid., pp. 213–14.
64   Cf. ibid., p. 215.
65   Ibid., p. 211.

Morality and Transcendence 75

Politics, taken un-rebuked, makes exploitation possible by envisaging a humanity of reciprocal relations, a system of interchangeable people rather than a fraternity of unique persons.[66] It does not allow for the truth that the individual and the personal act independently of the impersonal universal which would mould them. It overlooks that the very first signification—the very upsurge—of the rational originates in the ethical appeal to my will of the face of the Other.[67]

This awareness of the Other as a surplus beyond the *a priori* resources of thought is an absolutely innovative experience. It realizes a metaphysical relation of separation between terms that are absolute yet in relation. It realizes a radical multiplicity irreducible to numerical multiplicity, an asymmetrical pluralism irreducible to any totality of mutually defining parts.[68] This asymmetry is realized through my ethical acknowledgment that I am not entitled to claim to be transcendent with regard to the Other in the same sense that the Other is transcendent with regard to me.[69] It is manifested positively in the moral resistance of the face of the Other to the violence of murder and in my being more in dread of committing murder than of death.[70]

"Goodness", Levinas remarks, "consists in taking up a position in being such that the Other counts more than myself."[71] Morality arises not as a calculus of equality but from the fact that infinite exigencies, concerning the service of others, converge at one point of the universe—myself.[72] It is centered on the responsibility of *my* subjectivity vis-à-vis the concrete appeal of the Other. This subjectivity finds itself under a judgment more severe than that of the historically visible outcome of actions in accordance with impersonal rational principles such as utilitarian maxims. It must reckon with the offence done to individuals in impersonal judgments issuing from universal principles. As Levinas puts it: "What is above all invisible is the offence universal history inflicts on particulars. To be I and not only an incarnation of reason is precisely to be capable of seeing the offence of the offended, or the face."[73]

For Levinas, the fundamental asymmetry of the ethical relationship between the Other and myself is irreducible. It does not arise within a totality nor does it establish an integrated totality.[74] It is not impersonally accessible to a third party but only in the personal face to face encounters which establish it, e.g. in my personal awareness of the obligating summons of the needy Other. It is produced in multiple singularities and not in a being exterior to them who could enumerate the totality of relationships. This personal pluralism of society precedes the impersonal universal of the State. It is the primordial phenomenon of reason and is the condition of all subsequent commerce, communication and community. As Levinas puts it:

---

66 Cf. ibid., p. 298.
67 Cf. ibid., p. 218.
68 Cf. ibid., pp. 219–22.
69 Cf. ibid., p. 225.
70 Cf. ibid., p. 246.
71 Ibid., p. 247.
72 Cf. ibid., p. 245.
73 Ibid., p. 247.
74 Cf. ibid., p. 251.

76 *The Sense of Creation*

Reason presupposes these singularities or particularities, not as individuals open to conceptualization, or divesting themselves of their particularity so as to find themselves to be identical, but precisely as interlocutors, irreplaceable beings, unique in their genus, faces. The difference between the two theses: "reason creates the relations between me and the other" and 'the Other's teaching me creates reason" is not purely theoretical. The consciousness of the tyranny of the State—though it be rational—makes the difference actual.[75]

According to Levinas, his account of the ethical asymmetry of the relationship between the Other and myself is the key to a correct appraisal of the nature of being, one which goes beyond *traditional* ontology to genuine metaphysics. Western philosophy in the form of ontology has typically aspired to a cognitive comprehension of being. It subordinates otherness and exteriority to sameness within a unifying luminous horizon or concept of being: "*Being* before the *existent*, ontology before metaphysics, is freedom (be it the freedom of theory) before justice. It is a movement within the same before obligation to the other."[76] But, as the ethical relationship shows, being in its deepest significance is exteriority, as exercised in a face-to-face conjuncture. It is situated in a subjective field but goes beyond vision or cognition to ethical acknowledgment and thus allows exteriority to express itself as command, authority, superiority. 'this curvature of inter-subjective space inflects distance into elevation, it does not falsify being, but makes its truth first possible."[77]

Levinas sees his endeavor as having broken with the philosophy of the Neuter whether in the form of Heidegger's impersonal Being or Hegel's impersonal Reason. Materialism, too, is a form of philosophy which affirms the primacy of the Neuter, the primacy of an impersonal dimension of being which would determine the being of persons. To begin with the ethical face-to-face encounter as the focal source of meaning is to affirm that in its deepest significance being is irreducibly personal and that metaphysics is not a calculus of needs but a logic of ethical desire for the good.[78]

This ethical face-to-face relation is the paradigm of being and goodness. It is the source of authentic pluralism and a repudiation of the anonymity of impersonal totality. It is a relation of peace which starts from an I and goes to the Other in desire and goodness, not an uneasy utilitarian truce issuing from a combat of needs and forces.[79] For Levinas: "to posit being as desire is to decline at the same time the ontology of isolated subjectivity and the ontology of impersonal reason realizing itself in history."[80] It is to acknowledge the metaphysical primacy of the ethical relation between the Other and me and to see political and utilitarian considerations as derivative. Politics, the domain of the State, institutions, and laws, which are the context of universality, is the outgrowth of the ethical relationship inasmuch as the face of the Other relates us with a third party and thus moves into the form of the We. But taken simply by itself politics bears a potential tyranny within itself inasmuch as it tends to subordinate the concrete ethical relationship between oneself and the

---

75 Ibid., p. 252.
76 Ibid., p. 47.
77 Ibid., p. 291.
78 Cf. ibid., p. 299.
79 Cf. ibid., p. 306.
80 Ibid., p. 305.

Morality and Transcendence   77

other person to impersonal universal or utilitarian rules. Metaphysics affirms the irreducibility of the ethical relationship as that which the work of the State must take as its model and in relation to which it must be situated.[81]

This brief outline of the central ideas of *Totality and Infinity* reveals a close similarity between Levinas's account of ethics and Nagel's account of how an ethical absolutist, in contrast to a utilitarian, will direct his actions with primary regard to the rights of other people to whom he personally is directly related, rather than with primary regard to the most beneficial outcome for humanity in general, impersonally considered.

Nagel is expressly aware that such an ethical viewpoint commits one to a very different metaphysical appraisal of the world and human subjectivity than that implied by utilitarianism. It does not accept the position that one's decisions should be evaluated ultimately from an exclusively external point of view, which sees oneself as just one instance among many and attends impersonally not to what one *does* but to whether the outcome of what one does is for the best overall. Instead it insists that, since the agent lives his life from where he is, it is what he intentionally *does* vis-à-vis others whom he directly encounters which is of primary ethical importance. The pursuit of what seems impersonally best must be subordinate to what one does from a personal agent-centered viewpoint. "Life is always the life of a particular person, and cannot be lived *sub specie aeternitatis*."[82]

However, unlike Nagel, who sees the agent-centered and the outcome-centered moralities as involving mutually irreducible and equally compelling world views which can leave a previously innocent person with no escape from doing wrong, Levinas is unequivocal in subordinating the latter to the former. The agent's direct personal relation with the Other is of more fundamental metaphysical significance than any subsequent utilitarian consideration. Moreover, and again unlike Nagel, Levinas links up this metaphysical viewpoint in a positive, though unsystematic way, with a religious affirmation of God. In the final sections of this chapter I would like to consider this feature of his thought and suggest how it might be developed more systematically than perhaps he himself would endorse.

Ethics and Religion

For Levinas, an authentic affirmation of God must respect both the separateness and autonomy of the human subject on the one hand, and the irreducible transcendence of God on the other. Consequently the affirmation is not to be achieved through some mystical technique of ecstatic participation whereby the separated knowing self is annihilated or transported outside himself and absorbed into a numinous divine being.[83] Such an approach would treat man as a mere circuit of rupture and reunification within the totality of divine life. It would not respect the truth that precisely as a created existence he is separate from God—enjoys an *esse proprium*,

---

81   Cf. ibid., p. 300.
82   Cf. Nagel, *Mortal Questions*, p. 205.
83   Cf. Levinas, *Totality and Infinity*, p. 77.

78   *The Sense of Creation*

a genuine autonomy.[84] But neither can God, the utterly transcendent, be directly comprehended or thematized as an object of human cognition. God, as he is in himself, infinitely transcends our cognitional resources. As Descartes appreciated he overflows absolutely any idea we may have of him.

Levinas maintains that in metaphysics—or ethics (he uses the terms interchangeably)— man enters a relationship with God, the relation of a separated being with what he cannot in the etymological sense of the word comprehend.[85] This relationship with God, inaccessible to either mystical participation or theoretical cogitation, is accomplished through the ethical relationships with other people such as are portrayed by him in *Totality and Infinity*.

He speaks of the dimension of the divine being manifest in the human face of the Stranger, the widow, and the orphan who solicit us in their destitution. God is supremely present as the ultimate significance of the justice which we render to other persons. Our relationship with him respects his directly inaccessible transcendence and is more effectively disclosed in our ethical welcome of the Other than by any attempt to comprehend him theoretically. Thus he remarks:

> Ethics is the spiritual optics ... Hence metaphysics is enacted where the social relation is enacted—in our relations with men. There can be no "knowledge" of God separated from the relationship with men. The Other is the very locus of metaphysical truth, and is indispensable for my relation with God.[86]

He sees the ethical relationship between men as the primary irreducible structure upon which all metaphysics rests and as conferring upon theological concepts the only significance they have. This ethical relationship in which a separated self acknowledges concretely the irreducible moral claims of the Other is in its deepest significance the relationship between a person and the utterly transcendent God, and as thus envisaged is what we call religion. Religion is the bond between the same and the Other which is not a function of a totality and does not crystallize into a system.[87]

This claim that a religious relationship with God is achieved through ethical relationships with other people is an appealing but not immediately evident thesis. It strikes a responsive chord in anyone already committed to the Judaeo-Christian teaching that access to God cannot be disassociated from the loving welcome of the neighbor. But how might somebody, who is not explicitly a theist or even who is explicitly an atheist, but accepting Levinas's account of ethics, be persuaded that it implies the religious significance which he ascribes to it?

Levinas's text is not entirely helpful on this delicate point. He is generally dismissive of theoretical arguments for the existence of God and tends to assert the relationship between ethics and religion in rather striking terms rather than argue it systematically. His reticence about arguing this religious claim stems from his mistrust of traditional ontology and his conviction that the relationship at issue is unamenable to the totalizing movement of thought: 'the relationship between

---

84   Cf. ibid., pp. 104–5.
85   Cf. ibid., p. 80.
86   Ibid., p. 78.
87   Cf. ibid., pp. 79–80.

Morality and Transcendence 79

separated beings does not totalize them; it is a "Relation without relation" which no one can encompass or thematize."[88] He simply asserts that "the Other, in his signification prior to my initiative resembles God."[89] Again, speaking of "the curvature of inter-subjective space" which expresses metaphorically the relationship in which the other person is placed "higher" than me—in the sense that my ethical responsibility for him is more than I can require of him for myself—he says "this 'curvature of space' is, perhaps, the very presence of God."[90]

Nevertheless, some rational justification of this theistic interpretation is called for if it is not to appear arbitrary or even superfluous. The ethical relation must be shown to imply the alleged theistic interpretation as its ultimate rationale. Although he does not elucidate how this might be shown he does make some perceptive observations which open up an interesting line of reflection.

Ethics and Metaphysical Argument

According to Levinas, the idea of creation from nothing provides the best expression of his idea of the ethical relationship in which the transcendence of the other person is affirmed as irreducible to any kind of totality.[91]

Following up this idea (and recalling the kind of argument advanced by Kant which we indicated above) one might argue that the ethical relationship as envisaged by Levinas requires as its theoretical or metaphysical truth condition the theistic claim that the persons involved in the relationship are created beings. If this were shown to be the case one would have achieved at once a moral and a causal argument for the existence of God as the transcendent creator of moral beings. The argument would be an *a posteriori* and indirect one. It would argue that the concretely experienced ethical relationship turns out upon reflection to be unintelligible and even contradictory unless the terms of the relationship are acknowledged to be created beings.

Such an argument might begin with a consideration of the irreducible significance ascribed to the other person as an absolute and self-possessed source of moral obligation. Each other person appears even, and indeed principally, in their destitution and vulnerability as a being of surpassing worth to whom I find myself obligated.[92] He or she so appears that the only appropriate response in their regard is goodness—even to the point of very great sacrifice, which I cannot on that account reciprocally require of them. (Think of Kant's example of the honest man who is prepared to endure death rather than conspire in the execution of an innocent powerless person.)[93] The other person appears as expressing an absolute moral claim upon my conduct which may not be subordinated to my pursuit of personal happiness or to any global utilitarian ideal.

---

88   Ibid., p. 295.
89   Ibid., p. 293.
90   Ibid., p. 291.
91   Cf. ibid., p. 293.
92   Cf. ibid., p. 75 and p. 291.
93   Cf. Kant, *Critique of Practical Reason*, par. 305.

80 *The Sense of Creation*

This ethical relationship, if taken as veridical and not illusory, has metaphysical implications. The order of things must be ultimately such that the other person can validly exercise the irreducible ethical claim upon me which I acknowledge that he or she does—particularly since what might otherwise appear a better outcome from an impersonal viewpoint is subordinated to this claim. If how things are is not ultimately consonant with, and possibly even wholly inadequate and recalcitrant to, the exigencies of morality then the ethical life, at least as described by Levinas, is rendered rationally suspect. The absolute claims of the other person and the often very demanding constraints imposed thereby on my action could not be rationally defended—particularly when they appear to impede an objective maximization of good or minimization of evil. If absolutist checks cannot be cashed out metaphysically in ontological currency, i.e. in a compatible and dependable account of reality, then the ultimate subordination of utilitarian considerations to absolutist constraints is, as Nagel contends, rationally indefensible.

How then ultimately must reality be understood to be if the experienced ethical relationship, as described by Levinas, is to be metaphysically confirmed? The most significant features of this relationship are its asymmetrical character and the irreducibility of its terms to any encompassing totality. As Levinas puts it: "Multiplicity in being, which refuses totalization but takes form as fraternity and discourse, is situated in a 'space' essentially asymmetrical."[94] In the ethical relationship the other is placed higher than me. I respond freely to the other person as a transcendent and absolute source of obligation exercising a unique, ineluctable, and non-mutual claim upon my service.[95]

Here we come up against what Nagel refers to elsewhere as the sense of incredulity that one should be somebody in particular whose direct interpersonal relationships with other unique individuals constitute the irreducible bedrock of morality.[96] Especially paradoxical is the self-possessed superior ethical status ascribed in the relationship to the other person. This exalted transcendence, irreducible to any totality, orientates our thinking about the structure of reality. It indicates that we should envisage beings as standing in a relationship precisely as separate and independent, as both axiologically and ontologically diverse.

For Levinas, beings are characterized by a radical heterogeneity which is resistant to any attempt to totalize them as equivalent instances of the same kind. This radical independence and non-homogeneity of beings (in more traditional idiom the analogical character of finite beings) surpasses comprehension in terms of a naturally dispersed and variously configured break-up of a primordial common stuff. Hence he remarks:

> This impossibility of conciliation among beings, this radical heterogeneity, in fact indicates a mode of being produced and an ontology that is not equivalent to panoramic existence and its disclosure. ... The exteriority of being does not, in fact, mean that multiplicity is

---

94 Levinas, *Totality and Infinity*, p. 216, cf. also pp. 35–6 and pp. 290–92.
95 Cf. ibid., pp. 86–7.
96 Cf. Nagel, *Mortal Questions*, p. 206, also Levinas, *Totality and Infinity*, pp. 304–6.

Morality and Transcendence 81

without relation. However, the relation that binds this multiplicity does not fill the abyss of separation; it confirms it.[97]

In effect the ethical acknowledgment of the other person as asymmetrically transcendent impels us to ask how it can be that he thus exists? This exalted transcendence, this curvature of inter-subjective space, is unintelligible in terms of our ordinary scientific understanding of our shared human nature to which utilitarian considerations are so well adapted. It does not make sense considered from below, as it were, in terms of our common appearance as comparable members of the same biological species. We are speaking here more of an innovative emergence of ethically related unique individual subjects than a resultant appearance of objectively equivalent instances of a common physico-chemical structure. As Levinas puts it:

> That the Other is placed higher than me would be a pure and simple error if the welcome I make him consisted in "perceiving" a nature. Sociology, psychology, physiology are thus deaf to exteriority. Man as Other comes to us from the outside, a separated—or holy—face. His exteriority, that is, his appeal to me, is his truth.[98]

An account is called for of how this remarkable state of affairs can obtain—this coming to be of ethically related individuals possessing conscious moral capabilities irreducible to and underivable from their physico-chemical micro-parts or any connecting or compounding of these micro-parts. As in the case of theoretical knowledge, any attempt to provide a complete account of this interpersonal ethical relationship in cultural, psychological, evolutionary, or biological terms is self-defeating. It fails precisely to encompass the radical emergence of the interpersonal dimension of transcendence which characterizes the relationship. This dimension of transcendence, expressed in relationships of ethical obligation vis-à-vis the Other, is of a formality disparate from and exceeding the various scientifically comprehensible totalities in which the individuals involved are enmeshed.

How then can the other person, notwithstanding all his manifest limitations and dependencies, present himself to me, a particular non-interchangable someone, as a unique and innovative being, an absolute upsurge of self-possessed value—coming as it were at once from nowhere and from above in relation to where I stand vis-à-vis him? This paradoxical condition of a contingent existent, transcending scientific comprehension in terms of the network of totalities in which he is implicated, suggests that it might be better considered in a different, more metaphysical way, perhaps in terms of the classical account of creation. Let us consider what this suggestion involves.

According to the account of creation, which we have indicated in Chapter 2, finite human beings are not mere emanations of a divine substance. Although wholly dependent they exist and act as distinct substances in their own right. Their self-possessed being, and their activity and achievements as natural causes, depend upon the sustaining power of God's decision to originate them absolutely into communication with his transcendent infinite perfection and goodness. They and

---

97 Levinas, ibid., pp. 294–5.
98 Ibid., p. 291.

82 *The Sense of Creation*

their sustaining context are originated, not as the dispersion or transformation of some primordial uncreated stuff, but wholly from nothing—in other words, not from or out of anything. As thus originated to exist and act in their own right each finite human being possesses an ontological exteriority and distinction not only vis-à-vis God but also vis-à-vis other human beings. As created individual beings they stand related to each other not only as similar but also, across the chasm of their respective origin from nothing, as radically separate and diverse.

This exteriority or transcendence which characterizes human beings follows from their condition of each having come to be, as the particular incarnate ethical subject he or she is, through creation from nothing and maintained in being, action, and interaction by this same act of creation. They relate to each other as personal beings and to the transcendent God across the void of non-being, as it were, of their absolute origin *ex nihilo*. As Levinas puts it:

> To affirm origin from nothing by creation is to contest the prior community of all things within eternity, from which philosophical thought, guided by ontology, makes things arise as from a common matrix. The absolute gap of separation which transcendence implies could not be better expressed than by the term creation, in which the kinship of beings among themselves is affirmed, but at the same time their radical heterogeneity also, their reciprocal exteriority coming from nothingness. One may speak of creation to characterize entities situated in a transcendence that does not close over into a totality.[99]

Now this idea of creation, although it itself raises several deep issues, does make sense of the otherwise unintelligible ethical acknowledgment of the asymmetrical transcendence of the other person, which was the point of departure of our reflections. Ethics, as we have said, achieves a conscious relationship with the other person precisely as other and higher than me in the sense of requiring of me more than I can on that account require of that person for myself. Though it commences from my separated self-possessed subjectivity it challenges the tendency to seek the foundation of this self within itself envisaged as *pour-soi* or absolute freedom. Beyond the plane of natural need and arbitrary self-assertion it invests my freedom as desire for the good of the Other.[100] It locates my center of gravity outside myself at the service of the obligating encounter of the Other.[101]

The Other thus envisaged is separate, unique, transcendent—an absolute upsurge of meaning and value. Although manifestly implicated in all the causality and vicissitudes of a spatio-temporal nature he is welcomed as one whose existence surpasses comprehension in these terms. Thus Levinas remarks:

> The Other remains infinitely transcendent, infinitely foreign; his face in which his epiphany is produced and appeals to me breaks with the world that can be common to us, whose virtualities are inscribed in our *nature* and developed by our existence.[102]

---

99 Ibid., p. 293.
100 Cf. ibid., pp. 83–90.
101 Cf. ibid., p. 183.
102 Ibid., p. 194.

Morality and Transcendence

He is welcomed ethically by me as a separate self-referring existence arising from nothing in the world yet ineluctably summoning me to goodness in his regard. He is welcomed as a being who comes to be as existing in his own right, as dependent yet autonomous, as vulnerable to murder yet an expression of authoritative transcendent ethical significance. This ethical acknowledgment of the other person as asymmetrically transcendent, as being from nowhere and above—which is quite unintelligible in terms of any totality or natural process—exemplifies in a concrete way what is reflectively characterized by the abstract notion of a created being.

Thus the concrete ethical experience of the transcendence of the other person constitutes a privileged practical foundation for a metaphysical account of creation. Moreover, this experience appears to require such an account as its ultimate truth condition. It generates a line of metaphysical reflection which contests the totalizing tendency of much traditional philosophy and proposes a very different account—a basically religious account of the fundamental structure of being.

In other words, the asymmetrical transcendence of the ethically envisaged other person adduces, as its implicit ontological correlative or ultimate rationale, the theistic account of creation which envisages all finite beings as asymmetrically related to each other and to the transcendent God. Endorsing this contention Levinas writes:

> The dimension of the divine opens forth from the human face. ... God rises to his supreme and ultimate presence as correlative to the justice rendered unto men ... The Other is not the incarnation of God, but precisely by his face, in which he is disincarnate, is the very manifestation of the height in which God is revealed. ... Totality and the embrace of being, or ontology, do not contain the final secret of being. Religion, where relationships subsist between the same and the other despite the impossibility of the Whole—the idea of Infinity—is the ultimate structure.[103]

Incidentally, for Levinas, the ethical relation which acknowledges the asymmetrical transcendence of the other person not only provides the unique access to a true metaphysical conception of reality. It also provides an elucidation his original contention that "the moral consciousness can sustain the mocking gaze of the political man only if the certitude of peace dominates the evidence of war."[104]

The assurance of peace rests, not on an uncertain victorious outcome to war, but upon a prior, pre-political, ethical relationship whereby I subordinate my egoism to benevolent desire for the well-being of the other person:

> Peace therefore cannot be identified with the end of combats that cease for want of combatants, by the defeat of some and the victory of the others, that is, with cemeteries or future universal empires. Peace must be my peace, in a relation that starts from an I and goes to the other, in desire and goodness, where the I both maintains itself and exists without egoism. It is conceived starting from an I assured of the convergence of morality and reality ...[105]

---

103 Ibid., pp. 78–80.

104 Ibid., p. 22.

105 Ibid., p. 306.

84   *The Sense of Creation*

Implicit in this is a repudiation of utilitarian considerations sometimes invoked to justify atrocities.

Conclusion

This long discussion can be summarized and concluded. Our aim was to explore the possibility, in the context of contemporary ethical debate, of a moral argument for the existence of God, comparable to that advanced by Kant over two centuries ago. We considered the competing claims of two distinct and influential moral viewpoints, the utilitarian and the absolutist. We saw how Thomas Nagel, considering these viewpoints in terms of a non-theistic viewpoint, judged them to be incommensurable and irreducible. He argued that the conflict between them could involve a previously innocent person in unavoidable morally abominable action—a conclusion which disposed him to the pessimistic conclusion that the world is intrinsically evil.

Resisting this moral *impasse* we examined the striking presentation of the overriding claims of the absolutist viewpoint presented by Emmanuel Levinas. Elaborating his account to its ultimate metaphysical rationale we saw how our original aim of developing a moral argument for the existence of God might be realized. It is an argument which claims that the asymmetrical transcendence of the other person vis-à-vis oneself affirmed in the fundamental ethical relationship implies, as its metaphysical counterpart, the asymmetrical transcendence of God vis-à-vis creatures asserted in the classical view of creation. (This argument is analogous to that of the previous chapter where the asymmetrical relationship between our knowledge and what we know implies as its ultimate rationale, the asymmetrical relationship between God and the world. It is analogous in structure but probably also more debatable inasmuch as the exercise of practical reason about moral requirements is more intimately personal, self-involving, and hazardous than the exercise of theoretical reason about how things are.)

The conclusion of this argument is that the basic ethical relationship—unselfish desire for the good of the unique other person—is a cipher in human terms of God's creative benevolence which freely originates finite human persons into communication with his goodness. Moreover, it discloses that in its deepest structure being is not a bound system or totality of co-relative parts but an open order of autonomous existents sustained as such in an irreducible relation of infinity or goodness. This irreducible relationship in its ultimate expression is the relationship of divine creation. To leave the last word to Levinas:

> The Place of the Good above every essence is the most profound teaching, the definitive teaching, not of theology, but of philosophy. The paradox of an Infinity admitting a being outside of itself which it does not encompass,—in a word, the paradox of creation— thenceforth loses something of its audacity.[106]

---

106 Ibid., p. 103.

CHAPTER 7

Analogy and Transcendence

Introduction

In this chapter we propose a further argument for the existence of God based upon another cipher of transcendence disclosed within our experience. This is an explicitly metaphysical argument based upon our awareness of the analogical character of the objects of our experience. By their analogical character we mean, as we shall indicate more fully, the way in which they are at once both similar and dissimilar in their very being. The argument is, in effect, an interpretation of one of Aquinas's arguments for the existence of God, namely, his much disputed fourth argument.

In his Fourth Way of proving the existence of God, Aquinas argues to the existence of an Absolutely Supreme Being from the degrees of perfection which we observe in the things about us:

> The fourth way is taken from the degrees which are found in things. For amongst things it is found that some are more and some less good, true, noble and the like. But *more* and *less* are predicated of different things according as they approximate in their different ways to something which is the maximum: as something is said to be hotter according as it approximates more closely to that which is most hot. There is therefore something which is most true, best and noblest, and consequently which is most being, for what are greatest in truth are greatest in being as is remarked in *II Metaph.* But what is said to be the maximum in any genus is the cause of everything in that genus: as fire which is the maximum of heat is the cause of all hot things as is said in the same book. There is therefore something which to all beings is the cause of their being and goodness and other such perfections.[1]

This Fourth Way is generally viewed as the most controversial and dubious of his "proofs" and certainly, at first sight, the argument is neither very clear nor very convincing. Philosophers differ not only in their elaboration of it, but also in their interpretation of the text in which it is outlined. For instance, those who favour an argument in terms of exemplar causation (e.g. who claim that a reference to God's infinite perfection is directly involved in our ability to make comparative judgments about the relative perfection of the finite objects of our experience) maintain that the final part of the text which contains an appeal to efficient causation, i.e. to a source which causes or creates the various finite levels of perfection, is of secondary importance and not essential to the proof.[2]

---

1   Aquinas, *S.T.* (my trans.), 1, q. 2, a. 3.

2   Cf. E. Gilson, *The Christian Philosophy of St Thomas Aquinas*, London, 1957, pp. 70–74. And, more recently, J. Wipple remarks: there seems to be no justification in Thomas's text for the claim that his proof for the existence of a maximum rests on or

86   *The Sense of Creation*

The question is not simplified by the presence of similar proofs in other writings of Aquinas. For example, in *De Potentia*, q. 3, a. 5, three proofs are proposed, each of which has been suggested as the correct interpretation of the Fourth Way. There is the further complication that some consider the proof to be essentially Platonic while others are equally convinced of its Aristotelian character.

The aim of this chapter is to determine the nature of the Fourth Way as it is outlined in *Summa Theologiae*, I, q. 2, a. 3, and to suggest how it might be developed, not just in line with the general orientation of Aquinas's philosophy, but also as an illustration of the argument from asymmetry which we have discussed in the two previous chapters. As an introduction it will be helpful to formulate briefly some general remarks about what, in line with Aquinas's general approach to the topic, is involved in any "proof" for the existence of God.

"Proofs" for God – General Remarks

We cannot argue *a priori* from the notion of God to his actual existence. In order to do so it would be necessary to have a direct understanding of the divine nature (i.e. to know *what* God is as distinct from knowing what the term "God" means), and this is impossible. Indeed if we had a direct understanding of God's nature it would be unnecessary to prove his existence for we would either be immediately aware of it as in ontologism, or at least aware, *a priori*, of its positive possibility, which we are not, as we have argued in Chapter 3.[3]

An argument for God must, therefore, be *a posteriori* and indirect, and this means that we must show that the objects of which we are directly aware appear, in the light of philosophical analysis, to be contradictory unless he exists. In this way we seek to show, by indirect argument, the dependence of all finite being on the causality of Infinite Being.

Moreover, a philosophical argument must be philosophical throughout. This means, as we shall illustrate, that when a metaphysical argument is proposed it must be elaborated in the light of basic considerations and principles. These include our primary intuition of being as existing independently of our representation of it. Also, the principle of non-contradiction which maintains that contradictory statements about existing things cannot both be true. And, importantly for the argument to be developed here, that principle which is proper to metaphysics, namely, the intuition of finite being as analogical. Consequently, arguments which satisfy the mind at an infra-philosophical level of enquiry are inadequate in a philosophical argument for the existence of God. For philosophical argument seeks to establish well founded conviction and should be capable of withstanding rigorous criticism.

Since we have no *a priori* knowledge of God, and since the nominal definition of God, which precedes an argument for his existence, is that of Infinite Creator

---

presupposes reasoning from efficient causation. It follows, therefore, that if we wish to present the argument as it appears in his text, it can only be based on extrinsic formal causality, i.e., on exemplar causality. (J. Wipple, *The Metaphysical Thought of Thomas Aquinas*, Washington, DC, 2000, pp. 473–4)

3   Cf. Aquinas, *S.T.*, 1, q. 2, a.1, ad 2.

Analogy and Transcendence 87

of the universe, and since, causation in one manner or another is the only relation which can exist between the universe and God, it follows that one can "demonstrate" the existence of God only by showing that his existence, as the First Cause of the universe, is a necessary consequence of the philosophical analysis of finite being. If we express this by saying that we prove the existence of God through the principle of causation, applied to finite being as metaphysically conceived, it is necessary to make clear the role of the principle of causation in this context.

In the first place, the principle of causation cannot be applied to the datum of a proof as a universally true self-evident principle. To assume that finite being, or degrees of being, must have an extrinsic cause is equivalent to assuming the existence of God. For the extrinsic cause of finite being, as such, can only be Infinite Being. Furthermore, the principle of causation is not a self-evident principle. Admittedly, at an uncritical level of thought, we are instinctively inclined to accept that there must be a cause of whatever exists or happens. However, Hume denied the principle and this denial has been endorsed by others. Considered philosophically it lacks the self-evidence of an absolutely first principle and, therefore, it needs to be validated.

Nor can we argue inductively to the universal validity of the principle from its particular *de facto* applications in the empirical sciences. Any such attempt would involve the confusion of various levels of science, and would look defective in the light of metaphysical criticism. It could not, for example, withstand the criticism which Kant leveled against the transcendental validity of causation. Indeed far from facilitating a proof for the existence of God, the inductive generalization of the principle of causation would seem to render such a proof impossible. For it implies that causation is univocal, whereas for an argument for the existence of God to work it is necessary that causation be analogical, since the dependence of creatures on divine causation is an absolutely unique relationship. To identify causation *simpliciter* with the kind of causation we affirm in the finite world is to exclude the possibility of discovering the unique relation through which we might argue to the existence of God.

From these considerations it appears that the significance of the principle of causation must be evaluated in each particular context in which it is affirmed. Its truth in different cases cannot be affirmed merely as an instance of a universally true principle. In order to affirm the principle in a particular context we must prove the truth of the principle in that context.[4]

Admittedly the principle cannot be proved directly. Nevertheless, since it lacks the self-evidence of an absolutely first principle, it must be proved indirectly by revealing the contradiction involved in its denial. Therefore, in an argument for the existence of God, the principle of causation is not introduced from without as a self-evident principle or as a principle already proved. Rather the argument for the existence of God consists in seeking to prove this principle in a particular context. One seeks to show that the datum of the proof, considered in its metaphysical

---

4 "It follows that we cannot know the truth of the principle *apart from its application in the proof*, and this means that we can only know its truth by proving it to be true in this application." J. Horgan, "The Proofs for the Existence of God," *Philosophical Studies*, Maynooth, 1951, vol. 1, p. 52.

88 *The Sense of Creation*

significance, is contradictory unless this datum is understood as radically dependent upon an Infinite Cause.

It will be appreciated therefore, that metaphysical argument for the existence of God is critical and indirect. The only adequate criterion of such an argument is its actual success. Its positive possibility or impossibility cannot be established *a priori*. Moreover, the cogency of such an argument must be evaluated philosophically and not rejected because it cannot be expressed by means of the same self-evident clarity of principles, the same linear elegance of reasoning, or the same compelling conviction as, for example, a mathematical demonstration which is not concerned with the ultimate nature of reality. Metaphysics *does* seek an ultimate understanding of being as such, which is exceedingly complex and, to our finite minds, profoundly mysterious. It is unreasonable to look for an argument about the ultimate nature of things and then reject it because its context requires a more discursive and contemplative elaboration than the argument of a more specialized science.

Nor should a metaphysical argument be rejected because it is merely metaphysical. There is a prevalent tendency to discount such a proof because it lacks popular appeal, or because it does not evoke a religious response, or because it is insignificant in comparison with knowledge obtained by faith. Such objections are irrelevant to a discussion of the validity of a metaphysical argument. The purpose of such an argument is to establish with as much rational certitude as the undertaking admits the total dependence of finite beings on an Infinite Cause. It should be evaluated according to its success in this endeavor. To dismiss it because it does not exceed the scope of its aim is a misguided criticism.

In the light of these general introductory remarks let us now give specific attention to Aquinas's Fourth Way. Before developing an interpretation of the argument we will consider some significant features of the text. For the text does not claim to provide a fully articulated proof for the existence of God, but rather a "way" in which an argument for his existence might be developed. By seeking to decipher the "way" suggested by the text we will be in a better position to propose how it might be developed into a convincing argument.

Text of the Fourth Way

In the opening sentences of the text Aquinas draws our attention to the different degrees of certain perfections or properties which are found in things. The perfections with which he is concerned are those which he held to be predicable of all things. There are some perfections which are limited by their very nature to a particular kind of reality. For example, the perfection or property of heat can be found only in a material reality. There are also those perfections or properties such as human nature or triangularity which are not realized in different degrees—notwithstanding the often repeated perverse claim that particular classes of people are less human than those proposed as paradigmatically human.[5]

---

5   For there are specific forms which are not susceptible to inequality in such a way that one instance would be an intrinsically superior version of the specific form to another. Nor could the form exist in some subjects in a superior way to others. And this is true of all

Analogy and Transcendence 89

There are, however, certain perfections which are found in different degrees and which are not confined to a particular category or level of reality. These are termed the transcendental perfections such as "being" and its various properties, in terms of which we can consider it, such as truth, goodness, beauty, and unity.[6] Unlike intrinsically limited perfections these perfections are apprehended as co-extensive with whatever exists, even a reality of which we may have no direct experience.

It is important to bear in mind that it is with degrees of such transcendental perfections that Aquinas is concerned in the Fourth Way, for the cogency of the argument depends to a large extent on the unconfined character of such perfections. Further, since they are all understood by him to be identical with the fundamental perfection of being, as expressing various aspects under which it can be validly considered (e.g. as intelligible, desirable, delightful, and the like), it will suffice to consider the argument in terms of being, and what can be established in terms of it, may be applicable to the others.[7]

The next and perhaps most controversial feature of the text is the statement that objects are described in terms of more and less in virtue of their varying approximations to a maximum. In Platonic thought this statement was accepted as a universal and uncontroversial truth. Moreover, it maintained that we could not compare objects as more and less perfect in some respect unless the supreme exemplar of the perfection in question was somehow present to our minds when we made such judgments.[8] This point of view is also involved in the strict Aristotelian doctrine of measure which maintains that the most perfect expression of a perfection must be known in order to compare other objects as more or less perfect expressions of it.[9]

Aquinas, however, did not accept this view in an unqualified sense. He did not maintain that to know degrees of some perfection we must somehow be aware of its supreme expression. For if this were so, some knowledge of God as the absolute measure of being would be required in order to know degrees of being. This position would render a proof for God from degrees of being impossible. For it is not clear how one could come to know the existence of God as a consequence of knowing degrees of being, if some knowledge of God is required in order to know these degrees.

Aquinas insists that the intellectual ability with which we are naturally endowed adequately enables us to make comparative judgments:

---

substantial forms. (Aquinas, *Quaestio disputata de virtutibus cardinalibus*, a. 3 (my trans.). Cf. also *S.T.*, 1–II, q. 52, 1)

6   There is no reason why some name cannot be predicated analogously of God and creature … To this kind belong all attributes which include no defect nor depend on matter for their act of existence, for example, being, the good and similar things. (Aquinas, *Quaestiones disputatae de veritate/ Truth*, trans. R Mulligan, Chicago, 1952, q. 2, a. 11)

7   For a helpful discussion of these transcendental properties of being see O. Blanchette, *Philosophy of Being: A Reconstructive Essay in Metaphysics*, Washington, DC, 2003.

8   Cf. Plato, *Phaedo*, par. 100, trans. B. Jowett, Oxford, 1982.

9   Cf. Aristotle, *Metaphysica*, trans. W. Ross, Oxford, 1928, Bk X, ch. 1, 1052b.

90   *The Sense of Creation*

It is not to be understood that the uncreated truth itself is the proximate principle by which we understand and form judgments, but that we understand and judge by a light we are endowed with, which is similar to it.[10]

Therefore, when he refers to God as the measure of degrees of being he does not do so in the strict and epistemological sense according to which a measure is that by which we come to know degrees of perfection. He uses the term rather in the ontological sense, according to which a measure is whatever causes or accounts for a particular order of perfection. Thus, if or when we have proved God's existence, he can be called the measure which accounts for the degrees of being of which we were aware before we knew of his existence.[11]

Further, Aquinas did not hold that the principle *wherever there is a more and a less there must be a most* is a self-evident universally true principle, which can be automatically applied in the same sense wherever a *more and less* is affirmed. He realized that the purely logical relation of more and less is an abstraction from reality, and consequently inadequate in metaphysical reasoning which is concerned with real being as such.[12] He appreciated that in its real application the notion of more and less is an analogical notion, whose significance differs in the various contexts in which it is found.[13]

Obviously we are aware that objects are related in terms of more and less. We say that this water is warmer than that, that one person is healthier than another, that a man is a more perfect animal than a tortoise, that a flower is a more perfect being than a stone. These are all cases in which objects are truly related in terms of more and less. But the precise nature of *more and less* in each of these cases differs, and is determined by the particular conditions in which it is realized.

It will not do simply to assert that wherever there is an instance of *more and less* there must exist a *most* which is the principle of this order. Aquinas was well aware of this, for he subjected the notion of more and less to a detailed and critical analysis.[14] Further, frequently in his writings, he expressly reveals the fallacy of attempting to interpret all real instances of more and less as implying the real existence as distinct from the logical concept of a most. Thus, for example, he points out that we cannot argue from degrees of evil to the existence of a supreme principle

---

10   Aquinas, *In librum Boethii de Trinitate Expositio*, , q. 1, a. 3, ad 1.

11   "Now nothing is commensurate with God; though he is called the measure of all things, inasmuch as the nearer things come to God, the more fully they exist." Aquinas, *S.T.*, 1, q. 3, a. 5, ad 2. Blackfriars edn, London, 1964–74.

12   "For the logician considers the way in which terms are predicated and not the existence of a thing." Aquinas, *In XII libros Metaphysicorum Aristotelis Expositio/ Commentary on the Metaphysics of Aristotle*, trans. J. Rowan, Chicago, 1961, Bk 7, Lectio 17, n. 1658.

13   En stricte logique on doit donc dire que la dialectique vaut vi materiae, et non en raison des seules lois formelles. Il n''est pas vrai de dire que partout ou il y a plus et moins il y a un maximum, si on entend donner toujours au maximum le meme densite ontologique. (L.B. Geiger, *La Participation dans la Philosophie de S. Thomas d''Aquin*, Paris, 1953, p. 285)

14   Cf. Aquinas, *Quaest. Un. de virtutibus cardinalibus*, a. 3, *S.T.*; I–II, q. 52, a. 1; *De potentia*, q. 7, a. 7, ad. 3.

Analogy and Transcendence 91

of evil.[15] Likewise he observes that degrees of accidental qualities, such as various degrees of a particular color, do not warrant the affirmation of the existence of a supreme exemplar of the quality.[16] Again he remarks that although we may compare individuals of the same species or genus as more and less accomplished instances of it we cannot therefore affirm the existence of a supreme expression of the specific or generic form.[17] In this realistic approach to our experience of degrees of perfection there is an implied criticism of Platonic exemplarism.

We may conclude, therefore, that according to Aquinas the principle *more and less are predicated of different things according as they approximate differently to a maximum* cannot be applied universally as self-evidently true. It may be known to obtain under certain conditions. For example, the ranking of scores in a golf competition involves a reference to their relative approximation to the best score. However, it cannot be assumed as a principle of universal metaphysical validity. In particular he realized that it cannot be assumed, or accepted on the basis of some inductive generalization, in the case of degrees of being. His conviction that we may not conclude directly from degrees of being to the existence of a supreme being is also manifested by the fact that he considered it necessary to elaborate an indirect argument against the possibility of an infinite hierarchy of beings.[18]

How then should we understand his statement in the Fourth Way that things are spoken of in terms of more and less in virtue of their approximation to a most? In the first place this statement must be understood in the context of those perfections with which he is concerned in the proof, namely, transcendental perfections, which are not limited to a particular domain, but are predicable of whatever exists. He is not making a statement about more and less in general, but is speaking about degrees of perfections such as being, truth, goodness.

Secondly, he is not *assuming* that because there are degrees of transcendental perfections, there must be a supreme instance of transcendental perfection. For we have seen that he did not consider this to be self-evidently true and an argument for the existence of God, since it aims to be rationally probative, should avoid unjustified assumptions. It would appear, therefore, when he affirms in the Fourth Way that objects are called more and less in virtue of their approximation to a most, Aquinas means that if we wish to establish the existence of God from degrees of perfection *we must prove* that, because there are degrees of being, there necessarily exists a supreme being. In other words the statement should be understood, not as a self-evident principle to be applied to the datum of the proof, but rather as a principle which is constitutive of the proof and which must be established in the particular context of the proof. This is the "way" in which we should proceed.

---

15 Cf. Aquinas, *Quaestiones disputatae de potentia Dei/ On the Power of God*, trans. English Dominicans, London, 1932, q. 1, a. 6 ad 4, and q. 3, a. 6 ad 6, ad 8, and ad 14.

16 Cf. ibid., q. 7, a. 4, ad 7.

17 Cf. Aquinas, *Quaestiones disputatio de malo*, q. 2, a. 9, ad 16, also *Scriptum super IV libros Sententiarum/ Commentary on the Sentences*, Bk 1, disp. 35, q. 1, a. 4.

18 But in the case of some infinite thing in which there is neither a first nor a last part, no one part can be closer to or further away from what is either first or what is last. Therefore all parts are intermediates to the same degree right down to the one you designate now. (Aquinas, *Commentary on the Metaphysics of Aristotle*, Bk 2, Lectio 3, n. 304)

92   *The Sense of Creation*

At this stage an obvious objection arises. It is the objection that even were we to establish the existence of a supreme degree of being it is not evident that this must be an absolutely Supreme Being. It could be maintained, without obvious contradiction, that the supreme degree of being is merely relatively supreme, a being amongst other finite beings and, as such, really related to them as they are to it. Thus, for example, it might be claimed that humans or some finite spiritual being could be the most perfect kind of being. If this objection is false and contradictory, we must show that it is so; it is certainly not evidently so.

We could overcome this difficulty by proving the existence of a supreme being in such a way that the proof itself reveals that the supreme being is supreme in an absolute and non-relative way. This in effect what Aquinas proposes in the second part of the text of the Fourth Way. He points out that the principle of proof involved is a particular form of the principle of causation, namely, that the supreme expression of a perfection, in which a range of objects participate, is the cause of that perfection in the other members. Thus he argues that we establish the existence of an absolutely supreme being by proving the existence of a cause of degrees of finite being as such.

It is important to bear in mind our general remarks on the principle of causation when we come to consider this particular formulation of it. It cannot be assumed as self-evident, or accepted on the basis of an inductive generalization. It would be obviously unconvincing to argue that because there are some cases in which the greatest instance of a perfection in some sense causes the lesser instances of it to be such—that therefore there is a supreme instance of being which causes the lesser instances of it. Aquinas was well aware that the greatest instance of a perfection does not always cause the lesser instances of it.[19] And while he borrows from the physics of his day the example of heat, which he cites by way of illustration in the text of the proof, it is not evident, at least metaphysically, that the hottest body is the cause of heat in all other bodies. We may conclude, therefore, that since the causality of the maximum is not obviously true in all particular cases, *a fortiori* it cannot be assumed to be true in the case of degrees of being.

From these considerations we can now suggest the real significance of the principle of causation in the Fourth Way. When Aquinas affirms that the most perfect instance of a perfection is the cause of the perfection all other instances, and when he applies this principle to the transcendental perfections, he is not assuming the principle of causation. What he is affirming is that the Fourth Way consists in *proving* the principle in its application to the degrees of the transcendental perfection of being. In other words, we establish the existence of God by proving that the differing levels or degrees of being of which we have experience are radically dependent upon the causality of an Absolutely Supreme Being. As we have pointed out, the example of degrees of heat, which are caused by fire, allegedly the hottest object, should not give the illusion of illustrating a self-evident principle. It is merely a useful illustration, borrowed from Aristotelian physics, with the intention of indicating the

---

19   Cf. Aquinas, *Truth*, q. 1, a. 2 and *Summa Contra Gentiles*, trans. English Dominicans, London, 1934, Bk 1, ch. 34.

Analogy and Transcendence 93

kind of principle to be established at a metaphysical level in the case of transcendental perfections.[20]

Several considerations tend to verify this interpretation of the text. For example, unlike some other explanations, it maintains that there is a logical continuity of thought throughout the proof, the first part showing that we must argue from degrees of transcendental perfection to a supreme perfection, and the second one indicating how we may do this in such a way as to establish the existence of a supreme perfection which is such in an absolute manner and not simply the relatively supreme instance of perfection within the order of finite beings. This interpretation, which attaches real significance to the entire text, seems more accurate than any account which divides the proof into two quite distinct parts, the second being discounted as extrinsic to the proof itself.[21]

Moreover, this interpretation provides an explanation for the unusual manner in which Aristotle is quoted in the text. Aristotle had enunciated the principle that what causes a quality in other things possesses that quality in the most perfect way. Aquinas, however, quotes him as saying that what possesses a quality in the most perfect way is the cause of that quality in other things. There is a certain historical basis in the writings of Anselm and Averroes for this inverted quotation. However, there is also a more philosophical explanation inasmuch as, in our interpretation of the Fourth Way, the existence of a supreme perfection and its causality in relation to lower grades of perfection are established simultaneously as part of one movement of thought. There is no question of knowing that there is a supreme perfection and then adducing an inverted Aristotelian principle in order to deduce its causality. On the contrary, when Aquinas speaks of the causality of the maximum, he means that we prove that there is an absolutely supreme perfection by demonstrating its necessary existence as the cause of all lesser perfections.[22]

Analogy of Being – the Datum of the "Proof"

Having indicated our general interpretation of the text, let us now consider, in the light of this interpretation, how the argument itself might be developed. The problem posed by the datum of the Fourth Way is essentially the fundamental problem posed by the analogy of being. It is the problem of determining whether the various degrees or levels of being, which are formally diverse and irreducible—for example, a human being, a flower, a stone— are metaphysically unintelligible unless they necessarily

---

20 Cf. V. de Couesnongle, "Mesure et Causalité dans la Quarta Via," *Revue Thomiste*, LVIII, 1958, p. 253.

21 Such an explanation is usually suggested by those who interpret the proof in terms of exemplarism. For example, Gilson remarked that "the appeal to the principle of causality which terminates the demonstration of the *Summa Theologica*, is not at all intended to establish the existence of the Supreme Being." Gilson, *The Christian Philosophy of St Thomas Aquinas*, p. 73.

22 "Dans une seule et meme demarche l"esprit prouve l"existence du maximum et son role causal." de Couesnongle, "Mesure et Causalite dans la Quarta Via," p. 276, also Geiger, *La Participation dans la Philosophie de S. Thomas d"Aquin*, p. 294.

94 *The Sense of Creation*

imply the existence of Infinite Being as their First Cause upon whom they totally depend for their being.

The analogy of finite being means that the various levels or degrees of being are both similar and dissimilar in being. For since being, i.e. that which exists, cannot be differentiated by anything extrinsic to it, but must contain its differences within itself, it follows that any two beings are not only similar in being but also dissimilar in being. They are one in the sense that each is comprehensively identified as something which exists, yet they differ individually, specifically, generically, and in degree of perfection. Is it necessary that this unity and diversity, this similarity and dissimilarity, should have an ultimate basis outside the whole range of finite being?

If we assume the existence of God as Infinite Being we can explain the analogy of finite being in terms of the common relation of dependence of creatures upon God. They can be understood to possess their diverse and limited forms of actual existence (*esse*) as dependent participations in his unique unlimited perfection of existence. However, in an argument for God we cannot assume his existence. We must, therefore, approach the problem indirectly. Instead of showing how the existence of God might render the analogy of finite being intelligible, we have to show rather that, unless God exists, the analogy of finite being is ultimately unintelligible and even contradictory. We must show that unless God exists, our knowledge of being, which for us is the source of all intelligibility, is itself unintelligible. We can seek to do this by showing that our knowledge of being involves a fundamental unity which cannot be explained by the analogical order of finite beings considered simply in itself.

Our properly metaphysical concept of being is analogical. It is predicated only proportionally of different individuals, and signifies at once both their similarity and dissimilarity in being.[23] In each individual predication it signifies "this particular form or expression of being" and signifies it as proportionally similar to other really distinct forms or expressions of being. It is a concept of being as penetrated by different relations of essence and existence which constitute a diversified order of being. In other words the unity of our elaborated metaphysical concept of being is an imperfect unity involving both similarity and dissimilarity which cannot be adequately disassociated one from the other.

Nevertheless, this metaphysical concept presupposes a more fundamental, pre-philosophical apprehension or concept of being, which is perfectly one and which has important metaphysical implications. This basic concept, the expression of our basic intuition of being, is one *simpliciter*. It expresses a simple, undifferentiated, and unambiguous unity, always retaining the same objective meaning, namely, *that which exists*. We signify this concept through the term *being* and in predicating this term of all objects we affirm their unity, logically in the term *being*, psychologically in the concept *being*, and ontologically in *real being*. This unity of being is the primary unity which is required if our knowledge of beings is to be intelligible.

The unity signified by this basic concept represents an absolute and irreducible characteristic of being, namely its real existence. As one writer observes:

---

23 Cf. Aquinas, *Commentary on the Metaphysics of Aristotle*, Bk 4, Lectio 1, n. 535.

Analogy and Transcendence 95

> The idea of being, implying the absolute affirmation of being, is the foundation and stuff, as it were, of all intellection. It is transcendental in the sense that it is applicable to everything .... Everywhere being reveals itself as an absolute value, neither more nor less, for a thing is or it is not; there is no middle ground. [24]

When we predicate being of anything in this sense we affirm it in its entirety; we identify it as belonging to the transcendental order of real existence. Undoubtedly upon further reflection we can say that *this* is being in its own particular way, and that *that* is being in its own way. But this does not deny, but rather presupposes, that of each of them it is true to say simply "this exists" and in so doing we signify precisely one and the same truth, namely, that they pertain in all that they are to the transcendental absolute order of being.

Aquinas calls this basic concept of being the *primum cognitum.* "That which first appears is the *real*, and some insight into this is included in whatsoever is apprehended."[25] However, this priority signifies not merely a temporal or psychological priority but also, and more importantly, an epistemological priority. For this concept constitutes an absolutely basic foundation of a realist philosophy. It expresses the fundamental unity in all our knowledge of real being, because it is that through which all real being is known as such. This primary intellectual apprehension that things exist is basic and irreducible. In the light of it one knows whatever one knows and without it one does not know anything. As one writer remarks: "Knowing takes place only as it refers to being. It cannot be understood except as an act of attaining being, or in which being is disclosed, whether it be in common sense, in empirical science, or in metaphysics."[26]

When we speak here of the perfect unity of this concept of being it must be remembered that we are not referring to the fully elaborated metaphysical concept of being. For clearly this is an analogical concept and is not perfectly one but imperfectly one, involving both similarity and dissimilarity. We are referring rather to the pre-philosophical concept of being through which every object of knowledge, if it is to be an object of knowledge, must be known.

Whatever we know directly is known primarily and simply as a given which exists. In our intuition of any object, be it a man, a flower, a stone, or a table, we become aware of it as something which exists. Subsequently we may achieve a more precise and specific knowledge of its nature. But the feature which primarily constitutes it as an object of our knowledge is our pre-reflective awareness of it as something which really exists independently of our awareness of it. It is this apprehension of something as existing which discloses, as it were, the ontological import of our knowledge as attaining what exists independently of it.

The outcome of this revealing intuition (whose intrinsic foundational preconditions of possibility is an abiding concern of Heidegger's philosophy), is a concept of being (*ens*), a concept of *that which exists*, predicable of everything directly given in experience. It is a concept through which we grasp the unity of being, not as

---

24 L. de Raeymaeker, *The Philosophy of Being*, trans. E. Ziegelmeyer, New York, 1954, pp. 26–9.

25 Aquinas, *S.T.*, I–II, q. 94, a. 2; cf. also *Truth* q. 1, a. 1.

26 Blanchette, *Philosophy of Being*, Washington, DC, 2003, p. 29.

96 *The Sense of Creation*

the product of a summation, but as an englobing whole anterior to its parts which it permeates. Everything of which we have experience is totally identified by this concept. It is not obtained by abstraction from, or by comparison with, any other concept. Rather it is attained directly by the mind, in virtue of its natural light or spontaneous activity, in the presence of whatever being we may experience. It is a first principle of knowledge in the strictest sense of the term.

Although our affirmation of being, accessible through the intuitively generated concept of being, is an act of consciousness, what is affirmed in the existential judgment to which it gives rise is more than an object of consciousness. A relationship to consciousness is *exercised* through the concept of being but is not what is *signified* by it. What the concept of "being" signifies is more fundamental than "object of consciousness." It signifies the absolute or "non-relative" character of being, its independent status as "that which actually exists" and of which everything we progressively experience is a determination.

In virtue of this primary apprehension of being we appreciate that what we attain through it as conscious subjects is not simply an awareness of objects which we spontaneously constitute for ourselves, but the independent order of extra-mental being which is given to us and to which we are oriented in the pursuit of truth. In contemporary post-modern idiom one might say that the basic intentionality of our subjectivity finds that it is not, as phenomenology is disposed to claim, the containing measure of its given object of consciousness. Rather it finds itself, to borrow the illuminating image of the poet Seamus Heaney, under "the gravitational pull of the actual."[27] It is "saturated" by an overflow of givenness to which it finds itself "ex-statically" oriented. This gift or donation, this "overflow of givenness" issues in our primary all-embracing concept of being as that which exists independently and extra-mentally.[28] It is a concept which expresses the encompassing unity of that which exists. It is not just the product of a summation of its particular phenomenological manifestations to which it is anterior and irreducible.

To summarize, we have a pre-philosophical concept of being which is the basic unifying principle of all our knowledge. In our primary intuition of being we attain a concept which is perfectly one. Considered quite simply it signifies "that which exists" and it is within the unity of this fundamental concept, which wholly identifies everything we acknowledge as existing independently of our consciousness, that we elaborate all our scientific knowledge.[29]

---

27 S. Heaney, *The Redress of Poetry*, Oxford, 1990.

28 This way of expressing the matter is an adaptation of Marion's discussion of givenness although I doubt that he would endorse this application of it in the context of being. Cf. J.-L. Marion, *Reduction and Givenness: Investigations of Husserl, Heidegger, and Phenomenology*, trans. T. Carlson, Evanston, 1988.

29 Now in saying that being is the first intelligible and that "the understanding of being is included in all things whatsoever a man apprehends" (*S.T.*, I–II, q. 94, a. 2) what is being claimed is that the viewing of things under the concept of being is the very condition of cognition or intelligible discourse … For the Thomist, what is always being sought is the concrete existent in its place within the absolute unconditional order of being. (D. Tulloch, "The Logic of Positive Terms and the Transcendental Notion of Being," *Mind*, 66, 1957, pp. 358–9) Cf. also Geiger, *La Participation dans la Philosophie de S. Thomas d"Aquin*,

Analogy and Transcendence   97

These considerations bring us to the important issue of the objective basis of the unity of being. Truth means that being *is* as we know and declare it to be.[30] Hence in predicating *being* of all beings, we predicate their unity in being, since we know that the one concept *being*, fruit of our primary intuition, is predicable of all.

Therefore, in saying being is one, we know that all beings are somehow really one in being. Yet in virtue of this judgment alone, our only basis for claiming to know that all beings are one is the subjective unity of our concept. Thus Kant, who saw the necessity of postulating a principle to account for the unity of our knowledge, sought to find it in the unity of the knowing subject, and to this end he elaborated his doctrine of the transcendental unity of apperception.[31] Here, however, we have accepted, as more persuasive, the moderate realism espoused by Aquinas which requires that our objective concepts should represent objective being, and that to the basic unity signified by the concept there should correspond unity of being. Hence, to the epistemological unity of the concept *being* through which we know that all beings are one, there must correspond the ontological unity of being in itself. Otherwise the judgment *being is one*, would be not only defective, but in a manner contradictory metaphysically, since in saying that being is one we would at the same time claim to know that being is one, and yet could not justifiably claim to know that being is one unless we can, in principle, identify the ontological principle of its unity.

Let us see, therefore, whether we can discover in the objects of our experience an adequate basis for the unity in question. Let us consider, for example, a man and a stone as two representatives of beings in general. Each of these is totally identified within the comprehensive unity of the predicate being. When we affirm of a stone that it is a being we have, in a real sense, said all that there is to be said about it. Likewise, when we affirm that a man is a being, we affirm his entire reality. What objective basis is there in these two objects for their identity within the unity of the predicate being?

It will not do to suggest that the unity of the predicate is based on the abstraction of a nature common to every individual, just as a specific concept is based on the abstraction of a nature common to many individuals. The univocal concepts, through which we come to know specific or generic natures, are obtained by abstracting from whatever differentiates individuals as such, and considering only a universal form common to many. Thus the concept *human nature* is obtained by considering that in which Socrates and Plato and Aristotle are formally alike, and ignoring that in which, as individuals, they differ. Likewise the generic concept *animal* is the concept of *living sensitive substance* and it abstracts from the specific differences *rational* and *irrational*. Ultimately all specific and generic concepts are formed by

---

pp. 342–64 and F. O"Rourke, *Pseudo-Dionysius & the Metaphysics of Aquinas*, Leiden, 1992, pp. 109–13.

30 "When however it [the intellect] judges that a thing corresponds to the form which it apprehends about that thing, then first it knows and expresses truth", *S.T.*, I, q. 16, a. 2.

31 Cf. I. Kant, *Critique of Pure Reason*, trans. N. Kemp Smith, London, 1968, par. A 105–par. A114.

98 *The Sense of Creation*

abstracting from the individual as such, and representing its reality only partially and in a universal way.

However, the universal nature, as universal, has no real existence. It is real only in the individual objects with which it is identical. It is the similarity of the individual as such with other individuals, which is the real source of the formal unity of our specific concepts. These concepts, however, do not express this basic unity, for they are formed by abstracting from the individual. Consequently, a realist philosophy, which maintains that all knowledge is fundamentally based on the apprehension of real similarity between individuals as such, implies the epistemological primacy of a concept which totally contains every individual in a transcendental unity. This primary concept is the concept of being.[32] The predicate being identifies and transcends every individual and abstracts in no way from their reality.[33] It affirms the fundamental unity of each individual with every other individual, implied by the formal unity of our univocal concepts.

The concept *being*, therefore, cannot be based on abstraction from anything which really differentiates one individual from another, because such real differences are themselves being and are, therefore, included in the concept *being*. Thus, whereas specific concepts are abstract by excluding real differences, the concept of being includes all differences. We express this technically by saying that the intension and extension of specific concepts vary inversely (i.e. the less specific the concept the wider its range of application), but that the concept *being* has both the greatest intension and the greatest extension.[34] We conclude, therefore, that the unity of the concept *being* cannot be explained as an abstraction which includes merely a particular aspect of objects in a universal way. The concept of being encompasses the total reality of every object of our experience and, when we consider these objects as a possible basis of its unity, we must consider them, not in a partial aspect of their reality, but in their entirety.

However, considered in their totality, these objects seem incapable of providing a real basis for the unity of the concept *being*. Although any two individuals, such as a man and a stone, are alike in that each is *being* in all that it is, nevertheless, as

---

32   That which the intellect first conceives as, in a way, the most evident, and to which it reduces all its concepts is being. Consequently, all other conceptions of the intellect are had by additions to being. But nothing can be added to being as though it were something not included in being—in the way that a difference is added to a genus or an accident to a subject—for every reality is essentially a being. (Aquinas, *Truth*, q. 1, a. 1, also, *Commentary on the Metaphysics of Aristotle*, Bk 5, Lectio 9, n. 889)

33   To view an object under the concept of being is necessarily to place it, even if we cannot give positive identification marks of this place, in an order which is transcendental and from which nothing can escape. (Tulloch, "The Logic of Positive Terms and the Transcendental Notion of Being," p. 359)

Similiarly:Only the concept of being is absolutely universal in that it includes whatever *is* in what we shall call its transcendental order as distinct from the predicamental order of categories. The concept of being differs from a categorical concept in yet another way. As a concrete universal, or as common to many, it is inclusive of the very differences in which it is diversified. (Blanchette, *Philosophy of Being*, p. 85)

34   Cf. Aquinas, *Commentary on the Metaphysics of Aristotle*, Bk 5, Lectio 9, n. 889.

being, they are also completely different. Their unity in being is an imperfect unity, not the perfect unity of numerical identity, nor the perfect similarity of the species. It is a unity which is also a diversity, for they differ as individuals, in kind, and in degree of being. It is this unity and diversity to which Aquinas draws attention in his Fourth Way.

It is evident that beings are different as individuals. Although we predicate being of both a person and a stone, we are aware that the object we call a stone is a completely different individual from the object we call a person. Likewise it is obvious that a person and a stone are essentially different kinds of being. We say that one is a stone, the other a person, and thereby signify a fundamental difference in the nature of their being.

Furthermore, individual beings differ not only in kind but also in degree or level of being. The being of some objects is obviously more comprehensive and inclusive than that of others. Precisely as beings, different individuals constitute a hierarchy, a more and less, of perfection. Thus, whereas a stone is limited to an exclusively material mode of being, one comprehensible solely in terms of physics and chemistry, a person transcends such limitation and enjoys an essentially more comprehensive and perfect mode of being which cannot be adequately comprehended in exclusively physico-chemical terms. Here we speak of biological and cognitive structures which (like an intelligible text in respect of its component ink molecules, but unlike a radio in respect of its parts) are neither reducible to, nor predictable from, the physico-chemical components in which they subsist. Human persons, as intelligent beings, are emergent from their micro-matter and possess active powers not possessed by their micro-parts.[35]

It is significant that the datum of the proof is not simply our experience of multiple or different individual beings, but rather this experience of beings existing at different degrees or levels or intensity of being. It is this feature of "more and less" of beings *as being* which precludes us from seeking the basis of the unity and diversity of being in terms of the dispersion of some uniform primordial stuff or quanta. The difference we are considering is not like an epiphenomenal ripple of different waves on a common uniform substrate of being. Nor is the analogy of being explicable as simply a lattice of equivalent features in which individual beings agree and differ. Even if, over time, an increasingly complex evolution of some basic uniform stuff manifests the capacity to sustain the analogical diversity of being which interests us, it certainly does not explain it.

For, as indicated above, our affirmation of the analogical character of finite being, i.e. of its diversity of level or degree, involves the claim that certain realizations of being, for example, intelligent beings (and perhaps living beings in general), have active powers not possessed by their physico-chemical micro-parts. Intelligent life which humans enjoy, is an irreducibly distinct way of being from inanimate material

---

35   Cf. J. Ross, "Christians Get the Better of Evolution," in *Evolution and Creation*, ed. E. McMullin, Notre Dame, 1985, p. 223. The whole of this article (pp. 223–51) provides useful insights into the relationship between "emergence" and "analogy of being." Cf. also B. Purcell, "Reflections on Evolution in the Light of a Philosophical Biology," in *Thomas Aquinas: Approaches to Truth*, ed. J. McEvoy and M. Dunne, Dublin, 2002, pp. 77–113.

100 *The Sense of Creation*

being. Intelligent human beings are such (as we have seen in previous chapters) as can discern objective meaning, truth, and value. This ability cannot be fully explained in terms of the micro-matter pertaining to humans because the determining laws of such micro-matter cannot distinguish meaning from nonsense and the valuable from the empty, or account for our claims to objective truth and moral insight.[36]

A rational debate between two people presumably involves two sets of electro-chemical neural events. But neither of these neural events is right or wrong or more or less persuasive. They simply happen—even if their specific occurrence is a precondition of the rational debate which operates by way of logical implication rather than through physical causation. As Merleau-Ponty remarks more graphically:

> I am not the outcome or intersection of multiple causalities which determine my body or my "psyche". I cannot think of myself as a bit of the world, ... nor enclose myself within the universe of science. All that I know of the world, even by science, I know from a viewpoint which is mine, or from an experience of the world without which the symbols of science have nothing to say. ... scientific views according to which I am a moment of the world are always naïve and hypocritical, because they imply, without mentioning it, this other view, that of consciousness, by virtue of which in the first place a world disposes itself about me and begins to exist for me.[37]

Human beings are subjects who exist, intrinsically and necessarily, in a medium of micro-matter. However, their nature or structure as intelligent human beings is irreducible to, and unpredictable from, their micro-matter—all the aptitude of which is, in principle, comprehended by physical laws. It has merely an "obediential capacity" to sustain this intelligent human form, much as molecules of ink have an obediential capacity to sustain the works of Shakespeare. As James Ross observes: "The principles, the structures for intelligent material being, cannot be derived from the principles, the structures for material being, within any consistent formal system."[38] In their activity humans instantiate universal laws of intelligibility, purpose, and value which exceed the range of the physical laws governing the activities of matter everywhere including their own carbon-based systems of micro-matter in which they subsist. They emerge as new intrinsically unified compositions of micro-matter manifesting irreducibly new properties and characteristic activities.[39] As such they are a distinctively more comprehensive or perfect manifestation of being than those material beings explicable in exclusively physico-chemical terms.[40]

---

36 Cf. Ross, "Christians Get the Better of Evolution," p. 225.

37 M. Merleau-Ponty, *Phenomenology of Perception*, trans. C. Smith, London, 1962, p. ix.

38 Ross, "Christians Get the Better of Evolution," p. 233.

39 Cf. W. Norris Clarke, *The One and the Many: A Contemporary Thomistic Metaphysics*, Notre Dame, 2001, pp. 60–71.

40 As James Ross remarks:

Take the "region" of universal laws of physics and chemistry concerning, say the cosmos regarded as quanta: there may be another "region" say, laws of intelligent being, that is not transformationally accessible from the first. The one kind of laws might be underivable, formally, from the other. In that case the phenomena satisfying the one kind of laws would be absolutely emergent with respect to the phenomena satisfying the other. (Ross, "Christians Get the Better of Evolution," p. 232)

Analogy and Transcendence   101

Hopefully, this explicates to some extent the assertion that being differentiates analogously through different irreducible forms of existence. *To be* for a human is a different and irreducible level of *to be* from the *to be* of a stone. There is here a certain asymmetry between degrees of finite being which precludes a reductionist or monistic interpretation of the unity of being and gives rise rather to the consideration that the principle or basis of this unity should be sought outside the range of analogical finite beings. Indeed this asymmetry, which obtains between the degrees of being themselves, can be viewed as a cipher of the asymmetry between the diversified perfection of finite beings in general and the transcendent infinitely perfect God, whose existence Aquinas seeks to prove in this *Quarta Via* or fourth argument.

The Argument of the Fourth Way

The problem posed by the datum of the Fourth Way is now clearer. In our basic intuition of reality we form a concept of being which is perfectly one. It is through this concept, the concept of that which exists, that we apprehend the being of each individual in its entirety. This simple pre-philosophical concept of being discloses the fundamental unity required for objective knowledge to be possible. It is presupposed by all particular concepts and virtually contains these concepts. Yet when we consider the various individuals signified by this concept they seem to provide no basis for its unity. Whatever appears to be a source of their real unity is equally a source of their complete diversity. If the being of a stone, and the being of a man, can be called a source of their ontological unity, to the same extent it must be called a source of their ontological diversity, for the whole being of each is distinct from the whole being of the other. For the same reason any number of beings are at once one and diverse in their entire being. As intrinsically finite beings they differ one from another.[41] There is nothing perfectly identical in different objects, which could be isolated as a principle of their unity alone.

Nor can we perfectly abstract the similarity of different beings from their dissimilarity, for these features are intrinsic to each other. To say, without further qualification, that two beings are similar in being because of feature A, and dissimilar in being because of feature B, involves a misunderstanding of the analogy of being and is in fact an attempt to conceive it in terms proper to univocal predication. For the features which suggest similarity in any two beings are also different, and those which suggest difference are also similar. Thus it cannot be said that *existence* (*esse*) is a principle of unity only and that *essence* or *nature* (*essentia*) is a principle of diversity only, for *existence* in different beings is not only one but also diverse because *this* existence is not *that*, and *essence* is not only diverse but also one, because each individual essence or nature is, like any other, an aspect of being.

Further, we cannot, from an internal analysis of finite beings, say of similarity and dissimilarity in being that one is primary and the other secondary, for both seem equally fundamental. All beings are one and diverse *secundum se tota*, in all that

---

41 "A thing is made a being according as it is made one, undivided in itself and distinct from others." Aquinas, *Summa Contra Gentiles*, Bk 2, ch. 40. Cf. also *Summa Contra Gentiles*, Bk 1, ch. 42; also D. Turner, *Faith, Reason and the Existence of God*, Cambridge, 2004, ch. 9.

102   *The Sense of Creation*

they are, i.e. they are one in that in which they are diverse and diverse in that in which they are one.

We are drawn to the conclusion, therefore, that in themselves the objects of our experience contain no fundamental principle of unity in being, and provide no objective basis for the unity of our primary concept of being. From this it would seem to follow that reality and our knowledge of it are unintelligible and even contradictory. For while we affirm the unity of what our concept of being discloses we find no fundamental basis in individual beings for this affirmation. Thus the unity signified by this concept, which is the first principle of objective knowledge, itself appears to lack objective foundation. An analysis of the objects of experience fails to reveal a principle either of their unity in being, or of the unity of our concept. Such considerations would tend to suggest that reality is ultimately unintelligible and even contradictory—that it has not the fundamental unity which we affirm it to have in claiming objective knowledge of it.

We cannot, however, rationally terminate our enquiry by simply accepting this seemingly contradictory nature of being. Undoubtedly the notion of contradiction is a complex and contextually dependent notion. What appears contradictory from one point of view may not evidently be so from another. For example, what may seem contradictory in terms of the aspirations and ideals of our lived experience may not manifest a radical incoherence from a deeper philosophical point of view, as is instanced by Kant's affirmation of God as a solution to the paradoxes of morality— even though he had precluded such an affirmation by way of purely speculative thought alone.

However, while admitting the complexity of the notion of contradiction, it does seem certain that the affirmation that being is metaphysically contradictory is itself contradictory. For if the affirmation "being is metaphysically contradictory" is true, it is so, according to a realist view, because it corresponds to how being is objectively.[42] But, strictly speaking, what is metaphysically contradictory is what cannot exist, whereas being is precisely that which exists. Thus we reach the absurd conclusion that the assertion "being is metaphysically contradictory" is true only if being really exists and is, therefore, not metaphysically contradictory. Consequently, it is difficult to accept as ultimate the apparently contradictory character of being which the finite objects of our experience suggest when considered simply in themselves.

We are drawn, therefore, to envisage beyond the objects of our experience, and beyond all finite being, the existence of Infinite Being by relation to whom the analogical or imperfect unity of finite beings is rendered ultimately intelligible.[43]

This appeal to a transcendent source of the unity of finite beings is not simply an empty device by which we seek to resolve a contradiction which we meet in

---

42   Or as Aquinas remarks, "A thing's being is the cause of any true judgment which the mind makes about a thing." *Commentary on the Metaphysics of Aristotle*, Bk 2, Lectio 2, n. 298.

43   The one thing to which the different relationships are referred to in the case of analogical things is numerically one and not just one in meaning, which is the kind of oneness designated by a univocal term. Hence, ... although the term being has several senses, still it is not predicated univocally but in reference to one thing; not to one thing which is one merely in meaning but to one which is one as a single definite nature. (Ibid., Bk 4, Lectio 1, n. 5360)

Analogy and Transcendence   103

experience, by arbitrary appeal to a realm which, by definition, transcends our experience. For the appeal to a transcendent is based not merely on the seeming contradiction of the finite order, but also on our assurance that reality cannot be ultimately contradictory. These two aspects taken together explain our translating the problem to a level transcending experience, and justify our assertion that here we may find a real resolution, and not merely a restatement, of the contradiction. For the sole purpose of appealing to a transcendent principle is precisely to find a real resolution which we are compelled to seek in virtue of our assurance that the world of our experience cannot be ultimately contradictory even though it appears so when considered as the only and all inclusive order of being.

This transcendent Being is not affirmed merely as a Platonic exemplar, remote from the objects which it is invoked to explain. It is affirmed as Infinite Being, which, possessing the perfection of existence in an unlimited and simple unity, accomplishes, through creation *ex nihilo*, both the unity and diversity of finite beings. "God must be understood as existing outside the order of beings as a cause producing the whole of being and its differences."[44] Thus understood, the universe ceases to appear as a collection of individuals, whose intrinsic diversity in being seems to render the affirmation of their intrinsic unity in being unintelligible. For now we appreciate that a full metaphysical account of such beings must include their total and common dependence upon a unique First Cause.[45]

Through this relation of total dependence their unity and diversity in being become intelligible. They are one because each derives its being from the same principle which possesses in perfect unity and infinite actuality the plenitude of existence in which each finite individual participates in its determinate way as a finite reflection of this unique infinite perfection. They are diverse beings not just because they are variously configured bits of some common primordial stuff but, more fundamentally, because they are created as individual beings really distinct from each other and from their Creator, whom they resemble each in their own particular way and degree of being.[46]

In this manner, while taking due account of diversity, we render the unity of being intelligible in terms of its origin from a principle which is perfectly one and which pre-contains in its infinite unified perfection whatever finite perfections find expression in creation.[47] We see also that being is primarily one and secondarily diverse, that its unity is metaphysically prior to its diversity, for diversity too derives from the perfect unity of one First Cause. This First Cause could exist in the absence

---

44 Aquinas, *On Interpretation: Perehermeneias*, trans. J. Osterle, Milwaukee, 1962, lectio 14, par. 22.

45 Cf. Aquinas, *On the Power of God*, q. 3, a. 5. also *S.T.*, I, q. 44, a.1, ad 1.

46 Cf. Aquinas, *On the Power of God*, q. 3, a. 5, *S.T.*, I, q. 44, a. 1; *Summa Contra Gentiles*, Bk 1, ch. 22; *Commentary on the Sentences*, Bk 1, d. 8, q. 4, a. 2, ad 3.

47 For in themselves all caused things are finite, in God however they are infinite because they are identical with the divine essence ... Again, in themselves they are characterised by opposition and diversity, but in God they are combined together ... Again, in themselves they constitute a multitude, in God, however, they are one. (Aquinas, *In de divinis nominibus/ On the Divine Names* (my trans.), ch. 5, lect. 1, n. 641)

104   *The Sense of Creation*

of diversity, but diversity can only exist in total dependence on the perfect unity of a First Cause.[48]

By way of this argument for a unique source of degrees of being we affirm the ontological basis for the unity of our concept of being. This does not mean that God is the object of our concept of being, or that in knowing finite beings we have some obscure direct knowledge of their source. It simply means that since this concept comprehends the total reality of every object of our experience, it comprehends *by metaphysical implication* their real dependence on a First Cause.[49] Our concept of being, however, does not *explicitly* reveal this dependence. It is only by metaphysical reflection upon both the different degrees of being, and the implications of our primary pre-philosophical concept of being, that we discover this dependence of finite being on a First Cause.

By way of indirect argument we establish that all finite beings are one because they derive from one source, Infinite Being. We show that the same term *being* is predicable of different beings because it is fundamentally and primarily predicable of Infinite Being, which transcends our experience and is the Cause of all finite being. Because this Being transcends our experience we have no direct or proper knowledge of it, and our manner of signifying it is indirect and inadequate. However, we do establish that what the term *being* signifies, i.e. that which exists, is predicated of him primarily and most properly as act of existence without any restrictive determination and, as such, incommensurable with the analogical order of finite beings which depend upon him for their determinate existence.

Thus it might be said that our limited but direct knowledge of the unity of being is the foundation of an indirect argument by which we affirm the existence of God, and the affirmation of the existence of God enables us to affirm the ultimate principle of the unity of being and of our knowledge of it.

We have argued that there is a unique Cause of the degrees of being of which we have experience. Are we justified in affirming that this Cause is Infinite? We are; because only an Infinite Being can create, i.e. can cause other objects to be both similar to and different from itself. A finite being cannot cause the being of another being *as other*. It presupposes an object or medium in which to exercise its causality. Its causality consists in bringing about a change, which induces a certain effect in an object which is presupposed. It brings it about that an object x comes to exist as y. It does not bring it about that there exists an x such that x is y. In finite causality it is the object acted upon which is the proximate principle of individuality or otherness in the being of the effect. For a finite agent cannot produce an effect *ex nihilo*, i.e. cannot produce an effect *as other*. A lighted match can produce fire only in an object that already exists. It cannot produce the whole being of another fire including the

---

48   "All of the ways in which the terms prior and subsequent are used can be reduced to … the first of these inasmuch the term prior means something which can exist without other things, but not the reverse." Aquinas, *Commentary on the Metaphysics of Aristotle*, Bk 5, Lectio 13, n. 953.

49   Cf. Aquinas, *Truth*, q. 10, a. 11, ad 10.

Analogy and Transcendence 105

particular material in which it is generated, which is its principle of individuation and by which it is distinct from other individuals.[50]

Only Infinite Being is capable of creating other beings as other, different from himself and from one another. This causation is *creatio ex nihilo*, which brings it about that there exists a universe of diverse finite beings of greater and lesser degrees of existential perfection. Such causation can be effected only by exercising being in a manner not restricted to the operation characteristic of finite beings which can only bring it about that an already existing object or material comes to be in a different way.[51] It is this creative causation on the part of Infinite Being which is required to account for the existence of the analogical order, the unity and diversity and degrees or comparative levels of finite being, of which we have experience and which Aquinas takes as the datum of his Fourth Way of presenting an argument for the existence of God.

This analogical order of finite being, when considered simply in itself, provides no adequate ontological basis for the unity of our primary concept of being through which we affirm that the unity of being, of *that which exists*, is more fundamental than its diversity. For the analogical order of *finite being* is one in which diversity or otherness is just as fundamental and irreducible as unity. Its unity is always an imperfect unity intrinsically involving diversity.

The affirmation of God as Supreme or Infinite Being is achieved by way of argument that such Being is required as the creative cause of the analogical order of finite being which otherwise appears to contradict our most basic affirmation about the unity of being. Seen in this light, as arising totally by way of the creative act of Infinite Being, the intrinsic unity and diversity of the order of finite being becomes intelligible, or at least less mysterious, as does the conviction that being is primarily one and only secondarily diverse.

From these considerations we can conclude that in his Fourth Way when Aquinas proposes that we can argue to the existence of God as Supreme Being from the degrees of finite being he is not substituting a version of Platonic exemplarism for the appeal to the principle of efficient causation which characterizes his other arguments. On the contrary, he is proposing that by indirect argument from the paradoxical character of the analogy or degrees of finite being we can achieve an affirmation of the existence of God as the unique non-finite creative cause of this analogical order of being.

Finally, it is worth recalling that the profound asymmetry between the degrees of finite being themselves, as instanced by the irreducible asymmetry between human and simply physical being, is a cipher or trace of the radical asymmetry between this

---

50 Nothing, therefore, that has a finite being, can by its action be the cause of another, except as regards it having some genus or species—not as regards it subsisting as distinct from others. Therefore, every finite agent postulates before its action that whereby its effect subsists as an individual. Therefore it does not create. And this belongs exclusively to an agent whose being is infinite. (Aquinas, *Summa Contra Gentiles*, Bk 2, ch. 21, Cf. also *S.T.*, 1, q. 104, a. 1)

51 Cf. Aquinas, *In de divinis nominibus*, ch. 5, lect. 1, n. 629.

finite order and its transcendent Creator. And reciprocally it is this radical asymmetry characteristic of creation which makes ultimate sense of the asymmetry manifested by the degrees of being.

CHAPTER 8

Co-Existence and Transcendence

Introduction

Three broad lines of enquiry arise in a philosophical discussion about God. There is a question of meaning, a question of existence, and a question of co-existence. In the preceding chapters an outline of answers to the first two questions has been offered.

On the question of meaning, adopting indications provided by Anselm and Aquinas, a philosophical conception of God was proposed which, though compatible with, is more abstract than that envisaged pre-philosophically in the main monotheistic religions. It is a conception of God as infinitely perfect transcendent creator of the universe, an unlimited act of existence in relation to whom the universe of finite beings stands in a non-mutual relationship of real dependence.

On the question of existence, various arguments were offered in support of the claim that God, as thus envisaged, does indeed exist. These arguments proceeded from ciphers, or indications, within experience of the sort of transcendence and asymmetrical relationship involved in the account of divine creation. Examples of such ciphers of transcendence which we considered were the transcendence of what we know objectively vis-à-vis our knowing, the ethical transcendence of the other person vis-à-vis our freedom, and the transcendence or asymmetry involved in the analogical character of the finite beings of our experience. The arguments from these ciphers of transcendence led to the affirmation of the existence of God— required as their creative source if they are not to be judged unintelligible and even contradictory.

In this chapter some issues which arise in the context of the third question, the question of co-existence, will be considered. Here one asks whether the claims concerning the nature and existence of God which have been advanced as providing an ultimate foundation for human experience and a dependable outcome of philosophical enquiry really fulfill that role or whether, on the contrary, these claims themselves give rise to further difficulties which seem to undermine them.

Such difficulties do indeed arise and they form a significant feature of the profile of contemporary atheism. To consider them adequately would require a separate and extensive study. Here we will confine our attention and remarks to a series of "afterthoughts" (which may serve also as "foreword" to further study) indicating the sort of difficulties involved and lines along which they might be usefully addressed.

Contemporary Atheism

One helpful way of considering these difficulties is to view them from the perspective of contemporary philosophical atheism. There are at least two animating strands of such atheism. One is a form of scientific humanism which maintains that the limits of theoretical knowledge and the scope of human fulfillment are determined by the possibilities of empirical science and the technological developments to which it can give rise. The other may be described as a humanism of liberty which, emphasizing human autonomy, claims that the meaning and value of human existence is not somehow predetermined but rather self-determined through the exercise of freedom. This is a freedom which can not only liberate us from various oppressions such as disease, famine, and ignorance, but also liberate us to determine what our future meaning and value shall be.

These two strands of atheism, though distinct, can coincide as a scientific and technological project to achieve a form of human autonomy or self-sufficiency extending to the springs of human life itself, in which humanity through its own scientific and technological achievement will be adequate to its own freely adopted goals. A culture of human autonomy and self-determination replaces one of human destiny.

The claim that the existence of God as transcendent creator can be rationally affirmed is judged to be altogether incompatible with and alien to both of these humanistic viewpoints. This incompatibility can be illustrated in various ways.

Firstly, there is the positivistic objection that an affirmation of God is not available to the methods of empirical science which progresses by way of abstract hypotheses that can in principle, however indirectly, be objectively and impersonally verified by repeatable experiment. The loop of scientific explanation is one that operates exclusively within the natural order, originating from and terminating in some form of experience.

This objection, as such, is undoubtedly valid. For there is no experiment which could possibly provide the requisite empirically scientific verification of the hypothesis of the existence of God. God is not a component, however deeply hidden, of the empirical world and therefore his existence cannot be verified by procedures of empirical science.

However, as has often been pointed out in discussions of positivism, the further claim that therefore the existence of God is absolutely unknowable and even meaningless goes beyond the domain of what can be known by empirical science. It is to absolutize one way of knowing by means of an assumption which that way of knowing cannot itself justify, namely, the assumption that only what can be known empirically, either directly or indirectly, really exists. It is to make a meta-empirical or metaphysical claim whose validity must be evaluated accordingly. To thus exclude the possibility of a rational affirmation of God and to claim to know *a priori* that the idea of God is meaningless and contradictory, is equivalent to adopting a form of Ontological Argument for his non-existence. As such it is open to the same kind of objections which can be formulated against any such proof for his existence.

I think that this kind of response to the more doctrinaire forms of positivism is justified. However, it does not address various particular misgivings which underlie the presumption of positivism.

Explaining God?

One such misgiving often expressed, and not only by positivists, is that the affirmation of God as an ultimate explanatory cause of our experience is not really an ultimate explanation. For the question at once arises: "What causes or explains God?" In popular terminology: "If God made the world, who made God?" Or, as Thomas Nagel puts it more philosophically:

> The idea of God seems to be the idea of something that can explain everything else, without having to be explained itself. But it is very hard to understand how there could be such a thing. If we ask the question "Why is the world like this?" and are offered a religious answer, how can we be prevented from asking again, "And why is that true?"[1]

This misgiving should give the theist reason to be circumspect in statements about God and not to engage in a foolish exercise of explaining the why and wherefore of the necessary and self-explanatory existence of God as though one had some positive insight into the divine nature.

Instead one should seek to develop the assertion that since God is affirmed, by way of argument from experience, as the requisite cause or explanation of whatever requires an extrinsic cause or explanation, he cannot, precisely as such, be said to pertain to this hetero-explicable order. Rather he must be affirmed, even though not directly understood, to be self-explanatory. To ask for his cause or explanation is to go on the sort of linguistic holiday involved in asking what is north of the North Pole.

We have no direct understanding of the necessary and self-explanatory nature of God but only indirect analogical knowledge that it is so. We come to know this by way of indirect argument from features of objects of our experience, such as their causally dependent character, which ultimately require his existence as their creative transcendent source. In coming to affirm his existence as the ultimate explanation of whatever requires an extrinsic explanation he must be affirmed as not requiring such explanation himself.

Hence, although one can appreciate the puzzlement about why an explanation for the existence of God should not be sought, we can still maintain that it should not, even though we do not understand his self-explanatory nature. As one writer, James Ross, puts it: "we do not see it to be self-explanatory that God exists, and in fact we cannot see it to be so during our earthly lifetime, but from the things we know we can infer it to be self-accounting."[2] Aquinas makes a cognate point when he observes that although it follows from the nature of the beings of our experience that they are caused, to be caused is not part of the meaning of whatever exists and, therefore, there can exist an uncaused being.[3]

---

1   T. Nagel, *What Does It All Mean?*, Oxford, 1987, p. 99.

2   J. Ross, *Philosophical Theology*, New York, 1969, p. 91.

3   Although the relationship to a cause does not enter into the definition of a being which is caused nevertheless it may follow from that which pertains to it. Thus it follows that because something has being by participation that it is caused by another. Such a being cannot exist without being caused any more than a human being can exist without a capacity for

110 *The Sense of Creation*

Our claim to know that the existence of God is self-explanatory is based upon the nature of the arguments which affirm his necessary existence as the transcendent cause of whatever it can be shown must be explained in terms of something other than itself. Were he himself part of this order which needs to be explained in terms of something else he could not be the cause of this order which we claim him to be. The necessary existence of an infinite creator cannot be explained in terms of anything other than himself. Although implied by, it is not relative to his creation, or to any other extrinsic factor.

Undoubtedly we naturally seek some further account of how or why this necessary existence of God obtains—if only to alleviate the puzzling conclusion that for us it is simply an incomprehensible fact. However, as we have noted, to claim any positive understanding of it would imply direct insight into the divine nature, which we do not possess.

Perhaps the best we can do is argue indirectly that God's necessary existence obtains in virtue of his infinite perfection and desirable goodness. What is infinitely perfect and desirable would, as such, seem to be uniquely that of which it would be misconceived to ask why or "by what right" does it exist. We reason that what is infinitely perfect and desirable, if such could exist, would necessarily exist. Hence, it is because God is infinitely perfect and desirable that he necessarily exists. This idea that God's infinite perfection and desirability somehow makes sense of and "explains" his necessary existence is the perceptive insight of Anselm which we discussed in previous chapters—an insight which retains its value even though it does not, as Anselm believed, provide a proof of God's necessary existence, or any positive understanding of the self-explanatory perfection and goodness which implies it.

Such observations may commend themselves to theists but we should recognize that they cannot be presumed to resolve the profoundly held misgivings of atheists about the existence and self-explanatory nature of God.

Proofs that Don't

Another misgiving on the part of atheists is that the so-called proofs for the existence of God do not generally convince people except perhaps some of those who already believe in his existence. This observation about "the proofs that do not prove" requires more detailed consideration than can be provided here. However, the following remarks are offered as the outline of an initial response.

Someone proposing these disputed arguments for the existence of God must try to chart a way between on the one hand, conceding that the arguments lack cogency and, on the other, claiming that they should convince any impartial intelligent person. The latter claim is particularly dubious since it is obvious that there are many atheists who are altogether unconvinced by the proposed proofs and it is clearly false, not to mention patronizing and ridiculous, to imply that they are in bad faith or lack the

---

laughter. However, since to be caused is not essential to the meaning of being one can arrive at a being which is uncaused. (Aquinas, *S.T.*, I, q. 44, a. 1, ad 1 (my trans.))

Co-Existence and Transcendence 111

requisite philosophical competence to understand them. The relationship between "convincing" and "cogent" arguments is a loose one!

It is not the main purpose of a good or cogent argument to convince everyone acquainted with it of the truth of its conclusion. If this were so the arguments for the existence of God would be notorious failures. Moreover, in evaluating an argument one can, without having a cogent argument, be convinced of the truth of its conclusion because it follows from premises which one (erroneously) holds to be true. Again, an argument constructed precisely to establish a conclusion of which one is already convinced may well be, or indeed may not be, a good argument—not all reasoning about one's beliefs is rationalization. And one may understand but not be convinced by an argument which is in fact cogent—because the experiential premises of a good argument do not have to be either universally agreed or self-evident truths. The truth of the premises will be evident to the person proposing them and he will believe them to be verifiable by others, though this may well turn out not to be universally the case. Moreover, these premises do not have to be, indeed perhaps cannot be, self-evident since self-evident propositions are those which are true independently of any observation.

These remarks illustrate the fact that the intrinsic purpose of a good or cogent argument bearing upon the world of our experience is to establish the truth of its conclusion—whether or not it convinces or "converts" anybody. People of good will and philosophical sophistication will differ on whether or not a given argument establishes the truth of its conclusion.

We can propose arguments that we claim to be cogent. We can indicate that they are proposed as establishing the truth of their conclusion from independently known true premises and that they conform to objective or interpersonal criteria of accessibility and assessability. As such they satisfy and convince their proponent that they are good arguments. But one cannot claim indubitably that they must be so or that everyone who understands them must be convinced by them. Such absence of assent or conviction may be motivated by a non-acceptance of the premises, or of the argument, or of the conclusion, or perhaps even of all three.[4]

It is perhaps not surprising then that arguments for the existence of God as transcendent creator of the world, which are proposed as good arguments, usually do not convince people who do not already believe in such a Being. For this way of appraising what exists might well not have arisen had it not been indicated or prefigured at the pre-philosophical level of religious belief of the major monotheistic religions. People who do not adhere to such religious belief will, understandably, tend to confine their quest for explanation and understanding to within the context of the experienced world. As Anthony Flew remarked:

> The presumption, defeasible of course by adverse argument, must be that all qualities observed in things are qualities belonging by natural right to those things themselves; and hence that whatever characteristics we think ourselves able to discern in the universe as a whole are the underivative characteristics of the universe itself. This is, for us, atheism.[5]

---

4   For a perceptive and more detailed elaboration of these remarks cf. Ross, *Philosophical Theology*, pp. 3–34.

5   A. Flew, *God and Philosophy*, London, 1966, p. 69.

112 *The Sense of Creation*

Likewise for Bertrand Russell: "I should say that the universe is just there, and that is all."[6] And according to the early Wittgenstein of the *Tractatus*: "we feel that even if all possible scientific questions be answered, the problems of life have still not been touched at all. Of course there is then no question left, and just this is the answer."[7]

This was the natural way of viewing things in the context of non-Judaeo-Christian Greek thought where, even when gods were affirmed, they were still part and parcel of the universe. It is also very much the outlook of more recent philosophical culture as indicated by the above quotations.

In the pre-modern world outlook, animated by a culture of religious faith, an affirmation of God was the confidently anticipated conclusion of any philosophical appraisal of experience. The situation is very different today where the prevailing intellectual climate, characterized by achievements of science and technology and the claims of human autonomy, is predisposed to an atheistic, or at least a robustly agnostic, appraisal of experience. Even where the validity of some form of metaphysical argument is admitted the range of its application is usually presumed to lie within the limits of the experienced world.

Thus the de facto cultural conditions in which a proposed argument for the existence of God will be appraised have changed significantly and this change must be taken into account in the presentation of the argument. The age of innocence, some would say of "naiveté," is in the past.

Self-Involvement

What makes these considerations particularly relevant to any argument allegedly leading to an affirmation of God is the essentially self-involving character of such an affirmation. This idea of the self-involving character of an affirmation of God has been highlighted by Donald Evans in his illuminating adaptation of J.L. Austin's account of performative utterances to the special context of theistic discourse.[8]

Evans defines a self-involving assertion as "one which commits the person who asserts it or accepts it to further action, or implies that he has an attitude for or against whatever the assertion is about, or which expresses such an attitude."[9] As examples of such assertions he mentions: "I promise to return this book tomorrow." "I commend Jones for his restraint." "I look upon you as a father." Self-involvement is a logical feature of the meaning of such assertions and not simply a psychological accompaniment. The public linguistic conventions governing the force of such speech acts preclude a denial of the attitude or course of action asserted.

Broadly, one can distinguish amongst speech acts (a) those that are self-involving in the sense of committing one to a course of action or implying an attitude, and (b) constative speech acts which are not self-involving in the sense indicated but merely

---

6   B. Russell, "A Debate on the Existence of God," in *The Existence of God*, ed. J. Hick, London, 1965, p. 175.

7   L. Wittgenstein, *Tractatus Logico Philosophicus*, London, 1933, 6.25.

8   Cf. D. Evans, *The Logic of Self-Involvement*, New York, 1969.

9   D. Evans, "Differences between Scientific and Religious Assertions", in *Science and Religion*, ed. I. Barbour, London, 1968, p. 112.

express a factual content which is either true or false. As examples of constatives one could mention: "Smith made the table." "The litmus paper has turned red." "Water boils at one hundred degrees centigrade at sea level." Such assertions do not logically commit one to action or imply an attitude, even though they may be of great personal interest to the person uttering them.

The illocutionary force of a speech act may be self-involving in one context and merely constative in another. Consider the assertion "That woman is my mother." Asserted as a response to a question "Why did you embrace that woman?" the speech act is obviously self-involving in the sense that it implies an attitude of filial love. Asserted as a response to the question "Who is that woman in the garden?" the speech act may have merely constative force.

Let us now consider the speech act "I affirm that God is the Creator of the world." This speech act may look similar to a mere constative such as "Smith made the table," and therefore it may seem that, in some contexts at least, it might have merely constative force. However, upon reflection it appears undeniable that the speech act "I affirm that God is the Creator of the world" cannot have merely constative force. For it is part of the meaning of this speech act that it involves its users to the very core of their being. It means that they acknowledge their creaturely status and role. It is not simply a matter of saying impersonally how things are, as is the case when one says "Smith made the table." It implies as part of its meaning an attitude to the world and to oneself which regards them as radically dependent in their being upon a transcendent source. It involves accepting to look upon the world and oneself in a certain way—a God-dependent way. In virtue of its meaning there is no context in which it would not have logically practical consequences for attitude and action.

From this brief outline of the logically self-involving character of the affirmation of God we can develop certain considerations about the crucial importance of the theme of self-involvement in contemporary philosophy of God. The basic consideration to be taken note of is that for many people today it is the self-involving implications of this affirmation which motivate their atheism. Their basic objection is not to a merely speculative assertion of a divine first principle of everything but to the relativization of human autonomy which such an assertion involves. The self-involving dependence implied in an assertion of God no longer spontaneously recommends itself to human consciousness as a dependence upon the truly dependable. Rather it is seen as undermining a hard-won conception of human understanding and freedom.

One may say that since its origin in the Cartesian cogito the course of modern philosophy has witnessed to a progressive triumph of a humanism of liberty which calls in question in a radical manner the possibility of the co-existence of man and God. How can the ever more impressive claims of human subjectivity to be an irreducible source of a world of meaning and value be rendered compatible with the claims involved in the theistic conception of God as absolute creator of the existence nature and activity of all finite beings? The traditional conviction that the alienated person is the person who does not acknowledge God has given way to the view that the affirmation of God is a profound source of human alienation.

The development of this view can be traced from its origins in modern science and Cartesian philosophy, through Kant's vindication of the autonomy of science and

114 *The Sense of Creation*

morality and his critique of revealed religion, in Hegel's rejection of the traditional understanding of divine transcendence, In Feuerbach's atheistic anthropology, and in Marxist and Positivist rejection of God in favor of an exclusively secular humanism. In atheistic forms of existentialism one finds the rejection of God in defense of the transcendence, creativity, and freedom of man. Thus Sartre remarks:

> It took two centuries of crisis—a crisis of Faith and a crisis of Science—for man to regain the creative freedom that Descartes placed in God, and for anyone finally to suspect the following truth, which is an essential basis of humanism: man is the being as a result of whose appearance a world exists.[10]

Fidelity to a phenomenological conception of authentic though precarious human subjectivity is deemed to preclude any quest for a trans-human ontological principle of meaning and value such as a divine being.

Subsequent structuralist and post-modern thought has somewhat modified the exuberant claims made on behalf of human subjectivity. However, this often involves not so much a renewed theistic perspective as a reflection upon "otherness" which tends to devalue the claims of subjectivity in the direction of relativism or agnosticism.

In such a cultural ambience there appears to be no meeting point between the self-assertive logic of the irreducible autonomy attributed to man and the self-involving logic of an affirmation of God.

Human Autonomy

The foregoing observations illustrate the relevance of the theme of self-involvement to contemporary philosophical discussion of the co-existence of finite and infinite, of man and God. The logically self-involving character of an affirmation of God is judged to be incompatible with the sort of autonomy ascribed to human existence. As Anthony Flew puts it: "In short: if creation is in, autonomy is out."[11] And likewise for Merleau-Ponty: "Theology adverts to human contingency only to derive it from a necessary Being, in other words to undermine it."[12]

Hence, at a deeper existential level than impersonal argumentation concerning whether or not in the absence of God the world would be fundamentally unintelligible and our discussion of it ultimately incoherent, there is a principled repudiation of the self-involving consequences of any allegedly rational affirmation of God. This repudiation, made on behalf of a conception of human autonomy, would acquiesce in the ultimate unintelligibility and absurdity of the universe rather than accept the self-involving consequences of an affirmation of God. Thus James Ross remarks: "I have met philosophers who have said that if I could show them that the existence of

---

10 J.P. Sartre, "Cartesian Freedom", in *Literary and Philosophical Essays*, trans. A. Michelson, London, 1969, p. 184.

11 Flew, *God and Philosophy*, p. 47.

12 M. Merleau-Ponty, *Éloge de la Philosophie* (my trans.), Paris, 1953, p. 61.

Co-Existence and Transcendence 115

God followed from the fact that contradictions are always false, they would abandon their belief that the latter is a fact."[13]

This would suggest that, in some cases at least, Kierkegaard's insistence that profound truth is achieved only by way of resolute commitment to the promptings and passion of one's innermost subjectivity rather than by impersonal attention to allegedly cogent argument from objective evidence, has been adopted in its own support by contemporary atheism.[14]

From these considerations we can see that the logically self-involving character of an affirmation of God has a psychological counterpart affecting, though not necessarily determining, one's view of an argument for his existence. In the case of a religious believer the argument will tend to reinforce their belief. For unbelievers their atheism can pose a psychological obstacle to assent to any philosophical argument with such self-involving implications. Such unbelievers do not merely deny the existence of God. They fear or dislike its religious or self-involving implications and want there not to be a God. As Thomas Nagel, whom we have often cited, puts it:

> I speak from experience, being strongly subject to this fear [of religion] myself: I want atheism to be true and am made uneasy by the fact that some of the most intelligent and well-informed people I know are religious believers. It isn't just that I don't believe in God and, naturally, hope that I am right in my belief. It's that I hope there is no God I don't want the universe to be like that.[15]

In the light of such sincerely held conviction one can readily appreciate that an argument which for one person is cogent and convincing may for another be uncompelling and unconvincing. It is not always easy to disentangle the motivations, reasons, and causes of our beliefs.[16] The certainty attributed to the premises of an argument or the extent to which a rational elucidation of them is pursued may differ from one person to another partly because of profound existential or culturally conditioned commitment. Thus, for example the account proposed in previous chapters of epistemological realism, or of the ethical claim of the other person, or of the paradoxical character of the analogy of being, will certainly not be universally convincing. Nor will the argument that an ultimate account of them must be sought beyond the context of the world of lived experience.

All of this should not deter one from seeking to present cogent arguments for the existence of God, or from maintaining their cogency, or from disputing that they serve

---

13   Ross, *Philosophical Theology*, pp. 15–16.

14   Only in subjectivity is there decisiveness, to seek objectivity is to be in error. It is the passion of the infinite that is the decisive factor and not its content, for its content is precisely itself. In this manner subjectivity and the subjective "how" constitute truth. ... Here is such a definition of truth: *an objective uncertainty held fast in an appropriation-process of the most passionate inwardness is the truth*, the highest truth attainable for an *existing* individual. (S. Kierkegaard, *Concluding Unscientific Postscript*, trans. D. Swenson and W. Lowrie, Princeton, 1968, pp. 181–2)

15   T. Nagel, *The Last Word*, Oxford, 1997, p. 130.

16   Cf. P. Geach, *Reason and Argument*, Oxford, 1976, pp. 1–4.

116   *The Sense of Creation*

no useful purpose because their self-involving conclusion encounters difficult issues concerning the contemporary denial of the possible co-existence of man and God.

Rather it should motivate one to explain more effectively why the argument is held to be cogent. This may involve a more comprehensive and phenomenologically perceptive account of the experiential basis of the argument, and of the rationally persuasive nature of the reflection which leads to the affirmation of the existence of God as the ultimate explanation of this experience. However, it will also have to involve some account of why the affirmation of God as transcendent creator does not undermine the autonomy of human persons which, as we have noted, is a defining claim of contemporary atheism.

This is a demanding requirement and one must be careful to avoid the folly of expecting to provide a comprehensive explanation of what, in the final analysis, is profoundly mysterious. Nevertheless, certain clarifications and indications of potential misunderstandings to be avoided on this topic of the co-existence of God and human autonomy can be suggested.

In the first place, it is important to note that the co-existence of God and the human person should not be envisaged as a case of two beings exercising competing or conflicting claims of autonomy and efficacy within a common sphere of action. God is not a being amongst beings. A being amongst beings is this being rather than that being, a member of a differentiated system of distinct, and co-relative finite entities. God, considered as transcendent creator, is the unlimited source of all such finite beings including human persons and, as such, is not affected by them or co-relative to them. They, however, are really related to him as wholly dependent for every aspect of their existence and activity.

But being so dependent does not change their nature or activity. It originates them to exist as the nature and activity they are—not to become something different. Their created nature and activity is the same nature and activity that we can think about without any reference to creation. Being a created dog does not mean to be a different kind of thing to being a dog! As Aquinas remarked: "the relation to its cause is not part of the definition of a thing caused."[17]

Hence, when things are considered, not as created, but simply as the sort of things that they are one can properly say, without further reference, that it is simply in their nature to act as they do. Thus it is true, for example, that something such as fire "naturally" boils a pot of water applied to it—even though it is also true to say that both the fire and water exist and act as they do in virtue of God's act of creation. Different but compatible orders of causality are involved. As Herbert McCabe puts it:

> In the Jewish/Christian/Islamic tradition ... the one God we can worship, who is the cause of all that is, allows us to speak of causes of particular things at another level, at the level we examine scientifically. There is no quarrel between the scientific project and worship of the creator; there is only sometimes a quarrel between science and the religion of the gods.[18]

Similarly, if one admits the existence of a transcendent creator, one can affirm the compatible co-existence of God and human autonomy. God's causal activity

---

17   Aquinas, *S.T.*, I, q. 44, art. 1, ad 1.

18   H. McCabe, *God Still Matters*, London, 2002, pp. 33–4.

Co-Existence and Transcendence

in respect of my nature and activity does not interact with them to make them *become* dependent upon him. Acknowledging that one is a created person is not like becoming a slave deprived of a previously independently possessed freedom or dignity. God's causal activity does not compromise one's free action as can a countervailing force such as alcohol. Rather, as already mentioned, creation makes all beings—including human beings—to exist and to continue to exist and to act as the sort of beings that they are. In the case of human beings, the affirmation that God's free act of creation causes the existence of their free autonomous activity does not signify that their autonomous activity becomes or means something else, e.g. that it is now to be understood simply as the instrument of God's activity, like the paintbrush becomes an instrument in the hand of the artist. Because the free activity of each agent, one human the other divine, pertains to a different kind and order of efficacy it can be said, without contradiction, that each brings about freely and properly the same particular effect.[19]

A coherent account of the co-existence of God and human freedom can be envisaged along the lines indicated above. However, it would be foolish to aspire to provide a comprehensive explanation of how this is so. There are no appropriate comparisons or parallels, or insight into the divine nature, to which one can appeal for adequate clarification and understanding of how this is so.

This compatibility of human freedom with an affirmation of the existence of God can be developed into an account of a divinely enabled human project of self-expression and self-realization through our scientific ingenuity, our aesthetic sensibility and our moral impulse. For atheists are not the only people influenced by the contemporary sense of our autonomous capacity and responsibility to fashion and humanize the world of our experience—to liberate humanity from various oppressions and create new possibilities of self-realization. This is a project which can commend itself equally to believers. Likewise the primacy of personal conscience, the freedom to do what *we* judge to be right, is not a sentiment unique to contemporary atheism. Even in his time Aquinas maintained that "we should state quite simply that every act of will against reason, whether in the right or in the wrong is always bad."[20] He drives home this view with a couple of striking examples. A man would act wrongly if having judged it evil to abstain from fornication he in fact abstained. Likewise he would act wrongly if having judged it evil to accept the Christian faith he in fact accepted it.[21]

However, the difficulty persists that whereas for believers the co-existence of God and human autonomy need not be a problem, for atheists, even if the reasoning involved is understood, it may remains theoretically unconvincing and/or aesthetically and morally repugnant.

---

19 Cf. Aquinas, *Summa Contra Gentiles*, trans. English Dominicans, London, 1924, Bk 3, ch. 70.

20 Aquinas, *S.T.*, I–II, q. 19, art. 5. Blackfriars edn, London, 1964–74.

21 Cf. ibid.

Open Dialogue

In view of this deep-seated difference one may be tempted to revert to a form of what is sometimes loosely, and disputedly, called Wittgensteinian Fideism, which argues that the unbeliever and the believer inhabit totally different and incommensurable worlds. However, we have already argued that this is an unsatisfactory explanation of the deep division between believers and unbelievers. The view that people inhabit different worlds wholly insulated from one another leads, in the final analysis, to a form of relativism which undermines any discussion of a true or rationally justified appraisal of experience.

Instead of claiming that people see different worlds, the least that must be affirmed to maintain the possibility of rational discussion is that people inhabit and understand the same world, albeit differently. This leaves some scope for rational debate about the relative merits of different accounts of the same shared world of experience.

A believer's pre-philosophical religious faith may predispose him to a more optimistic view of the significance of human experience, to a more agent-centered view of morality, and to a more confident view of the range and viability of metaphysical reflection. He will be disposed to seek an adequate metaphysical background for his apprehension of meaning and value and to defend a conception of freedom as more a matter of liberation from fantasy than absolute exercise of unrestricted free choice. He is likely to be responsive to claims such as that of Iris Murdoch who wrote:

> It is in the capacity to love, that is to see, that the liberation of the soul from fantasy consists. The freedom which is the proper human goal is the freedom from fantasy, that is the realism of compassion.[22]

The opposite may be the case for an unbeliever who may have a more circumspect view of the significance of human experience, a view that morality is more effectively advanced by utilitarian than by agent-centered considerations, and a conviction that the human desire for ever deeper knowledge is best served by ceaselessly pushing back, but remaining within, the boundaries of what is empirically verifiable.

These (and other) considerations illustrate the need for mutual attention to, and open debate about, what are very different overall perspectives or outlooks. They also illustrate the difficulty, but not the impossibility, of developing a theistic argument which proposes itself as one which not only corresponds to the anticipations of believers but which also takes into account (even if not altogether dissipating), the objections of unbelievers.

In effect, any such theistic explanation of experience will have to argue that its account and appraisal is more faithful to the indications and implications of experience than those adduced in various versions of atheism. In other words, it will have to argue that it is a more adequate, a more truth-full, account of how things are independently of our wishing or hoping or making them to be. This is a demanding, ongoing, worthwhile, and indeed necessary rational pursuit although it is unlikely to reach a definitive and universally accepted conclusion.

---

22 I. Murdoch, *The Sovereignty of Good*, London, 1970, p. 66.

Co-Existence and Transcendence

Attending to and seeking to address objections is not just a source of uncertainty and doubt but also a way of reaching a more refined and better reasoned presentation of a philosophical approach to the issues concerning the existence of God and our co-existence with him. This study is an attempt to contribute to this ongoing enquiry and will no doubt have the benefit of many perceptive objections which will give impetus to further reflection and hopefully further refinement of the ongoing process of enquiry and argument.

In the next chapter we will consider one further matter which also bears directly upon the issue of the co-existence of finite and infinite, of God's life and human life. It will no longer be a case of encountering some philosophical objections posed by atheists, but rather one of addressing a theistic account of human and divine co-existence which involves a very different conception of the God of monotheistic religions to that for which we have argued throughout this work.

CHAPTER 9

Phenomenology and Transcendence

The way of signifying God availed of throughout this work has been by means of an abstract philosophical conception of the creator God worshipped in the main monotheistic religions. It is a traditional conception of God as infinitely perfect being to whom the created world is related in a non-mutual real relationship of radical dependence. It signifies God as pure act of existence, whose unconstrained activity is not subject to any process of change or development and whose infinite perfection is not relativized or affected in any way by the existence of his freely created world.

The God Who May-Be

The view I wish to consider now is a version of the view that God is more properly envisaged in terms of possibility rather than in terms of actuality. This is a view that has family resemblances with strands of Neoplatonism, with Hegel's Absolute Spirit, and with the process theology of thinkers such as Whitehead and Hartshorne.

However, the version I wish to consider here is one formulated more recently by Richard Kearney, an Irish philosopher teaching at Boston College (a friend and former student and colleague). The view is developed in a book pointedly entitled *The God Who May Be*.[1] This work is proposed as a philosophical, rather than theological, treatise. It is written chiefly from a phenomenological and hermeneutical perspective in the tradition of contemporary continental European philosophy, drawing inspiration from philosophers such as Husserl, Heidegger, Levinas, Ricoeur, and Derrida.

From the outset Kearney states clearly that:

> God neither is nor is not but may be. That is my thesis in this volume. What I mean by this is that God, who is traditionally thought of as act or actuality, might be better rethought of as possibility. To this end I am proposing here a new hermeneutics of religion which explores and evaluates two rival ways of interpreting the divine—the eschatological and the onto-theological. The former, which I endorse, privileges a God who possibilizes our world from out of the future, from the hoped-for eschaton which several religious traditions have promised will one day come. … Instead of seeing possibility as some want or lack to be eradicated from the divine so that it be recognized as the perfectly fulfilled act that it supposedly is, I proffer the alternative view that it is divinity's very potentiality-to-be that is the most divine thing about it.[2]

And a little later: "God can be God only if we enable this to happen."[3]

---

1 R. Kearney, *The God Who May Be*, Bloomington, 2001.
2 Ibid., pp. 1–2.
3 Ibid., p. 2.

122   *The Sense of Creation*

This is a conception of God which differs greatly from that defended in this work. Let us consider, therefore, some of the reasons adduced by Kearney in favour of his conception and then offer some reflections by way of appraisal of it.

He tells us that: "In this wager, I subscribe to that new turn in contemporary philosophy of religion which strives to overcome the metaphysical God of pure act and asks the question: what kind of divinity comes after metaphysics?" His answer, in brief, is that God is more appropriately envisaged in terms of possibility rather than in terms of actuality:

> My ultimate suggestion is that we might do better to reinterpret the Transfiguring God of Exodus 3 neither as "I who am" nor as "I who am not" but rather as "I who may be."—that is as the possibility to be, which obviates the extremes of being and non-being. 'Ehyeh 'asher 'ehyeh might thus be read as signature of the God of the possible ...[4]

This move to considering God in terms of possibility rather than actuality is motivated, in part, by his acceptance of the contemporary rejection of what has been called, after Heidegger, "onto-theology", namely, the tendency "to reify God by reducing Him to a being (*Seinde*)—albeit the highest first and most indeterminate of all beings."[5]

This "reifying" idea of God is seen as a distorting reformulation of the biblical God into the ontological categories of Greek metaphysics. God is represented as an immutable, self-sufficient pure act of being, existing as an eternal now with no past or future, without movement desire or possibility.[6]

Instead of this conception of God in ontological terms, Kearney proposes a more dynamic conception of the divine as a transfiguring ethical possibility or may-be—an eschatological summons, exceeding our own capacity, which enables us to accomplish a re-created world of peace, justice, and love.[7]

Much of the book is devoted to illuminating interpretations of key biblical events (such as Moses and the burning bush, the Sulamite woman in the Song of Songs, the transfiguration and paschal apparitions of Christ) in terms of this transcendent divine transforming possibility. His "wager" that God should be envisaged in terms of possibility rather than actuality facilitates a perceptive ethical interpretation of such biblical incidents, which in turn lend credibility to the wager.

Likewise he uses his wager as a hermeneutical approach to provide probing elaborations of enigmatic treatments of "the Possible" by various contemporary philosophers such as Husserl, Heidegger, and Derrida, and uses them as signposts to strengthen the claims of his wager.[8]

His basic wager—that God should be understood as a transcendent enabling possibility of human transformation or transfiguration—is both subtle and elusive and certainly not adequately recounted in a few sentences. However, certain particular features of it should be highlighted.

---

4   Ibid., p. 22.
5   Ibid., p. 24.
6   Cf. ibid., p. 23.
7   Cf. ibid., pp. 37–8.
8   Cf. ibid., pp. 84–200.

Phenomenology and Transcendence 123

One significant feature is the insistence that God conceived as possibility is not to be understood simply as an immanent possibility of the historically evolving world. God, understood as possibility, has indeed a relationship to the historical world, but as a transfiguring possibility beyond its own intrinsic possibilities. It might be called, following Derrida's expression, an "impossible possible." "It is radically transcendent— guaranteed by the mask of its impossible-possibility."[9]

Here we are in the domain of eschatology not teleology, of ethical invocation not latent purpose. We are "where the infinite eschaton intersects with the finite order of being." [10] Or again:

from an eschatological perspective, divinity is reconceived as that posse or possest which calls and invites us to actualize its proffered possibles by our poetical and ethical actions, contributing to the transformation of the world to the extent that we respond to this invitation, but refusing this transfiguring task every time we do evil or injustice or commit ourselves to non-being.[11]

Another, even more striking, feature of this conception of God as possibility is the fact that although God has a bearing upon human history, human history has a comparable bearing upon God.

As we have noted, for Kearney, God can be God "only if we enable this to happen." This startling theme is repeated frequently throughout the work. He tells us that

God will be God at the eschaton. That is what is promised … But because God is posse (the possibility of being) rather than esse (the actuality of being as fait accompli), the promise remains powerless until and unless we respond to it. … God depends on us to be.[12]

He maintains that henceforth God may be recognized "as someone who becomes with us, someone as dependent on us as we are on Him."[13] He repeats this constant theme in his concluding paragraph:

The eschatological *possest* I have been endeavouring to sketch out in this volume promises something radically new and adventurous. For *possest* may be seen as advent rather than *arche*, as *eschaton* rather than *principium*. The realization of *possest*'s divine *esse* . . . refigured and transfigured in a mirror-play where it recognizes its other and not just the image of itself returning to itself … . Is such a thing possible? Not for us alone. But it is not impossible to God—if we help God to become God. How? By opening ourselves to the "loving possible" by acting each moment to make the impossible that bit more possible. [14]

Such, in broad outline, is the conception of God advocated in *The God Who May Be*— a conception involving a striking account of the co-existence of finite and infinite, of man and God. It is an account motivated by the contemporary claim that the onto-theological conception of God, developed in terms of Greek metaphysics,

---

9   Ibid., p. 100.
10   Ibid., p. 8.
11   Ibid., p. 105.
12   Ibid., p. 4.
13   Ibid., pp. 29–30.
14   Ibid., p. 111.

124 *The Sense of Creation*

has led to a distorted view of the biblical God and his relationship to humanity. Instead it proposes, as a wager, what it claims is a more biblically faithful conception of God— a more dynamic and ethically challenging conception.

This is a conception inspired by the interest of contemporary continental European philosophy in rethinking in post-metaphysical terms, the notion of the possible—a rethinking which, privileging the future, highlights the radical otherness, eventfulness, and innovative character of the possible vis-à-vis our natural human capabilities. Kearney weaves these ideas together into an original and distinctive conception of God as an eschatological ethically inspiring possibility which, transcending our intrinsic resources enables us to aspire to and attain an otherwise unattainable kingdom of peace, justice, and love. In so doing we make actual the unlimited divine possibility which is God.

This is an impressive work. It manifests notable religious sensitivity to key biblical texts, formidable hermeneutical skills, and an informed readiness to engage with the language and preoccupations of contemporary phenomenological and post-modern thought. In so doing it strives to re-present a conception of the co-existence of God and man in terms comprehensible to, and providing an illuminating development of, various features of contemporary thought.

Nevertheless, as it clearly differs from the conception of the co-existence of man and God defended in this study, some further examination of its implication are in order.

Phenomenology and Metaphysics

The work proposes itself as a post-metaphysical approach to philosophy of religion, one which rejects the onto-theological corruption of the dynamic biblical notion of God. "In short, interpreting God as posse rather than esse is a final "no" to theodicy."[15]

However, it seems to me, that although the discussion in the book may be said to be post-metaphysical in the sense that it is proposed at a time subsequent to the development of traditional theodicy, in another sense it may be more appropriately described as pre-metaphysical.

By this I mean that the expressly phenomenological-hermeneutical character of the work tends to confine its discussion and interpretations of the divine to the context of a descriptive account of Judeo-Christian religious experience and metaphors. This context is characteristically that of the interaction between man and God as described phenomenologically from the perspective of human religious attention. In this context the God so described, although undoubtedly portrayed as a "presence-absence," an "eschatological Otherness" transcending the limits of intentional consciousness, is nevertheless always envisaged in terms of God as he is for man. "God does not reveal himself, therefore, as an essence *in se* but as an I-Self for us ... This God of Mosaic manifestation cannot be God without relating to his other—humanity."[16]

---

15 Ibid., p. 5.
16 Ibid., pp. 29–30.

Phenomenology and Transcendence   125

The metaphysical consideration of God's own independent existence is not an issue. From a phenomenological viewpoint it is put out of play or "in parenthesis." It is his religious significance for man which is the englobing focus of attention and discussion.

Within this pre-metaphysical phenomenological context the co-existence of man and God is explored metaphorically as a dynamic two-way correlative interaction—the interaction of love of man for God and the love of God for man. "this new model of religious hermeneutics seeks a two-way production of metaphorical meaning—like Jacob's ladder with angels passing up and down."[17]

Inasmuch as this two-way interaction is viewed eschatologically as something not yet fully accomplished, one can readily comprehend how the correlative poles of the relationship, man and God, might be spoken of in terms of a possibility yet to be achieved, namely, the fulfillment of man's religious desire for God.

However, as we shall argue presently, this phenomenological and hermeneutical manner of speaking requires a metaphysical counterpoint which seeks to express what we can say of God himself, independently of the relationship of humanity to him. This metaphysical retrieval seeks to identify what God simply as such must be whether or not we exist, or recognize and acknowledge him. This self-possessed existence of God is not something which we bring about. It is presupposed to all such bringing about, as the Ninetieth Psalm intimates: "Before the mountains were brought forth, or ever thou hadst formed the earth and the world, even from everlasting to everlasting, thou art God."

It is, of course, true that he cannot be the God whom we religiously and ethically acknowledge as the enabling transformer of our lives unless we accept that he is so. This, however, refers to something about us rather than to something about him. In himself, he is neither actualized or not-actualized by us. It is the possibility which he represents for us which can be actualized by our response to it. This is the possibility which can be expressed by way of phenomenological description and metaphor. But such discourse is liable to occasion ambiguity and misrepresentation unless it can be grounded in an affirmation of the independent existence of God, affirmed as the metaphysical condition of its possibility.

Onto-Theology

Similar reservations should be expressed about the "post-metaphysical" dismissal of traditional philosophy of God as an onto-theology in which the biblical God of monotheistic religion is misrepresented by the intrusion of Greek metaphysics. This widely, and often uncritically, held view is a very one-sided view of the encounter of Judeo-Christian religion with Greek metaphysics.

Undoubtedly careful attention should be paid to the way in which Greek metaphysics contributes to an abstract and necessarily inadequate philosophical way of speaking about the biblical God. If this way of signifying God is proposed as an adequate account of the divine reality it signifies, as has indeed been the case in

---

17 Ibid., p. 7.

126 *The Sense of Creation*

popular manuals, then there are good grounds for speaking of a distorted objectifying understanding of God. However, from the outset, in the thought of major philosophers and theologians, the encounter of biblical religion and Greek philosophy has been guided by the awareness that what God is infinitely exceeds our representative way of thinking and our manner of signifying him. From medieval times it is a constant theme of philosophy of God that our way of signaling his perfection analogically involves negating that it is of the same order of perfection as that which characterizes the beings of our objective experience. His existential perfection is said to utterly transcend the manner of being of the beings which we do, to some extent, know and understand. We cannot know or understand either his existence or his nature—we can only signal it as existing in a way beyond our comprehension.[18]

Moreover, one should also take into account the impact which the biblical conception of God had upon the reinterpretation of Greek metaphysics. The suggestion, that because of the intrusion of Greek metaphysics, traditional philosophy of God has become an onto-theology tending to reify the biblical God as simply the highest and most indeterminate being in a system of beings is a serious oversimplification.[19] For, in fact, traditional theodicy transforms the Greek metaphysics which it employs through its insistence that the creator biblical God cannot be a being amongst other beings.

The divine unmoved "mover" of Aristotelian metaphysics is indeed a being amongst all other beings and related to them as their most perfect and influential instance. He accounts ultimately for their interactions and transformations but not for their existence.

When God is envisaged as creator this picture changes radically. Now, instead of not been seen as problematic, the very existence of finite beings is viewed as utterly contingent and dependent—as obtaining in a totally different way to their creative source. The question of the existence rather than the non-existence of such an order of beings transcends the level of explanation of their interactions and transformations in terms of natural causes. Natural causes explain how this instance of a particular kind of being (e.g. this particular man) becomes that instance of that particular kind of being (e.g. that particular corpse). God envisaged as creator is affirmed as explaining the existence of all such beings, which happen to exist but need not have—of why there are, rather than are not, any particular beings at all. Seen in this light God is not an inhabitant of the order of beings whose existence he originates and explains. "He said: Let there be light! Creation was not a shaping: it was a command, in response to which the creature sprang into being."[20] Thus envisaged, as Aquinas frequently remarks, he "must be understood as existing outside the order of beings, as a cause producing the whole of being and its differences."[21]

It is in virtue of this conception of God as creator that the categories of Greek metaphysics are revised to serve a new understanding of the significance of beings and of their ultimate foundation. The categories of act and potency, which hitherto

---

18   Cf. Aquinas, *S.T.*, I, q. 3, a. 4 ad 2, Blackfriars edn, London 1964–74.

19   Cf. Kearney, *The God Who May Be*, p. 24.

20   E. McMullin (ed.), *Evolution and Creation*, Notre Dame, 1985, p. 8.

21   Aquinas, *Perihermeneias*, trans. J. Oesterle, Milwaukee, 1962, lect. 14, par. 22.

Phenomenology and Transcendence 127

were confined to the analysis of the intrinsic structure of the nature and activity of finite beings (e.g. their composition of matter and form, of substance and accidents, their relations of cause and effect), are now adapted to address the issue of the existence of such beings and the divine source of this existence. The existence of finite beings (their esse) is seen as their actualizing perfection, which is limited in scope to the potentiality of the particular forms which it actualizes. (As Aquinas remarks: "esse is the actuality of all things including forms themselves.")[22] On the other hand, the divine reality is no longer seen as a co-relative participant in a system of such mutually defining determinate beings. Rather its existence is affirmed, though not comprehended, as utterly beyond and unrelated to this system of finite beings— an infinite plenitude of actual existence which freely originates their contingent and variously determined finite existence but is not in any way affected or limited by them.

Viewed in this light traditional theodicy can be seen, not as a metaphysical forgetfulness of the ontological difference between Being and beings, but rather as a recovery, in its own terms, of this very distinction through a de-hellenization of Greek rationality.[23]

Evaluation

In the light of these observations about the allegedly distorting impact of Greek metaphysics on traditional theodicy let us return to the central claims of *The God Who May Be*. These are the related claims: (1) That God should be envisaged as possibility. "God, who is traditionally thought of as act or actuality, might be better thought of as possibility."[24] (2) That to become God he is dependent upon our human endeavour. "God henceforth may be recognized as someone who becomes with us, someone as dependent on us as we are on Him."[25]

I think, as I have indicated above, that if one is to concede a measure of validity to this way of speaking about God one must understand that it is proposed as a phenomenological and hermeneutical account of historical ethico-religious consciousness. Kearney writes: "My approach remains, however, in spite of invoking several scriptural and patristic texts, that of a phenomenological-hermeneutic retrieval rather than that of a theological exegesis per se."[26] As such it will be an account of God with irreducible reference to our religious awareness, God as he is for co-existing humanity. "This God of Mosaic manifestation cannot be God without relating to his other—humanity."[27]

---

22 Aquinas, *S.T.* I, q, 8, art. 1.

23 Cf. A. Dondeyne, "Une discours philsophique sur Dieu est il encore possible?" in *Miscellanea Albert Dondeyne*, Leuven, 1974, pp. 417–18; also M. Westphal, "Overcoming Onto-theology," in *God, the Gift and Postmodernism*, ed. J. Caputo and M. Scanlan, Bloomington, 1999, pp. 146–69.

24 Kearney, *The God Who May Be*, p. 1.

25 Ibid., pp. 29–30.

26 Ibid., p. 39.

27 Ibid, p. 30.

128   *The Sense of Creation*

This phenomenological perspective abstracts from theological claims and precludes traditional metaphysical ones. Interpreting the religious sense of God phenomenologically *sub specie historiae* replaces metaphysical explanation. Kearney again:

> Most philosophical reflections on God are in need of revision. And certainly, the orthodox onto-theological categories of omnipotence, omniscience, and self-causality, originally forged sub specie aeternitatis, could do with a radical rethink sub specie historiae.[28]

From this phenomenological perspective one can see the point of speaking of God as a possible and possibilizing eschaton or finality of human aspiration, who is so affirmed precisely as the not yet accomplished fulfillment of religious desire. He is encountered as the "impossible-possible," transcending yet transfiguring human capacity by enabling it to achieve a kingdom of justice and love beyond its own intrinsic resources.

All of this unfolds, not as a process of causality, but as an ethical adventure of invocation and response. It is mediated through our response to the eschatological appeal of the "persona" of the other person, which brings home to us that we have no power over him or her, and initiates our desire for their good. Kearney writes:

> The phenomenon of the persona calls for a new or quasi-phenomenology, mobilized by ethics rather than eidetics. ... Persona is the in-finite other in the finite person before me. In and through that person. ... we refer to this persona as the sign of God. Not the other person as divine, mind you—that would be idolatory—but the divine in and through that person. The divine as trace, icon, visage, passage.[29]

This asymmetrical appeal, so well described by Levinas, is skillfully adapted by Kearney throughout the work both to interpret, and in turn be illuminated by, key biblical texts. It enables him to chart a hermeneutic path which affirms a transcendent God, present to experience as the absent eschaton or finality intimated in the ethical appeal of the other person to goodness in her regard.

This approach represents a "post-metaphysical" attempt to respect the radical transcendence of the divine while still envisaging it from a phenomenological perspective of concrete human experience. Hence the recourse to such enigmatic expressions as "presence-absence," "impossible-possibility," and "eschatological May-be." One has the impression of a demanding attempt to speak about divine transcendence in a way which, without betraying this transcendence, affirms that it impinges upon experience in a way which enables a legitimation of it by experience. One feels the tension of this requirement in the eschatological appeal to a "possible God," experienced, not as a direct object of intentional consciousness, but as an enabling ethical invocation.

This concern to somehow contain the discussion of divine transcendence within a phenomenological frame of reference is motivated not only by his "post-metaphysical" outlook and commitment. It is motivated also as providing a defense

---

28   Ibid., p. 30.
29   Ibid., pp. 16–18.

Phenomenology and Transcendence 129

against the view of influential deconstructionist philosophers such as Derrida and Caputo which insists that since transcendent "Otherness" is certainly never given phenomenologically we can know nothing whatsoever about its nature—however much we may pray and weep to do so. It recedes from every attempt to access it. For all we can know, or hope, this transcendent otherness, this *tout aûtre*, may well be monstrous rather than divine, *khora* rather than God.[30]

This consequence of a radically inaccessible *tout aûtre* poses, for Kearney, a serious threat to any ethical perspective. For if the foundational Otherness, which allegedly utterly transcends human experience, might well be demonic chaos rather than divine goodness, the ultimate significance of ethical endeavor is undermined and no atrocity can be effectively confronted. Hence, faced with the alternative of transcendent Otherness being either phenomenologically accessible, or else wholly inaccessible and possibly chaotic and evil, Kearney opts decisively for the former. For him, the alternative God or *khora* is answerable by a hermeneutically argued option for God as the phenomenologically accessible eschaton who possibilizes our ethical experience.[31]

But is it really satisfactory to seek to legitimize an experiential affirmation of divine transcendence within a phenomenological frame of reference, even one so tentatively envisaged in terms of eschatological possibility? Can divine transcendence be both unbounded by experience and yet situated within experience? Or rather, as I have suggested, should this way of thinking, however compatible with pre-philosophical religious sentiment, be philosophically repositioned by more metaphysical considerations?

The phenomenological perspective and its relevant discourse is all very well as far as it goes—provided it is not claimed that one can go no further. It is a way of talking about God as though what is meant by "God" involves necessarily and unavoidably his relationship to us as the "possible," or not yet achieved, goal of our ethical and religious desire.

In phenomenology of religion God appears inextricably, in however privileged, transcendent, or eschatological terms, as God for humanity—a co-relative component, together with human subjectivity, of human experience. Insofar as one remains within this phenomenological perspective one can accommodate the sort of claims, advocated by Kearney, about God as "possibility" and God as "dependent upon us to be God."

However, unless such discourse is open to reflective metaphysical qualification and reappraisal, one faces the objection of being exposed to a dilemma involving either idolatry or atheism. For a God inextricably inscribed in human experience is inextricably a human god, and a God not so inscribed must ultimately not even be a possibility from a strictly phenomenological viewpoint. On the one hand, the relative

---

30 Cf. J. Caputo, *The Prayers and Tears of Jacques Derrida: Religion without Religion*, Bloomington, 1997; also "Apostles of the Impossible. On God and the Gift in Derrida and Marion," in *God, the Gift and Postmodernism*, ed. Caputo and Scanlan, pp.185–222; R. Kearney, *Strangers, Gods and Monsters*, London, 2003, pp. 191–211.

31 Cf. Kearney, *Strangers, Gods and Monsters*, pp. 100–111, and *The God Who May Be*, pp. 69–79.

130 *The Sense of Creation*

dependence of God, described in phenomenological terms as a "possibility" co-relative to human desire (rather than in terms of his independently possessed actual existence—his esse), appears to compromise his alleged radical transcendence. On the other hand, insistence on the radical alterity of his transcendence calls in question the claim that he is most appropriately spoken of as "possibility" or "the God Who May-Be," which refers inextricably to his reality for mankind. As one perceptive exponent of phenomenology remarks: "It thus seems that we are at an impasse; to remain fully transcendent, the transcendent must lay claim upon us as unbounded by experience, but to retain the status of a phenomenon, it must be situated within experience."[32]

I would suggest that one can avoid this *impasse* if one appreciates that the transcendence which is apprehended or given in experience cannot be phenomenologically legitimated as an experience, however indistinct or eschatological, of divine transcendence. In other words, phenomenology even if a necessary or appropriate approach to the question of divine transcendence cannot be a sufficient one. For in order to claim that the transcendence which is the object of our affirmation is phenomenologically justified because given experientially, rather than simply postulated, one must affirm a pole of conscious subjectivity which allows or enables the phenomenon to appear as bearing the meaning which it has. Such phenomenologically given transcendence is essentially a transcendence accessible to my disclosing capacity for experience, a transcendence relativized as transcendence-for-humans. As Zarader remarks:

> If in the framework of phenomenality, one cannot do without a pole that guarantees the meaning of the phenomenon—then the transcendence of which this pole is a witness can only be relative: transcendence in immanence, an other for me. The phantasm of a pure or absolute alterity proves to be unachievable. Unachievable in phenomenology.[33]

This is why some authors such as J.L. Marion seek to preserve, unsuccessfully it seems to me, the unconditioned transcendence of the given by claiming that it empties human subjectivity of any active role in its saturating phenomenological appearance. (One is reminded of medieval debates about Averroes's denial of individual human intellects active or even passive, and Malebranche's affirmation of the pure passivity of human understanding which enables his assertion that God is the object of human consciousness and the locus of all objective knowledge.[34])

If an experience of transcendence, describable within a phenomenological frame of discourse, is the only legitimate way to discuss divine transcendence, one will be constrained in one's form of description. On the one hand, because

---

32 M. Zarader, "Phenomenology and Transcendence", *Transcendence in Philosophy and Religion*, ed. E. Faulconer, Bloomington, 2003, p. 110. My discussion of this topic has been facilitated by this clear and penetrating short account of an often obscurely presented issue. Cf. also D. Janicaud, *Phenomenology and the "Theological Turn,"* trans. B. Prusak, New York, 2000, pp. 16–103.

33 Zarader, "Phenomenology and Transcendence," pp. 116–17.

34 Cf. O. Leaman, *Averroes and his Philosophy*, Oxford, 1988, pp. 82–116. Cf. also D. Connell, " La passivite de l"entendement selon Malebranche," *Revue philosophique de Louvain*, 51,1953, pp. 543–65.

Phenomenology and Transcendence 131

of the inherent reference to the irreducible role of human subjectivity in allowing phenomena to appear one will have to speak of a certain interdependence between the phenomenologically described "divine transcendence" and human consciousness. On the other hand, in order to try to respect the radical alterity referred to in the experienced transcendence, one will be led to attenuate the ontological force of this interdependence by recourse to the idiom of "possibility"—a God Who May-Be attainable only through a possibilized transformation of human ethical desire. This, it seems to me, is the horizon within which Kearney operates—a horizon which accounts for the striking and unconventional terminology in which his discussion of the God who may-be unfolds.

However, if one accepts that an experientially inscribed transcendence, however numinous, "other," absent, or eschatological, cannot be phenomenologically legitimated as an experience of divine transcendence, a different approach to such experienced transcendence is required.

Such an approach is one which, while disclaiming that a human experience of transcendence can be legitimated phenomenologically as somehow an experience of God, nevertheless takes the experience as a significant occurrence requiring serious consideration. It will ask questions not just of meaning, but of existence and truth. It will ask for the conditions of the possibility of this experience of transcendence—an experience which appears to orientate our thought beyond the limits of experience.

There are various ways in which this experience of transcendence might be addressed. Adopting what Ricoeur calls "a hermeneutics of suspicion," one could consider it in entirely naturalistic terms from the perspective of various human sciences. For example, one could consider how from a psychoanalytic perspective the affirmation of God can be seen as a projection of childhood dependence. Or how from a Marxist perspective the affirmation is an expression of economic alienation. Or how from the viewpoint of anthropology of religion God may be seen as the key to route-finding activity through human compounds of intransigence. More generally, within phenomenology the experienced transcendence may be explicated in terms of an account of various intrinsic conditions, such as "subjectivity," "givenness," and "temporality" which are characteristic of any human experience. And discriminating phenomenological description of the sense of God can provide a valuable critique of some of the more reductionist interpretations of it provided within the human sciences.

However, beyond these explanations from within experience of our sense of God or divine transcendence, there remains the question whether, beyond the intrinsic conditions of the experience, anything exists independently which corresponds in some way to what is intimated, however inadequately, by our phenomenologically describable experience. Here one is seeking some light and truth about the ultimate ontological foundation of the phenomenologically given. The question presents itself might God be the source of our given sense of God?—a question which, we have argued, cannot itself be answered phenomenologically. For God, as such, is not a phenomenological "given"—neither psychologically, socially, culturally, or otherwise.

There are two ways in which this question might be addressed: one theological, the other philosophical.

132 *The Sense of Creation*

A theological approach would be based upon faith in a divine revelation accepted as such. The divine transcendence affirmed, for example, through faith in the eventful Judeo-Christian salvation history, is not given phenomenologically. It is an object of faith, not experience. But, for the believer, this faith legitimates the experienced salvation history as a genuinely revealing trace of what exceeds this-worldly human experience. It enables a theological interpretation of the dependable meaning and value and purpose of human existence in terms of its relation to a transcendent God affirmed in faith.

A philosophical approach to the ultimate foundation of the experientially given sense of divine transcendence must proceed very differently to a theological one. It should, I suggest, proceed by way of indirect metaphysical analysis of the implications of this experience to arrive finally at a non-experiential affirmation of God as its ultimate real foundation.

The following indications of what this analysis would involve utilize features of Aquinas's philosophical approach to the topic. The central idea is that a phenomenological intimation of divine transcendence can be shown to be existentially problematic, theoretically puzzling, and even contradictory unless it is understood as a created trace or likeness or cipher of God himself. Here one is in the realm, not of a God who may-be, but a God whose actual existence is a metaphysical presupposition of his phenomenological representation as an eschatological possibility for man.

Aquinas summarizes the idea very succinctly when he writes:

> it is not necessary that God considered in Himself be naturally known to man, but only a likeness of God. It remains, therefore, that man is to reach the knowledge of God through reasoning by way of the likeness of God found in His effects.[35]

Although, obviously, he did not have access to the perspective and terminology of contemporary phenomenology, he makes very relevant philosophical comments denying any experiential awareness of God himself and highlighting the necessity of metaphysical arguments for his existence:

> For the philosopher takes his arguments from the proper causes of things; ... In the teaching of philosophy, which considers creatures in themselves and leads us from them to a knowledge of God, the first consideration is about creatures; the last of God. But in the teaching of faith, which considers creatures only in their relation to God, the consideration of God comes first, that of creatures afterwards.[36]

It might be objected that if a philosophical consideration of the creatures we experience can lead us to knowledge of God then this experience must somehow involve, however minimally and indistinctly, some experience of God. However, a distinction must be made between knowing something indistinctly and knowing it implicitly. And this distinction distinguishes a phenomenological from a metaphysical approach to the question.

---

35 Aquinas, *Summa Contra Gentiles*, trans. English Dominicans, London, 1934, Bk 1, ch. 11.

36 Ibid., Bk 2, ch. 4.

Phenomenology and Transcendence 133

A phenomenological approach to our ethico-religious sense of divine transcendence tends to claim that this transcendent reality is somehow inscribed in experience. However, in order to safeguard its utter alterity it is affirmed as appearing very indistinctly, obscurely, enigmatically, or ambiguously, e.g. as a presence-absence, or an eschatological possibility, etc.

A metaphysical approach to the same ethico-religious sense of God claims that there is no, even indistinct, experience of God himself. Rather, his existence is only implicit in any experience and must be made non-experientially explicit by way of indirect argument. Thus one would be misled if one discerned a vague experience of God as Infinite Truth and Goodness in our seemingly limitless desire for knowledge and happiness. Aquinas does remark that we implicitly know and desire God the supreme truth and goodness in whatever we know and desire. However, in the same article he observes that the important point is that God is thus naturally known and desired only implicitly. What is implicit is known to be implicit only by being made explicit and this cannot be accomplished by any direct insight or immediate inference from the given of experience but only indirectly by causal argument.[37]

Levels of Explanation

These remarks indicate that, for Aquinas, in an account of the co-existence of man and God, one must distinguish various levels of discussion. In the first place there is what might be called a phenomenological account of the immediate and direct field of human experience. Although in various forms a certain sense of "the Transcendent" may be an aspect of such experience, an affirmation of the existence of God should not feature in a description of it either as something naturally known or given, or as a constituent principle, or as a self-evident truth. Dismissing any impression we may have to the contrary, Aquinas accounts for it in terms which Hume, and perhaps even Freud, would have appreciated, as merely a misleading psychological tendency to accept as experientially legitimated or self-evident what we are accustomed to hearing since childhood.[38]

This stage of phenomenological description of lived experience leads on methodologically to metaphysical analysis of both its immanent and transcendent ontological conditions— arriving ultimately by indirect causal argument at the affirmation of the existence of a transcendent creator.

The development of these stages of philosophical enquiry involves a progressive transition from what is prior according to our human experience to what is prior in an absolute sense, i.e. a transition from the *prius quoad nos* to the *prius quoad se*. The foundation of this itinerary from the *prius quoad nos* to the *prius quoad se* is the natural openness and capacity of the human mind to engage, on the basis of our experience of the world and ourselves, in metaphysical enquiry concerning the ultimate meaning and value of being in general and of human existence in particular.

---

37 Cf. ibid., Bk 1, ch. 11.
38 Cf. ibid.

134 *The Sense of Creation*

Such enquiry can be engaged by various features of experience which, in different ways, express within experience paradoxes of immanence and transcendence, of openness and constraint, of freedom and facticity, of meaning and value enmeshed in tragedy and contingency, of a numinous sense of divine transcendence inscribed within our fragile human frame of reference.

Such experiences evoke the metaphysical enquiry "How must reality ultimately be in itself if it is to manifest itself phenomenologically to us as it does?" And in virtue of a person's natural openness to such enquiry one can, through a rational process of reflective discourse, seek to provide in conceptual terms an account of the ontological conditions of one's lived experience. In a word, one can go beyond phenomenology to metaphysics. We claim our phenomenological discourse to be true inasmuch as and because it faithfully describes what is given in experience. It gives rise to metaphysical discourse which we claim to be true inasmuch as and because it describes what must be the case, even though not experienced, if the phenomenological discourse which gives rise it is not to be ultimately unintelligible and even contradictory.

I do not propose to enter here into a discussion of whether such a metaphysical argument for the existence of God can be developed from some phenomenologically described feature of specifically religious experience such as a numinous experience of the holy or the sacred. I believe that it might well and that the argument would parallel those of previous chapters of this work. These showed that paradoxical ciphers of transcendence manifested within our experience of objective truth, our experience of moral invocation, and our experience of the analogical character of finite being, are rendered metaphysically intelligible as reflections of the non-mutual real relationship which characterizes the created world vis-à-vis its divine creator.

Particular issues arise of course when the domain of phenomenological discourse is that of religious experience. The discussion will be influenced by whether, for example, the alleged experience is a naturally accessible "depth experience," such as existential dread, a sense of the sublime, a sense of the holy, etc., or on the other hand an experience arising in virtue of an alleged divine revelation.

Again, there is the very large issue of the relationship between the relatively austere space opened up by metaphysical reflection on the co-existence of man and God and the much richer and more salvific account of the matter disclosed through faith in revelation. Which should be interpreted in terms of which or do they throw light upon each other and if so in what way?

Such issues are for future consideration. What concerns us here, with reference to Kearney's evocative work, is our argument that a phenomenological and hermeneutical approach to the issue of divine transcendence is insufficient and must be complemented by metaphysical considerations in which the independently possessed actual existence of God and his causal role as transcendent creator are affirmed.

The attempt to confine discussion of the issue to the phenomenological level because of fear of the distorting influence of metaphysical considerations has, it seems to me, the opposite of the desired effect. For it proposes as definitive an experiential level of discourse which speaks of God in terms of interdependent relationships of "possibility" between himself and man. Such descriptive phenomenological discourse should be seen as only preliminary or partial. If seen as the only appropriate way

Phenomenology and Transcendence 135

of speaking about the co-existence of man and God, and as replacing metaphysical discourse, it will in fact be inappropriate in respect of each of them.

The discussion in *The God Who May Be* does indeed appear to confine its discussion in this way. It

> strives to overcome the metaphysical God of pure act and asks the question: what kind of divinity comes after metaphysics ... how we may overcome the old notion of God as disembodied cause, devoid of dynamism and desire, in favour of a more eschatological notion of God as possibility to come?[39]

The "radically new and adventurous" view of God as eschatological possibility or *possest* is seen as alternative rather than complementary to a metaphysical account of God as actually existing creator. "For *possest* may now be seen as advent rather than *arche*, as *eschaton* rather than *principium*."[40]

Such restriction of talk about God to the level of phenomenological and hermeneutical discourse about God as possibility, a "deity yet to come" who "depends on us to be" inevitably raises questions about whether such a God is only a future kingdom of God for us, an enabled ethical ideal which we in turn somehow make possible. In a word, a conditional God.

Kearney is aware of this possible objection and explicitly discounts it. "Does all this amount to a conditional God? No. For if God's future being is indeed conditional on our actions in history, God's infinite love is not. As a gift, God is unconditional giving. Divinity is constantly waiting."[41]

However, quite apart from how God's being can be dependent upon our historical actions, the point remains that God's love must actually exist unconditionally and independently of us in order to play a possibilizing role in our regard. And this implies a metaphysical claim which goes beyond discussion of how things appear to us. As one commentator remarks more generally:

> A God that has to become God, must first be God to become God, that which has to create itself, must first be itself to create itself. But why become itself if it is itself; why create itself if it is? ... We do not make, or enable God to be. God makes us to be. God must be to enable to be. ... God enables the kingdom to be, and we may be cooperators, perhaps even creative contributors, but God is not the kingdom of God.[42]

The upshot of all of this is that phenomenological description of religious experience, which speaks as though there is a mutually enriching interdependent encounter between man and God, must be complemented by a metaphysical level of discourse which explicates the implicit assertions about the independently possessed and absolute existence of God and the non-mutual relationship of dependence of creation upon him. If this complementary level of theological or metaphysical

---

39   Kearney, *The God Who May Be*, pp. 2–3.

40   Ibid., pp. 110–11.

41   Ibid., p. 37.

42   W. Desmond, "Maybe, Maybe Not: Richard Kearney on God," *Irish Theological Quarterly*, 66, 2003, pp. 114–15.

136   *The Sense of Creation*

elaboration is precluded one is exposed to defending an anthropomorphic or superficial conception of God.

Needless to say, there remain many issues to be addressed, some of them touched upon earlier in previous chapters, concerning the co-existence of man and God as metaphysically conceived. In particular, there is need to explore why features such as God's remoteness, immutability, independence, and absence of shared experience and suffering, do not imply a static, inert deity, lacking any understanding of or involvement with creatures. This may be what leads Kearney to observe: "if God is devoid of all historical being, is He not then deprived of the power to act and call and love—a God so distant as to be defunct?"[43]

Why this is not so should and can be elaborated notwithstanding the undeniable inadequacy and analogical character of any talk about God. It will involve reflection on the implications of the idea of creation and the non-mutual relation with creatures which it involves. It is precisely because of this that God should not be thought of as an inhabitant of the world, a being interacting with and affected by other beings. But not being able to learn by or be affected by experience does not preclude his understanding and love of creation. As one writer puts it:

> the question is not one of experience. God simply does not have any relation of dependence on his creatures but he understands, with an understanding more intimate than any knowledge from experience, the truth about the dependence of creatures on his knowledge and love.[44]

This brief indication of an approach to a very large issue is outlined here merely to emphasize the point that the question of the co-existence of finite and Infinite, of man and God, which is the theme of these pages, cannot be adequately addressed simply in phenomenological and hermeneutic terms. In particular, the attempt to describe their co-existence experientially in terms of mutually defining "possibilities" and abstracting from any reference to their actual existence, their *esse*, is necessarily incomplete. It must be complemented and re-situated by a metaphysical discourse which acknowledges the primacy of the independently possessed actual existence of God and his role as creator of whatever may be accessible to phenomenological description. To reverse this order and refer to God as primarily and fundamentally more possible than actual, a God Who May-Be rather than a God Who Exists, is it seems to me, to preclude any affirmation of God. For a God who does not (yet) exist, cannot exist and is therefore not a possibility but rather an impossibility.

Kearney, rightly it seems to me, seeks to rescue discourse about ultimate transcendence from the alarming implications of deconstructionist insistence upon its radical and potentially terrifying unknowability. He seeks to navigate hermeneutically a conscious reconciliation of transcendence and immanence, of God and man, by way of a phenomenological account of ethical openness in interpersonal relationships to a divine transfiguring possibility.

However, these ciphers of divine transcendence, disclosed in ethical endeavour, are not an indistinct awareness or experiential "presence through absence" of divine

---

43 Kearney, *The God Who May Be*, p. 26.
44 H. McCabe, "The Involvement of God," in *God Matters*, London, 1987, p. 45.

transcendence itself. Here, it seems to me, the deconstructionists are right. Radical "Otherness," or the utterly transcendent God is not accessible phenomenologically and if this is the only access to divine transcendence then it is indeed unknowable. My suggestion is that various ciphers of transcendence, including the ethical ciphers so engagingly delineated by Kearney, can be deciphered by metaphysical argument which enables a non-experiential but informative affirmation of a radically transcendent God.

Conclusion

In the course of this work we have considered three central questions in the philosophy of religion. These are a question of meaning, a question of existence, and a question of co-existence. They are closely interrelated. For to ask whether God exists one needs to have some understanding of what is meant by "God"; and if he does exist this will have self-involving implications for human existence.

The exploration of these questions has been inspired by a single idea and the work can be seen as an attempt to develop and test this idea. It is the philosophical idea that God can be truthfully said to exist as the creator of the world of finite beings which are really related to him in a non-mutual real relationship of dependence. This way of thinking about God is implicit in the Scripture-based beliefs and worship of the main monotheistic religions.

We noted how Anselm and Aquinas made significant contributions to the philosophical elaboration of this idea of God. Anselm's idea of God, as that than which nothing greater or better can be conceived, provided a philosophical conception which can avoid viewing God idolatrously as simply the best being there happens to be and emphasizes rather the infinite and self-sufficient nature of divine perfection. Aquinas develops this in his account of creation which, according to him, is neither necessitated, nor enhances, limits, or relativizes the divine perfection. This account implies the claim that, although the order of finite beings is really related to God in a relationship of total dependence, the transcendent perfection of God is not really involved in, or affected by, any inter-relativity with created beings—even though, because of the inter-relativity of the objects of our experience, we naturally tend to imagine it as so related, particularly in respect of God's knowledge and love of his creation.

We argued that in discussing the existence of this transcendent God two extremes should be avoided. On the one hand, the view attributed to Anselm and indeed many subsequent philosophers, including Descartes and Leibniz, that the existence of God is self-evident and that this can be shown *a priori* by reflection upon the idea of him as infinitely perfect being. We argued that although this idea is of great significance in framing a true account of what is meant by "God" it is not possible to derive an affirmation of his existence from an analysis of this idea of him.

The other extreme is one which claims that it is unnecessary to offer philosophical arguments for the existence of God because in fact it is impossible to do so. This view draws inspiration from certain theological reflections about nature and grace and more recently from the later philosophy of Wittgenstein. It argues that an affirmation of God is woven into the grammar of a religious form of life and cannot be rationally justified independently of this form of life, in which it is a source of meaning rather than a possible conclusion of rational argument. There is no trans-field domain of rationality by which various forms of life, including any affirming the existence of God, can be evaluated philosophically.

140   *The Sense of Creation*

I have argued that this approach tends to generate a form of relativism which insulates the affirmation of God from criticism at too great a cost. For it tends to undermine the independence of his self-possessed transcendent existence vis-à-vis our affirmation of him.

Instead of either of these extremes I argued that if the existence of God is accessible to philosophical reflection it is so by way of indirect argument from features of our experience to an affirmation of him as their creative source. The argument claims to show that certain features of experience turn out upon reflection to be unintelligible and even contradictory unless understood as owing their existence to a Transcendent Creator.

The common feature, in terms of which various arguments are developed in the study, is the discovery within the given of experience of various analogues, or traces, or ciphers of the non-mutual real relationship which characterizes the relationship envisaged between finite beings and their creator. In Chapters 5–7 I proposed three such arguments, each based upon such ciphers of transcendence within our experience.

The first argument was based on the transcendence of what is known objectively vis-à-vis the knowing subject. The second, more ethical argument, was based upon the asymmetrical moral claim of the vulnerable yet transcendent other person upon my action in his or her regard. The third, and more explicitly metaphysical argument, was based upon the asymmetry and relative transcendence discovered within our experience of the analogical order of finite being—an interpretation of Aquinas's Fourth Argument for the existence of God.

I believe that there are other contexts in which the possibility of such arguments could be fruitfully explored. I think, for example, of the aesthetic context of the experience of beauty. Here, of course, we are in a very different context to that of theoretical or moral discourse—we have no access to distinctive laws of thought or categorical principles which enable us to conclude that something is beautiful. Nevertheless, when we describe something as beautiful we mean more than that we find it agreeable or delightful. We believe that we discover an objective excellence, which we can discuss with others, because it obtains independently of our liking or affirming it.[1] A question which might be pursued, though not here, is whether such an experience of the transcendent objective reality of beauty might not be a cipher or analogue of the transcendent beauty of God even, and perhaps particularly, when this beauty can also, in a different way, be wholly ascribed to a human artist.

Another context in which such reflection might be developed is that of the relative transcendence affirmed within religious experience of the sublime or the holy.[2] It is important, however, not to confuse this experience of relative transcendence with a direct experience of the transcendent God.

In Chapter 8 we considered some issues which arise in the context of questions concerning the co-existence of God and man. We considered objections, arising from the context of contemporary atheism, which question not only the "proofs that don't prove" but also the compatibility of an affirmation of God with an affirmation of human autonomy. We tried to indicate how these difficulties might be addressed.

---

1   For a splendid treatment of this topic cf. M. Mothersill, *Beauty Restored*, Oxford., 1991.
2   On this topic cf. J. Bowker, *The Sense of God*, Oxford, 1973.

Conclusion 141

On the one hand, by not making exaggerated claims about the compelling nature of the proposed arguments. On the other hand, by arguing that God's creative causality, being of a wholly different non-empirical order to that of human causality, can be viewed as enabling human autonomy, rather than constituting inter-active conflict with it. It is because God's creative causality is not co-related inter-actively with his creation that human freedom retains its autonomy.

In the final chapter we considered a different approach to the co-existence of God and man—one also critical of metaphysical arguments for his existence and of any metaphysical account of his co-existence with man. This is an approach advocated by philosophers working in the contemporary phenomenological and hermeneutical tradition. The particular example which we considered is that advanced by a theist philosopher, Richard Kearney, in his book entitled *The God Who May Be*. It proposes a phenomenological account of God in terms of possibility rather than a metaphysical one in terms of actuality.

The main thrust of such phenomenological discussion is that divine transcendence is not to be discovered by metaphysical argument. Rather, it is inscribed within experience in a non-presentational manner but one capable of confirmation by sensitive phenomenological description and hermeneutic interpretation.

In our discussion of this viewpoint we argued that a phenomenological level of discourse must be complemented by a level of metaphysical discourse if we are not to confuse a created trace of divine transcendence with the transcendent God himself. Here again the guiding idea of the non-mutual relationship between the world and God plays a central role.

What is the impression with which one is left at the end of this philosophical itinerary? It is, I think, one of the significance but inadequacy of what has been related. From an incomparably more modest perspective, I can appreciate the sense of insufficiency which great intellectual innovators such as Newton and Aquinas express when they review their achievement. Thus Newton remarked:

> I seem to have been only like a boy playing on the seashore, and diverting myself in now and then finding a smoother pebble or prettier shell than ordinary, whilst the great ocean of truth lay all undiscovered before me.[3]

And Aquinas observes:

> When therefore we proceed towards God by the way of remotion, we first deny of him anything corporeal; and then we even deny of him anything intellectual, according as these are found in creatures, such as "goodness" and "wisdom"; and then there remains in our mind only the notion that he is, and nothing more: wherefore he exists in a certain confusion for us. Lastly, however, we remove from him even "being" itself as it is found in creatures; and then he remains in a kind of shadow of ignorance, by which ignorance, in so far as it pertains to this life, we are best united to God.[4]

---

3   I. Newton, in *The Columbia World of Quotations*, ed. R. Andrews, M. Biggs and M. Seidel, New York: Columbia University Press, 1996, n. 41419.

4   Translated from Aquinas, *Scriptum super IV libros Sententiarum*, ed. P. Mandonnet and P. Moos, Paris, 1929–47, Lib.1, d.8,q.1, art,1, ad 4.

142   *The Sense of Creation*

All three key issues in philosophy of religion which we have addressed require and are capable of much greater elaboration. However, any such undertaking must be tempered by a keen awareness of its limitation and inadequacy. It is a mistake to think that philosophy can provide a fully intelligible understanding of the attributes ascribed to God himself and of their bearing upon human existence. This is particularly true when we discuss divine attributes such as simplicity, immutability, infinity, eternity, knowledge, freedom, goodness, and love. Much of the disregard in which traditional natural theology is held today is due to the exaggerated claims which have been made on its behalf. Instead of emphasizing that it describes divine transcendence and perfection but in an indirect and imperfect manner, it is sometimes represented instead as a luminous and definitive system of rational thought parallel and even superior to the discourse of religious faith.[5]

This is why, it seems to me, there is particular need for greater dialogue between strictly theological, phenomenological, and metaphysical discourse about God with a view to achieving a better understanding of how they can complement and enrich one another, rather than appearing as conflicting alternatives. Each operates according to its own aim and guiding principles, e.g. elaboration of faith in divine revelation, descriptive elucidation of the intrinsic structure and content of the given of experience, discovery of the ultimate ontological foundations of being in general and of human existence in particular. In other words one can seek to give an ultimate account of things as revealed by God (theology), or as they appear to human consciousness (phenomenology), or as they are objectively (metaphysics).

The resultant explanatory systems will be partial and, one might say, asymmetrical. They require each other as complementary. The Hegelian ideal of integrating them into a higher unified system is illusory.

By comparison with the experientially rich, historically eventful, and existentially engaged discourse of phenomenology and theology, the abstract and impersonal deliverances of metaphysical enquiry can appear very meager. Indeed they seem to call for some more comprehensive disclosure about God than they themselves can reveal. For, on the one hand, metaphysical reflection about the existence, nature, and human significance of God develops from an illuminating phenomenological account of pre-philosophical lived experience which typically includes richly textured religious experience and belief. And, on the other hand, its affirmations are very exploratory and incomplete vis-à-vis the profound understanding of the grace-full and eventful relationship between man and God portrayed in faith-inspired theology. Metaphysical reflection appears to hover as an inconclusive abstraction between a subject-centered phenomenology of religious experience and a faith-inspired theology of divine revelation of mankind's supernatural vocation. It is perhaps not surprising that sometimes there is a tendency to question the need for any metaphysical phase in the discussion and to claim that discourse about God is adequately, and more appropriately, elaborated only through creative interaction between theological and phenomenological enquiry.

---

5   Cf. A. Dondeyne, "Un Discours philosophique sur Dieu: est il encore possible?" *Miscellanea Albert Dondeyne*, Leuven, 1974, pp. 417–48.

Conclusion 143

However, it has been central to the argument of this study that metaphysical reflection on the ultimate meaning and value of being in general and of human existence in particular has an indispensable role to play in the discussion. A theologically elaborated revelation can be a light and a message and a gift of salvation only for those who can see and hear and receive it as such. It presupposes a fundamental openness to what can be revealed.

This fundamental openness cannot be adequately expressed in terms of a phenomenological account of our intentional openness to the given of religious experience, even if this experience is described as an experience of divine transcendence. For the experience thus apprehended is a relative transcendence and not God's absolute self-possessed transcendence. It is, considered simply in itself, irreducibly a transcendence-for-us, a transcendence inscribed, however obliquely, within experience, a transcendence co-ordinate with human subjectivity. If one is confined to this level of discourse it would be difficult to reply to Merleau-Ponty's remark that one can never be sure whether it is God who sustains men in their human reality or vice versa, since his existence is affirmed only via their own.[6]

The phenomenological description of this experientially given transcendence must be complemented by a non-empirical metaphysical account of its ontological or theoretical truth conditions. Central to such an account will be an argument showing the non-mutual relation of dependence of the phenomenological order upon the creative causality of a radically transcendent creator. Various ciphers of this relationship are given phenomenologically in experience, but their ultimate rationale must be argued metaphysically. It is not given experientially.

Undoubtedly, the metaphysical view of the relationship of man and God as creature and Creator is very abstract and inadequate vis-à-vis the immensely richer view revealed in biblical theology—the God of Abraham, Isaac, Jacob, the God of Jesus Christ. Nevertheless, however abstract the manner in which God is thus signified metaphysically, it is the same God as the one signified, so much more comprehensively, in the light of biblical theology. Moreover, it is the metaphysical analysis of what it means to speak of God as Creator which enables such theology to elucidate the eventful biblical account of God as Creator in non-idolatrous terms—in terms which do not reduce the transcendent God to just one participant, however powerful, in history.

The further exploration of the ways in which phenomenology, metaphysics, and strictly theological enquiry can throw light upon each other is of the greatest interest and importance. But it is equally important to emphasize, as we have in this study, their distinctively irreducible contributions to this multi-disciplinary undertaking.

---

6   Cf. M. Merleau-Ponty, *Éloge de la Philosophie*, Paris, 1953, p. 38.

Bibliography

Anscombe, E., "Modern Moral Philosophy," *Philosophy*, London, 33, 1958, pp. 1–19.

Anselm, *Monologion*, in *Saint Anselm—Basic Writings*, trans. S. Deane, La Salle: Open Court, 1962.

—, *St Anselm's Prosologion*, trans. with introduction and commentary by Max Charlesworth, Notre Dame: University of Notre Dame Press, 1979.

Aquinas, *In librum Beati Dionysii de Divinis Nominibus*, Turin: Marietti, 1950.

—, *In librum Boethii de Trinitate Expositio*, Turin: Marietti, 1954.

—, *In XII libros Metaphysicorum Aristotelis Expositio*, Turin: Marietti, 1964. (*Commentary on the Metaphysics of Aristotle*, trans. J. Rowan, Chicago: Henry Regnery, 1961)

—, *In libros Peri Hemeneias Aristotelis Expositio*, Turin: Marietti, 1964. (*Aristotle on Interpretation: Perehermeneias*, trans. J. Osterle, Milwaukee: Marquette University Press, 1962)

—, *Quaestiones disputatae de malo*, Turin: Marietti, 1965.

—, *Quaestiones disputatae de potentia*, Turin: Marietti, 1965. (*On the Power of God*, trans. English Dominicans, London: Burns, Oates and Washbourne, 1932–4)

—, *Quaestiones disputatae de veritate*, Turin: Marietti, 1964. (*Truth*, trans. R. Mulligan, Chicago: Henry Regnery, 1952)

—, *Quaestio disputata de virtutibus cardinalibus*, Turin: Marietti, 1965.

—, *Scriptum super IV libros Sententiarum*, ed. P. Mandonnet and P. Moos, Paris: Lethielleux, 1929–47.

—, *Summa Contra Gentiles*, Turin: Marietti, 1967. (*Summa Contra Gentiles*, trans. English Dominicans, Burns, Oates and Washbourne, London, 1924)

—, *Summa Theologiae*, Turin: Marietti, 1952–62. (*Summa Theologiae*, Latin text and English translation, ed. T. Gilby, 60 vols., Blackfriars edn, London: Eyre and Spottiswoode, 1964–74)

Aristotle, *Metaphysica*, trans. W. Ross, Oxford: Clarendon Press, 1928.

—, *The Generation of Animals*, Loeb edition, trans. A.L. Peck, London: Heinemann, 1984.

Arp, R.,"Vindicating Kant's Morality," *International Philosophical Quarterly*, 47, 2007, pp. 5–22.

Baghramian, M., *Relativism*, London: Routledge, 2004.

Bambrough, R., "Introduction," in *Reason and Religion*, ed. S. Brown, Ithaca and London: Cornell University Press, 1977, pp. 13–19.

Barnes, J., *The Ontological Argument*, London: Macmillan, 1972.

Bhaskar, R., *A Realist Theory of Science*, 2nd edn, Hassocks: Harvester Press, 1977.

Blanchette, O., *Philosophy of Being: A Reconstructive Essay in Metaphysics*, Washington, DC: Catholic University of America Press, 2003.

Bowker, J., *The Sense of God*, Oxford: Clarendon Press, 1973.

146   *The Sense of Creation*

Brown, S., "Religion and the Limits of Language," in *Reason and Religion*, ed. S. Brown, Ithaca and London: Cornell University Press, 1977, pp. 233–55.

Caputo, J., "Apostles of the Impossible. On God and the Gift in Derrida and Marion," in *God, the Gift and Postmodernism*, ed. J. Caputo and M. Scanlan, Bloomington: Indiana University Press, 1999, pp.185–222.

—, *The Prayers and Tears of Jacques Derrida: Religion without Religion*, Bloomington: Indiana University Press, 1997.

Connell, D., "La passivite de l'enttendement selon Malebranche," *Revue philosophique de Louvain*, 51, 1953, pp. 534–65.

Copleston, F.C., *Medieval Philosophy*, New York: Harper, 1962.

Creel, R., "A Realist Argument for Belief in the Existence of God," *International Journal for Philosophy of Religion*, 10, 1979, pp. 233–53.

Davidson, D., *Enquiries into Truth and Interpretation*, Oxford: Oxford University Press, 1984.

Davies, B., *An Introduction to the Philosophy of Religion*, 3rd edn, Oxford: Oxford University Press, 2004.

de Couesnongle, V., "Mesure et Causalité dans la Quarta Via," *Revue Thomiste*, LVIII, 1958, pp. 55–75 and pp. 244–84.

de Raeymaeker, L., *The Philosophy of Being*, trans. E. Ziegelmeyer, New York: Herder, 1954.

Descartes, R., *The Philosophical Works of Descartes*, 2 vols., trans. E. Haldane and G. Ross, Cambridge: Cambridge University Press, 1967.

Desmond, W., "'Maybe Maybe Not.' Richard Kearney on God," *Irish Theological Quarterly*, Maynooth, 66, 2003, pp. 99–118.

Dondeyne, A., "Un discours philosophique sur Dieu est il encore possible?" *Miscellanea Albert Dondeyne*, Leuven: Leuven University Press, 1974, pp. 410–30.

Dummett, M., *Frege: Philosophy of Language*, London: Duckworth, 1973.

Evans, D., "Difference between Scientific and Religious Assertions," in *Science and Religion*, ed. I. Barbour, London: SCM Press, 1968, pp. 101–33.

—, *The Logic of Self-Involvement*, New York: Herder and Herder, 1969.

Findlay, J., "Can God's Existence be Disproved?" in *New Essays in Philosophical Theology*, ed. A. Flew and A. Macintyre, London: SCM Press, 1955, pp. 47–56.

Flew, A., *God and Philosophy*, London: Hutchinson, 1966.

Geach, P., "Aquinas," *Three Philosophers*, Oxford: Blackwell, 1961.

—, *God and the Soul*, London: Routledge & Kegan Paul, 1969.

—, "God's Relation to the World," in *Logic Matters*, Oxford: Blackwell, 1972, pp. 318–27.

—, *Providence and Evil*, Cambridge: Cambridge University Press, 1977.

—, *Reason and Argument*, Oxford: Blackwell, 1976.

Geiger, L.B., *La Participation dans la Philosophie de S. Thomas d'Aquin*, Paris: Vrin, 1953.

Gilson, E., *The Christian Philosophy of St Thomas Aquinas*, trans. L. Shook, London: Gollancz, 1957.

Heaney, S., *The Redress of Poetry*, Oxford: Oxford University Press, 1990.

Hegel, G.W., *Lectures on the Philosophy of Religion*, 3 vols., trans. E. Spiers and J. Saunderson, London: Routledge and Kegan Paul, 1962.

Bibliography

Heidegger, M., *An Introduction to Metaphysics*, trans. R. Manheim, New York: Anchor Books, 1961.

Henninger, M., *Relations: Mediaeval Theories, 1250–1325*, Oxford: Oxford University Press, 1989.

Hick, J. (ed.), *The Existence of God*, London: Macmillan, 1964.

— and A. McGill (eds.), *The Many-Faced Argument: Recent Studies on the Ontological Argument for the Existence of God*, London: Macmillan, 1968.

Horgan, J., "The Proofs for the Existence of God," *Philosophical Studies*, Maynooth, vol. 1, 1951, pp. 41–53.

Husserl, E., *Cartesian Meditations*, trans. D. Cairns, The Hague: Martinus Nijhoff, 1960.

—, *The Crisis of European Sciences and Transcendental Phenomenology*, trans. D. Carr, Evanston: Northwestern University Press, 1970.

Janicaud, D., *Phenomenology and the "Theological Turn,"* trans. B. Prusak, New York: Fordham University Press, 2000.

Kant, I., *Critique of Practical Reason*, trans. T. Abbott, London: Longman, 1963.

—, *Critique of Pure Reason*, trans. N. Kemp Smith, London: Macmillan, 1968.

—, *The Critique of Judgement*, trans. I. Bernard, New York: Haffner, 1968.

—, *Religion Within the Limits of Reason Alone*, trans. T. Green and H. Hudson, New York: Harper, 1960.

Kearney, R., *Strangers, Gods and Monsters*, London: Routledge, 2003.

—, *The God Who May Be*, Bloomington: Indiana University Press, 2001.

Kenny, A., "The Argument from Design," in *Reason and Religion—Essays in Philosophical Theology*, Oxford: Blackwell, 1987, pp. 69–84.

Kierkegaard, S., *Concluding Unscientific Postscript*, trans. D. Swenson and W. Lowrie, Princeton: Princeton University Press, 1968.

Kretzmann, N., *The Metaphysics of Theism*: *Aquinas's Natural Theology in* Summa Contra Gentiles I, Oxford: Oxford University Press, 1997.

Ladrière, J., "Preface" to C. Winckelmans de Cléty, *The World of Persons*, London: Burns & Oates, 1967, pp. vii–xxi.

Leaman, O., *Averroes and his Philosophy*, Oxford: Oxford University Press, 1988.

Leibniz, G., *Monadology*, in *Leibniz Selections*, ed. P. Weiner, New York: Charles Scribner, 1951.

Levinas, E., *Totality and Infinity*, trans. A. Lingis, Pittsburgh: Duquesne University Press, 1969.

Locke, J., *An Essay Concerning Human Understanding*, 2 vols., ed. A Fraser, New York: Dover, 1959.

Lyas, C., "The Groundlessness of Belief," in *Reason and Religion*, ed. S. Brown, Ithaca and London: Cornell University Press, 1977, pp. 158–80.

McCabe, H., *God Matters*, London: Geoffrey Chapman, 1987.

—, *God Still Matters*, London: Continuum, 2002.

McMullin, E. (ed.), *Evolution and Creation*, Notre Dame: University of Notre Dame Press, 1985.

Malcolm, N., "The Groundlessness of Belief," in *Reason and Religion*, ed. S. Brown, Ithaca and London: Cornell University Press, 1977, pp. 143–57.

148 *The Sense of Creation*

Marion, J.-L., *Reduction and Givenness: Investigations of Husserl, Heidegger, and Phenomenology*, trans. T. Carlson, Evanston: Northwestern University Press, 1998.

Masterson, P., *Atheism and Alienation: The Philosophical Sources of Contemporary Atheism*, Harmondsworth: Penguin, 1973.

Merleau-Ponty, M., *Éloge de la Philosophie*, Paris: Gallimard, 1953.

—, *Phenomenology of Perception*, trans. C. Smith, London: Routledge & Kegan Paul, 1962.

Mitchell, B., "Remarks," in *Reason and Religion*, ed. S. Brown, Ithaca and London: Cornell University Press, 1977, pp. 181–6.

Mothersill, M., *Beauty Restored*, Oxford: Oxford University Press, 1991.

Murdoch, I., *Metaphysics as a Guide to Morals*, London: Chatto & Windus, 1992.

—, *The Sovereignty of Good*, London: Routledge & Kegan Paul, 1970.

Nagel, T., *Concealment and Exposure and Other Essays*, Oxford: Oxford University Press, 2002.

—, *Mortal Questions*, Cambridge: Cambridge University Press, 1979.

—, "Secular Philosophy and the Religious Temperament," available from law.nyu.edu., accessed Sept. 11, 2005.

—, *The Last Word*, Oxford: Oxford University Press, 1997.

—, *The Possibility of Altruism*, Oxford: Clarendon Press, 1970.

—, *The View from Nowhere*, Oxford: Oxford University Press, 1986.

—, *What Does it All Mean*, Oxford: Oxford University Press, 1987.

Norris Clarke, W., *Explorations in Metaphysics*, Notre Dame: University of Notre Dame Press, 1994.

—, *The One and the Many: A Contemporary Thomistic Metaphysics*, Notre Dame: University of Notre Dame Press, 2001.

—, *The Philosophical Approach to God*, Winston-Salem: Wake Forest University Press, 1979.

O"Rourke, F., *Pseudo-Dionysius & the Metaphysics of Aquinas*, Leiden: Brill, 1992.

Phillips, D.Z., *Belief, Change and Forms of Life*, London: Macmillan, 1986.

—, *Death and Immortality*, London: Macmillan, 1970.

—, *Faith and Philosophical Enquiry*, London: Routledge & Kegan Paul, 1970.

—, *Religion and the Hermeneutics of Contemplation*, Cambridge: Cambridge University Press, 2001.

Plato, *Phaedo*, trans. B. Jowett, Oxford: Oxford University Press, 1982.

Purcell, B., "Reflections on Evolution in the Light of a Philosophical Biology," in *Thomas Aquinas: Approaches to Truth*, ed. J. McEvoy and M. Dunne, Dublin: Four Courts Press, 2002, pp. 77–113.

Ross, J., "Christians Get the Better of Evolution," in *Evolution and Creation*, ed. E. McMullin, Notre Dame: University of Notre Dame Press, 1985, pp. 223–51.

—, *Philosophical Theology*, New York: Bobbs Merrill, 1969.

Russell, B., "A Debate on the Existence of God," in *The Existence Of God*, ed. J. Hick, London, Macmillan, 1965, pp. 167–91.

Sartre, J.P., *Being and Nothingness*, trans. H. Barnes, New York: Washington Square Press, 1966.

—, "Cartesian Freedom," in *Literary and Philosophical Essays*, trans. A. Michelson, London: Hutchinson, 1969, pp. 169–98.

Bibliography

—, *The Flies*, trans. S. Gilbert, New York: Knopf, 1947.

Searle, J., *The Construction of Social of Reality*, London: Allen Lane, 1995.

Sertillanges, A.D., *L'Idée de Creation*, Paris: Aubier, 1945.

Sokolowski, R., *Christian Faith and Human Understanding*, Washington, DC: Catholic University of America Press, 2006.

—, *The God of Faith and Reason*, Notre Dame: University of Notre Dame Press, 1982.

Swinburne, R., *The Coherence of Theism*, Oxford: Clarendon Press, 1977.

Taylor, R., *Metaphysics*, Englewood Cliffs: Prentice-Hall, 1963.

Trigg, R., *Reason and Commitment*, Cambridge: Cambridge University Press, 1973.

Tulloch, D., "The Logic of Positive Terms and the Transcendental Notion of Being," *Mind*, London, 66, 1957, pp. 351–62.

Turner, D., *Faith, Reason and the Existence of God*, Cambridge: Cambridge University Press, 2004.

te Velde, R., *Aquinas on God*, Aldershot: Ashgate, 2006.

—, *Participation and Substantiality in Thomas Aquinas*, Leiden: Brill, 1995.

Weil, S., *First and Last Notebooks*, London: Oxford University Press, 1970.

Westphal, M., "Overcoming Onto-theology," in *God, the Gift and Postmodernism*, ed J. Caputo and M. Scanlan, Bloomington: Indiana University Press, 1999, pp. 146–69.

Winch, P., "Meaning and Religious Language," in *Reason and Religion*, Ithaca and London: Cornell University Press, 1971, pp. 193–221.

Wipple, J., *The Metaphysical Thought of Thomas Aquinas*, Washington, DC: Catholic University of America Press, 2000.

Wittgenstein, L., *Tractatus Logico Philosophicus*, London: Routledge & Kegan Paul, 1922.

Zarader, M., "Phenomenology and Transcendence," in *Transcendence in Philosophy and Religion*, ed. E. Faulconer, Bloomington: Indiana University Press, 2003, pp. 106–19.

Index

absolutism 63–9
analogy 55–6, 85–105
Anselm 2, 5–9, 11, 19–22, 93, 107, 110, 139
    description of God 5–9
    a priori argument for God 7, 19–22
Anscombe, E. 68
Aquinas 11–18, 22, 42, 56–7, 85–106,
        116–17, 126–7, 132–3, 141
    analogy 85–105
    creation 11–13, 55, 103, 116–17, 126–7
    fourth argument for existence of God
        85–106
    relation 13–17, 56–7
Aristotle 8, 47, 89
Arp, R. 60
asymmetry 2, 56–7, 71, 75–6, 101, 105–6, 140
atheism 108–12, 114–15, 128
Austin, J.L. 112
autonomy 60, 77–8, 108, 114–17
Averroes 93, 130

Baghramian, M. 42
Bambrough, R. 37
Barth, K. 20, 23
Barnes, J. 20
Being
    analogy of 94, 98–102
    greatest conceivable 6–8, 19–22
    measure of 89–90
    metaphysical concept of 94–5
    pre-philosophical concept of 94–6
    supreme 89–93
    unity of 94–106
Berkeley,G. 16, 59
Bhaskar, R. 42
Blanchette, O. 89, 98
Bowker, J. 140
Brown, S. 24, 35

Caputo, J. ix, 129
causation 55, 85–8, 92–3, 103–5
ciphers 2, 17, 107, 132, 134, 137

concept of being 70, 76, 94–105
Connell, D. 130
Copleston, F. 59
creation 1, 2, 8, 9, 11, 17, 79–82, 103–6,
        116–17, 139
Creel, R. 51

Davidson, D. 42
Davies, B. 13, 53
de Couesnongle, V. 93
de Raeymaeker, L. 95
Derrida, J. 122–3, 129
Descartes, R. 1, 20, 42, 51, 74, 78, 113, 139
Desmond, W. ix, 135
Dondeyne, A. 127, 142
Dummett, M. 22, 44

emergence 47, 81–2, 99–101
eschatology 69–70, 122–4
Evans, D. 112–13
evolution 47–8, 54, 99–101
explanation 50–57, 109–10

Feuerbach, L. 36, 37
Findlay, J. 21
Flew, A. 20, 111, 114
'fourth way' 85–106
freedom 11, 70–74, 82, 114–17
Freud, S. 36–7, 133

Gaunilo 20
Geach, P. 14–15, 21, 50, 54, 115
Geiger, L. 93, 96
Gilson, E. 85, 93
God
    arguments for existence of
        a priori argument 29–32, 86, 88,
            108
        a posteriori argument 11, 22, 79, 86
        fourth argument of Aquinas 88–106
        moral argument for 60–63, 79–83
    arguments that don't convince 110–12

152 *The Sense of Creation*

as creator 11–17, 104–6, 116–17, 126–7
description of 5–9
Greek and Roman conception of 8–9,
126–7
and grammar 23–39
as possibility 122–5, 135–6
his co-existence with creation 12–13,
107–19, 126–7, 140–41
his knowledge 12–13, 16
nominal definition 86–7
goodness 6–7, 30, 75–6, 83–4, 110
groundless belief 24–7

Hartshorne, C. 12, 20, 121
Heaney, S. 96
Hegel, G. 16, 32, 37–8, 121, 142
Heidegger, M. 95, 121–2
Henninger, M. 13
Hick, J. 6, 20, 46, 112
hope 61–2, 115, 118
Horgan, J. 87
Hume, D. 87, 133
Husserl, E. 35, 46, 121, 122,

infinite perfection 7–8, 12–13, 22, 30–31,
104–6, 110
intelligibility of being 12, 41–50

Janciaud, D. 130

Kant, I. 17, 19, 20, 60–63, 87, 97, 102
Kearney, R. 12, 121–37, 141
Kenny, A. 55
Kierkegaard, S. 23, 27, 115
knowledge 12, 16–17, 41–57, 89–90,
129–34
Kretzmann, N. 13

Ladriere, J. 44
Leibniz, G. 20, 56, 139,
Levinas, E. 69–84, 125, 128
Locke, J. 59
Lyas, C. 24–7, 34, 36

McCabe, H. 13, 116
McMullin, E. 126
Malcolm, N. 20, 24–5, 31
Malebranche, N. 130
Marion, J.L. 96, 130

Masterson, P. 1
Marx, K. 36, 37, 131
measure 70, 89–90
Merleau-Ponty, M. 35–6, 37, 100, 114, 143
metaphor 5, 124–5
metaphysics 46–57, 86–8, 124–7, 133–7,
141–3
and ethics 59–62, 79–84
Mitchell, B. 27
monotheism 1, 5, 16, 107, 121, 125
morality 59–84
'agent-centered' 63–9, 77, 80
and belief 59–60
and creation 79–84
Kant's 'moral argument' for the
existence of God 60–63
Levinas's account of 69–84
'outcome centered' (or utilitarian) 63–9,
77, 80
more and less 89–93, 99–101
Mothersill, M. 140
Murdoch, I. 6, 118

Nagel, T. 43, 44, 47–8, 63–9, 73, 77, 109, 115
Newton, I. 141
Norris Clarke, W. 12, 100

Ockham, W. 59
Ontological Argument 7, 19–22, 108
ontology 35–7, 69–84, 135–7
onto-theology 32, 122, 125–7
O'Rourke, F. 97
'Other'– 'other' 71–7, 128–9

phenomenology 35, 96, 121–37, 141–3
Phillips, D.Z. 23–4, 27–8, 31–6
Plantinga, A. 20
Plato 6–9, 86, 89, 103
positivism 108–9
principle of causation 87–8, 92–3
of non-contradiction 56, 87–8
of sufficient reason 56
Purcell, B. 99

rationality 23, 27–8, 43–53, 127
realism 36, 41–5, 52–3, 95–6
relations 13–17, 29–30
ethical 70–84
mutual 14–15

Index

non-mutual 14–17, 38–9, 56–7, 107, 135, 143
real and notional 14–15
Ricoeur, P. 121, 131
Ross, J. 99, 100, 109, 114–15
Russell, B. 20, 46, 112
Ryle, G. 20

Sartre, J.P. 11, 46, 72, 114
Schopenhaeur, A. 48
Searle, J. 42
self-involvement 62, 112–14
Sertillanges, A.D. 13
Sokolowski, R. 7, 8
summum bonum 60–62
Swinburne, R. 13

Taylor, R. 51–3
teleology 53–7, 123
te Velde, R. 13

theology 131–5, 142–3
transcendence 15–17, 38–9, 70–84, 102–4, 107, 116–17
transcendental perfections 88–9
Trigg, R. 42
truth 41–2, 96, 102
truth conditions 33–5, 38–9, 143
Tulloch, D. 98
Turner, D. 13, 21, 101

Utilitarianism 63–9

Weil, S. 29
Westphal, M. 127
Whitehead, A.N. 121
Winch, P. 24, 28–36
Wipple, J. 86
Wittgenstein, L. 23, 49–50, 112, 139

Zarader, M. 130